Design for Aging

International Case Studies of Building and Program

Design for Aging

International Case Studies of Building and Program

JEFFREY ANDERZHON, FAIA,
DAVID HUGHES, RIBA,
STEPHEN JUDD, PHD,
EMI KIYOTA, PHD,
MONIQUE WIJNTIES, B.O.T.

John Wiley & Sons, Inc.

This book is printed on acid-free paper. ♾

Published by John Wiley & Sons, Inc., Hoboken, New Jersey
Published simultaneously in Canada

Library of Congress Cataloging-in-Publication Data

Design for aging : international case studies of building and program / Jeffrey Anderzhon . . . [et al.].
p. cm. — (Wiley series in healthcare and senior living design)
Includes index.
ISBN 978-0-470-94672-5 (cloth : alk. paper); 978-1-118-17385-5 (ebk); 978-1-118-17386-2 (ebk); 978-1-118-17976-5 (ebk); 978-1-118-17977-2 (ebk); 978-1-118-17978-9 (ebk)
1. Barrier-free design for older people—Case studies. I. Anderzhon, Jeffrey W. II. Title: International case studies of building and program.
NA2545.A3D46 2012
720.84'6—dc23

2011031423

Printed in the United States of America

10 9 8 7 6 5 4 3 2 1

Contents

Foreword

By Mary Marshall, MBE, MA, DSA, DASS, Emeritus Professor, University of Stirling, Stirling, Scotland, United Kingdom

An aging population is something you can plan for. It need never be a surprise. As a person born at the start of the British baby boom in 1945, I have always known that I belonged to a very large cohort who put a strain initially on the schools and then on homes to live in and now on pensions. We are beginning to have all the impairments of aging such as deteriorating mobility, eyesight, and hearing, and this will get worse. As we age, we can also expect a good number of us to get dementia. This bulge of the population has been known about as long as we have been alive, although the cohort ahead of us have lived longer than expected, which means that if we do too, there will be a larger number of us reaching really old age than could have been planned until recently. This baby bulge is a phenomenon in all industrialized countries and will be seen in almost all countries of the world before long. What could not have been planned for is the fact that we had fewer children than our parents and this fall in the birth rate has continued.

The point I am trying to make is that we could and should have been planning for large numbers of older people for many years. Instead, people behave as if it is a sudden event—anything less sudden is hard to imagine. You have to assume that it has been in the "too difficult" basket of most decision makers for a long time. Certainly the fact that a lot of very old people get dementia has been. The sudden realization of the aging population means that it is often labeled a "problem" or a "burden" on society, which is nonsense. It is an amazing public health achievement. It means that babies started to survive infancy and all the illnesses that used to kill children. It also means that we now have a cohort of people who are skilled and experienced and can continue to make a real contribution to society. However, a proportion will find their impairments overwhelming and their families and friends will not be able to support them to remain at home, however much care in the community is available. Alternatives will be required, and this book is about the buildings in which they will live.

In all societies alternatives to home involve communal living of some sort going from small flats with intensive support to hospitals. The largest number of buildings will be care homes (a term we use in Scotland for our homes that combine residential and nursing homes). These are a challenge to design as well as a challenge to run. Communal living is the choice of very few people; perhaps only those who have lived communally all their lives. This book is about designing the best possible buildings that maximize privacy, choice, and independence while making it easy for peoples' needs to be met. They are also places where staff work, so they must provide a congenial work environment in which staff members feel valued and that their needs have been met, too. These buildings also have to be flexible since we are all so different in what we want from our home and each cohort using the building will have different attitudes and preferences.

Collections of examples of good buildings are a great way of influencing others. They provide an engaging story about a building and details for every kind of reader. As far as designing specifically for people with dementia, Cohen and Day produced their excellent book of case examples in 1993. This book had huge influence. I have, for example, taught in many design schools when we looked at examples from this book. It also inspired Peter Phippen, Stephen Judd, and me to collect 20 case studies for a book published in 1998 to be followed by Damian Utton's collection in 2007, when ours sold the full print run. These well-used books will now be enhanced by the collection in this book, which has a wider remit of covering buildings for older people generally as well as those with dementia. Given that the majority of older people in care homes have dementia (60 percent of residents in English nursing homes had dementia in 2007, National Audit Office), it is important that all facilities for older people are dementia-friendly.

There are many particularly interesting aspects to this collection. One is the range of countries from which examples are drawn. The Japanese examples in particular will underline the differences that arise from different cultural traditions. Another is the range of examples within countries. The Australian examples include one for indigenous Australians who need very different things from buildings and another for older homeless people who have particular needs. De Hogewejk in the Netherlands aims to provide for people from very different backgrounds in one building. This acknowledgment of lifestyle differences, as well as cultural differences, is rare and to be welcomed as an example to learn from. Another welcome focus is on outside space; the design of which is only beginning to get the attention it deserves.

This book will be immensely useful for a wide audience. The detail in the case studies will be helpful for commissioners, planners, and providers. Professions such as architects and designers will see it as an invaluable resource. Learning from the best can only enhance practice because it sets a benchmark. What we need more than anything in this field is higher expectations. This book makes an invaluable contribution.

REFERENCES

Cohen, U., and K. Day (1993). *Contemporary Environments for People with Dementia*, Maryland: John Hopkins University Press.

Judd, S., M. Marshall, and P. Phippen (1998). *Design for Dementia*. London: Hawker Publications Limited.

National Audit Office (2007). *Improving Services and Support for People with Dementia*. London, The Stationary Office.

Utton, D. (2007). "Designing Homes for People with Dementia." *Journal of Dementia Care*, London.

Acknowledgments

This book could not have been possible without the support of numerous individuals who graciously agreed to assist in both large and small ways. To all of these individuals we owe much gratitude.

The massive editing chores completed by Linda Anderzhon were "spot on." She added clarity and consistency to the work with little reward and less grumbling. Without that assistance, we would have words but certainly no book.

In England, Jane Hughes, Alison Thomas, Jane Mahon, Damian Utton, and Denise Giblin not only provided wonderful graphics and critical input, but were of wonderful assistance in the organization of multiple electronic files for the manuscript.

Kate Sarkodee has been a sterling support in the development and collation of the material and photographs for the Australian studies as well as for two of the Japanese case studies. Kirsty Bennett, Maureen Arch, Doug McManus, and John Wilson helped enormously with the Tjilpi Pampaku study. Kikuta and Himawari are two studies that could not have been published without the wonderful support of Hideo Abe. Rosemary Norris kept Stephen Judd on track, as always, for which we thank her.

Introduction

It is stating the obvious that the populations of the developing countries are aging and that this is having significant impacts on their economies and their societies. If the second half of the twentieth century focused on the education of the baby boomers, the first half of the twenty-first century will be about funding their health and aged care and about housing this population.

How countries will pay for the health and care costs of an aging society is a question that is occupying center stage within the political debate in many countries. In Japan, Long-term Care Insurance was introduced in 2000; in the United States, in early 2010 a signature and controversial health-care reform legislation for the Obama administration was initiated to broaden health insurance coverage; in Australia, the federal Labor government has wrestled with the states on how to pay for health and aged-care services. In Europe, the demographics are the same but the responses have been different: Governments that have previously fully funded health and aged care are now seeking greater private funding of these costs. The impending costs of health and aged care over the next 40 years are something that no country can ignore and for which all countries must now prepare.

This impending need has generated new ideas and new ways of providing aged care. There has been increasing choice in the type, nature, and complexity of services that are delivered within the home. This has meant that fewer people are being prematurely admitted into all forms of residential aged care. But while at-home community care is crucial, it cannot be the only option or solution. The demand for more residential aged care facilities, skilled nursing homes, assisted living, or similar congregate housing that are places where both accommodation and care services are delivered is increasing at a rapid rate and will undoubtedly continue to do so at least in the near term.

At the same time, as the numbers of older persons with higher dependencies are increasing dramatically, there has been a fundamental rethink about the style and nature of those services and the built environment in which those services are housed. There is recognition that these places are not medical institutions, though they need increasing medical supports to address the cognitive and physical conditions of their residents. There is increasing recognition that the "facilities" are not institutions but people's homes. Unlike a hospital or a hotel, people do not visit them for days, but they come to live, sometimes for years. But these are also places where the care staff work and are charged with providing quality care for the residents. The challenge we all have as designers, care providers, or simply members of society is how to express the competing needs of "home" and "care delivery" in both the physical and social environment, so that the residents feel they belong while at the same time delivering as effective and efficient care as possible.

It is not surprising that, in a search for answers to this challenge, there have been quite a number of *shibboleths* that methodologies have been peddled, and that "solutions" have been trademarked. The common thread has been a recognition that the physical and the social environment must work together to create an environment that facilitates better care for the older person within an environment that at least replicates home.

These are not abstract concepts. This is a question of where your mom or dad might live their last years or, indeed, where you might live your last years should you need care. These are realities that individuals and, indeed, societies, face on a daily basis and, with the world population demographics we face, will be realities that assume more urgency.

This book brings together 26 case studies of excellent aged-care environments from seven countries: Australia, Japan, Sweden, Denmark, the Netherlands, the United Kingdom and the United States. The authors do not suggest that it is an exhaustive selection or, indeed, that the 26 case studies are the very best services or designs from each country. We hope, however, that this work will stimulate further investigation, presentation, and discussion from around the world.

However, these examples do share two commitments. The first commitment is that the physical environment is an integral part of the care being delivered: Effective residential aged-care environments must be both therapeutic, promoting resident improvement, and prosthetic, compensating for physical or cognitive dysfunction.

The second commitment is to the idea of belonging. "Home" is a much used and abused word in aged care and in designing for older people. What do we mean by home? How do we know when we've found it?

The American author Frederick Buechner, in his book *The Longing for Home*, says:

> The word home summons up a place—more specifically a house within that place—which you have rich and complex feelings about, a place where you feel, or did feel once, uniquely at home, which is to say a place where you feel you belong and which in some sense belongs to you, a place where you feel that all is somehow ultimately well even if things aren't going all that well at any given moment.[1]

These case studies share a common commitment and focus on the person and an appreciation of what is important for that individual, within their culture, so that they have the greatest opportunity to feel that they belong. What suits the older American in an urban environment will most certainly not be appropriate for the Australian Aboriginal in the remote deserts of Australia. What has been designed as a memory village for 140 Dutch residents with dementia would most certainly be inappropriate for the residents of the group home in Japan. But while the designs and the care programs of all 26 case studies are very different, all of these case studies are environments in which older people belong and one in which they can feel truly at home. We hope that you are inspired by them.

[1] Buechner, F. (1996). *The Longing for Home, Recollections and Reflections*, San Francisco: Harper Collins, p. 7.

Part I

Australian Schemes

Chapter 1

A Study of Sir Montefiore Home Randwick

REASONS FOR INCLUSION OF THIS SCHEME

- Sir Moses Montefiore is committed to the respect of elders within a distinctly Jewish cultural tradition.
- This scheme is one of the largest and most expensive residential aged care services in Australia.
- The multistoried building was designed on a strict grid system.
- The scheme is a very large residential aged carebuilding that has minimal overtones of institutionalism.
- The facility boasts more than 500 volunteers who provide community engagement.

Building Description

Name of Scheme: Sir Montefiore Home Randwick
Owner: Sir Moses Montefiore Jewish Homes
Address:
Sir Moses Montefiore Home
36 Dangar Street
Randwick, New South Wales
Australia
Occupied since: 2007

FIGURE 1-1 Sir Moses Montefiore Home is a large service for 276 residents on five levels. *Brett Boardman Photography; Courtesy of Calder Flower Architects*

FIGURE 1-2 Scheme location. *Courtesy of Pozzoni LLP*

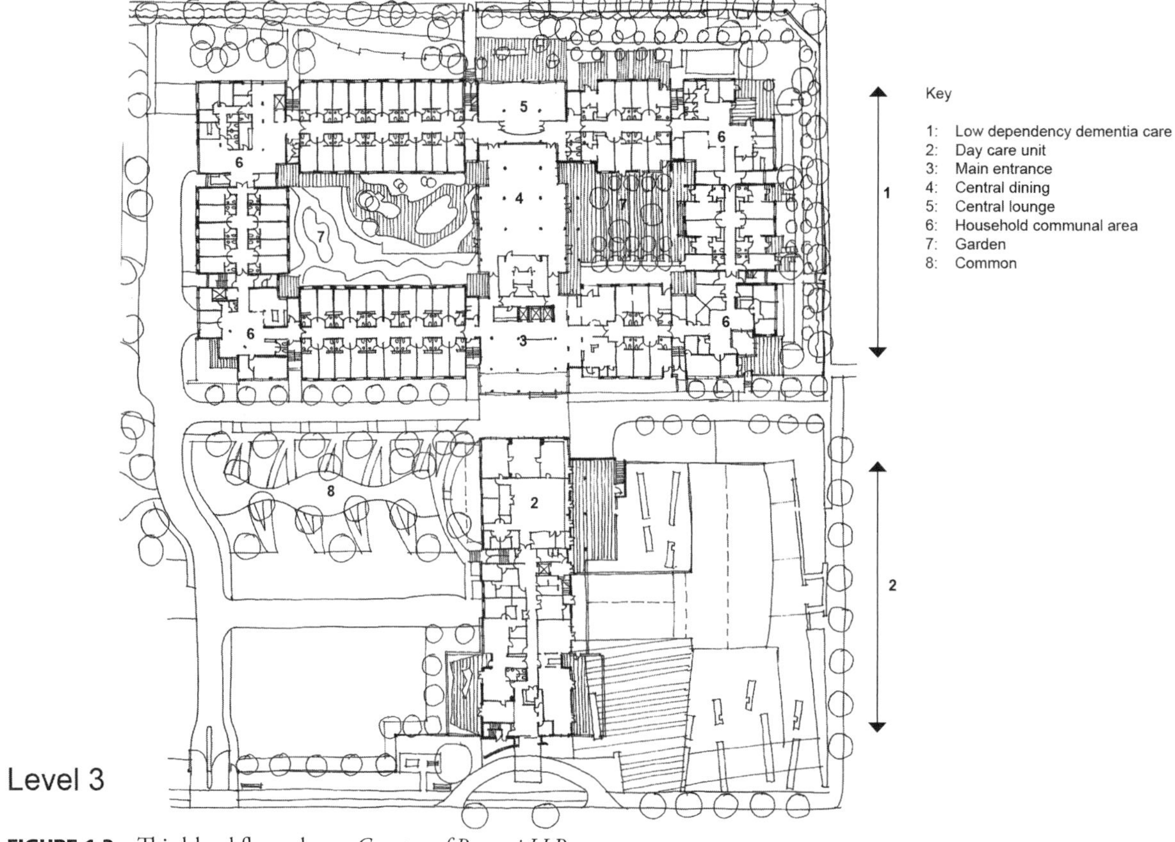

FIGURE 1-3 Third-level floor plan. *Courtesy of Pozzoni LLP*

Description of the Type of Community, Including Number of Residents

Sir Moses Montefiore Home Randwick is situated in eastern suburban Sydney. The multistory scheme is home to 276 frail, aged residents and older people with dementia. The operator, Sir Moses Montefiore Homes, has a long history of serving Sydney's Jewish community. The construction of this aged care scheme extends that service and reflects the cultural heritage and, importantly, the expectations of the Jewish residents and their families.

THE SCHEME IS DIVIDED AS FOLLOWS:

- Dementia-specific resident apartments:
  - 30 dementia-specific nursing residents
  - 30 dementia-specific assisted living residents
- Standard resident apartments:
  - 107 nursing apartments
  - 42 assisted living apartments
- Deluxe resident apartments:
  - 2 nursing apartments
  - 34 assisted living apartments
- Suite resident apartments:
  - 28 assisted living
- Respite apartments:
  - 3 assisted living apartments

The site development was planned as a two-stage phased development. Stage one has been completed with the construction of the residential aged care facility, a frail, aged and dementia-specific day center, hydrotherapy pool, and café. This first stage is the subject of this discussion. Stage two will see construction of additional dementia-specific apartments, a community plaza area, and a synagogue for the community.

The scheme is spread over five stories, the lowest is below ground and is the service area that includes a hotel-inspired kosher kitchen, a large industrial-scaled laundry, and the building's mechanical systems. In addition, there is under-building parking that is accessed at this level. The main entrance is located on the ground floor, as is the assisted living dementia-specific unit. The third level is made up of frail, aged assisted living places and a dementia-specific high care unit. The fourth floor is dedicated to frail, aged skilled nursing and the fifth floor to frail, aged assisted care. Each floor houses 15 residents, making up what is referred to as a "neighborhood." Twenty common room spaces are distributed across the four residential floors, usually located at the ends of the buildings to capture sunlight.

FIGURE 1-4 The façade is "patchworked" using brick, glass, and steel to reflect the surrounding streetscape and reduce the building's scale. *Brett Boardman Photography; Courtesy of Calder Flower Architects*

Geographics

Vernacular Design

How does the scheme/environment respond to the locality?

Although the Montefiore scheme is very large, the design team has attempted to deinstitutionalize its aesthetic. For example, a mixture of materials has been used on the building's façade and includes understated signage. Because the majority of the garden areas are inwardly focused, created by the building itself, there is no street view of resident activity. This provides a quiet setting for the community, but at the risk of the Home seemingly trying to protect itself from the surrounding world. This feeling is exacerbated by both the size of the building and by a surrounding fence and heavy landscaping creating an almost fortress-like feeling. So large is Montefiore that the operator and design team refer to it as an "urban precinct" rather than a building.

FIGURE 1-5 In the "Deluxe Room" residents have a separate lounge and access to a balcony. *Brett Boardman Photography; Courtesy of Calder Flower Architects*

Three distinctly different urban areas surround the Home's site. To the north is a low-scale historically protected residential area separated from the site by a narrow street. Medium-density housing of varying scales occupies the east and south. The western boundary of the site adjoins a precinct for large-scale development including low-rise housing and university workshops. The site's natural topography has been used to lessen the impact of the five-story structure. A two- or three-story building is presented to the residential flanks on the east depending on where the residential neighbor is located, south and north, while the five stories look over the university workshops. The scheme successfully negotiates between the changing contexts, and in this way respects the surrounding streetscape, but maximizes the development potential of the site.

The grid design used by the designers is the driving force behind the building's layout. This fairly rigid design has limited variety with a repetitive pattern of windows due to the module room design. The façade would have been relentlessly institutional if not for the clever mixed use of a variety of materials to reflect the streetscape and reduce the exterior scale of the façade. Brickwork and painted panels mirror the residential housing and the building corners relate in a more formal manner to the nearby university buildings using glass and metal mullions. A mark of its success is that a residential development adjacent to the site, which was designed after the Home, has clearly integrated the vernacular design of the Home into its own architecture.

Care

Philosophy of Care

What is the operators' philosophy and how does the building match this philosophy?

The philosophy of Sir Moses Montefiore Homes is "to enhance the Quality of Life of the Jewish Aged Community by providing an exceptional standard of service and care, and embracing the richness of Jewish Culture and Tradition." Quite simply, Montefiore Home is committed to respecting their elders and providing the very best for them within a Jewish cultural tradition. Therefore, the design brief included the charge to the architects to build a flagship for high-quality residential aged care in Australia. There was a strong focus on excellence and quality with costs being a tertiary consideration. The design process was lengthy, beginning in 2000, and saw a remarkable attention to detail by the design team. Design solutions and interior design approaches were explored in depth, including the construction of mock-up resident rooms in the basement of another of the operator's facilities in order to test sizing and finishes. Chief Executive Officer Robert Orie stated: "We wanted to get it right. We were building for 50 years, so we were asking ourselves, 'What would we want when we reach this stage of life?'" The result is perhaps the most expensive building of this type in Australia. Resident rooms are nearly double the required size as a way to preempt any future regulatory changes; interior design selections, finishes, and furnishings are "upscale" and of high quality; food services are comparable to any fine restaurant dining and there is a comprehensive social program.

The executive team was inspired by a research study[1] that significantly influenced the development of the philosophy of care, and, in its turn, the design of the building. The study found that there are 11 critical elements of quality of life: comfort, privacy, dignity, individuality, autonomy, spiritual well-being, security, relationships, functional competence, meaningful activity, and

[1] Kane et al., "Quality of Life Measures for Nursing Home Residents," *Journal of the Gerontological Society of America,* 2002.

FIGURE 1-6 Memory boxes inset beside residents' bedroom doors assist with wayfinding. *John Ambler Photography; Courtesy of Calder Flower Architects*

enjoyment. These quality of life elements were translated into a variety of design decisions. "Autonomy," for example, is expressed through the inclusion of lit memory boxes for display of photographs and mementoes outside resident rooms, affirming the unique history of each resident and assisting with wayfinding. "Meaningful activity" is realized through the location of residential scale therapy and activity kitchens in the neighborhoods for use by residents. "Dignity" is accomplished by the inclusion of private occupancy rooms with en-suite baths, as the design team firmly believed shared bathrooms compromise privacy.

There is perhaps a deeper, understated philosophy at work within the design of this scheme. It is a symbol showing honor for elders; a challenge to the wider Australian community to value older citizens by providing high standards of care and accommodation. For this reason alone, it should be viewed by Australians as exemplifying the culmination of good design and quality care provision.

Community and Belonging

How does the scheme design and operation support this ideal?

There are numerous case studies that point to a domestic style of architecture that serves to promote community and a sense of resident belonging. There is little that can be called "domestic" about the architectural design of the Montefiore scheme. Rather, it lies aesthetically somewhere between a contemporary hotel and a modern retirement complex. Wayfinding in the building is difficult, and even for a visitor with full cognition it is easy to lose your way. One would be forgiven for thinking that this, combined with 276 residents across five huge floors, is antithetical to the concept of belonging. Yet without a doubt, many of the residents feel they belong because, in the end, it is designed to be, or at least has become, so very Jewish. The Kosher kitchens, the elegant silver service, the Jewish symbols such as the mezuzah on bedroom doors, the celebrations of Jewish festivals, and the collaborations with Jewish schools and foundations all appeal to Sydney's Jewish community, but also fully integrates that culture into the Home.

A "sense of home" is integral to creating an environment conducive to residents feeling like they belong. The Montefiore scheme has concentrated on expressing "home" through its interior design selections. Of all the included Australian case studies, this scheme has the most expensive finishes and furnishings. There is a sense of the "grand," the color schemes are subtly modulated and the corridors have become galleries of original works by iconic Australian artists. In the entry foyer a large window valance suspended from the ceiling was painstakingly hand-covered with silver foil. The ceiling of the hydrotherapy center is pierced with fiber optic cables to give a very effective night sky effect. Timber woven into lattices is used extensively to screen off particular areas without closing them off. All of this reinforces and

FIGURE 1-7 The aesthetic detail in the grand entry foyer includes the valance suspended from the ceiling, hand-covered with silver foil as well as artworks from iconic Australian artists. *John Ambler Photography; Courtesy of Calder Flower Architects*

FIGURE 1-8 Montefiore's hydrotherapy center where the ceiling is pierced with fiber optic cables to give a "night sky" effect. *Brett Boardman Photography; Courtesy of Calder Flower Architects*

suggests the culture of honoring elders and the tremendous pride the community has in the Home.

To promote community, the design team attempted to break down the enormous scale and anonymity of the building using a neighborhood concept. Each neighborhood is made up of 15 single-occupancy resident rooms with a series of common areas located in the middle and at the corners of the building, connecting the neighborhoods. From the point of view of the built environment, the neighborhood concept is unconvincing: There is little to link the rooms other than their colocation in a corridor with themed signage and their convergence at the connecting common areas. However, the social program does much to make up for what the design fails to do to enhance the neighborhood concept. There is a separate social program for each neighborhood, guided by the interests and abilities of that particular resident group. There is even a friendly sense of competition between neighborhoods that serves to coalesce into a sense of community. The social program at the Home is strongly supported with 12 recreational activity officers on the floors, input from the Allied Health team and involvement of a very large volunteer group.

Innovation

If the operator pursues a policy of innovation and pursuit of excellence, how is this demonstrated?

The design approach underlying this scheme shows innovation. With such a large facility, the operator was determined that the design should have capacity for future flexibility. The design has communal spaces at its corners with residential blocks between. The residential blocks have been designed on a strict grid system that allows for three different types of modular residential suites. The "Classic Room" is a single grid width, the "Deluxe Room" one and a half, and the "Suite Room" two widths. This gives a range of accommodation sizes and standards infinitely flexible in combination. During the design phase, and even the construction phase, the operator was able to reorganize the mix of suites to develop the ideal combination for the incoming resident requirements. As the building is a framed structure with non-load-bearing walls, these modules can be revisited and revised in the future to respond to emerging needs and resident market demands. For example, though never included in the master plan, the Home has introduced a dental clinic to address the challenge many aged care providers experience in accessing appropriate and convenient dental care for their residents. The dental clinic initiative came through a partnership with an international fraternity of Jewish dentists, and the Home was quickly able to provide an adequate clinic by converting a deluxe suite into the dental clinic.

The Home's design has also cleverly disguised the service areas. The scheme is actually made up of 16 separate buildings, each joined by narrow service links that can be accessed directly from the exterior. This reduces the presence of servicing activity in resident areas and, at least in a small way, promotes a more residential ambience.

The Home has also taken an innovative approach to the shared past of many of its residents. Australia is home to approximately 35,000 European survivors of the Holocaust, the largest number of survivors per capita of any country's population outside of Israel. About one-third of the residents at Montefiore are Holocaust survivors and there are, in addition, those who make up the "second generation," or children of survivors, who feel that the Holocaust is the single event that has had the

FIGURE 1-9 The "Classic" or entry-level room has an en-suite bathroom and kitchenette. *Brett Boardman Photography; Courtesy of Calder Flower Architects*

most critical effect on their lives. Some suffer from post-traumatic stress disorder, a factor that can have a compounding effect in the management and onset of dementia. A training program has been initiated that is designed to equip staff with an understanding of the Holocaust, its impact on individual residents, and potential care issues that might ensue. Six hundred staff from the Home have visited Sydney's Jewish museum to hear the Holocaust history directly from survivors. This training program assists staff in identifying possible triggers for distress and strategies to diffuse situations that may arise from these experiences of the residents. The architects were particularly aware of this history, and consciously tried to avoid materials or design decisions that would suggest feelings of imprisonment or institutionalization. The graceful, light-filled common rooms contribute considerably to negating these feelings.

Neighborhood Integration

Community Involvement

Is the scheme and service designed to integrate successfully with the local community?

Montefiore Home enjoys very strong support from Sydney's Jewish community, which is strongly present in Sydney's eastern suburbs. Nowhere is this more apparent than in the Volunteer Program, which boasts around 500 individuals of all ages devoting their time and resources to the Home. However, it is the colocation of services that really embed and anchor Montefiore in the community. During the early design stage of the building, a child care center, Moriah College Preschool, temporarily occupied land in a corner of the site. Since the opening of the Home, the benefits the preschool has brought have ensured that it became a permanent part of the master plan. The director of care services stated, "The preschool has provided so many wonderful opportunities for intergenerational interaction. We can't see it going anytime soon." A Sabbath program each Friday sees the children from the preschool visit the dementia-specific unit to light Sabbath day candles and join in a ritual blessing over bread and wine. Older children from the Moriah College Preschool participated in the Zikron V'Tikvah project, painting ceramic butterflies with residents in honor of the 1.5 million children who died in the Holocaust. Some of these preschool children have returned to the Home as volunteers. The Home saw this as a particularly important interaction as some residents are childless Holocaust survivors or have very small family networks. With the preschool, as well as other outreach programs, the Home has affirmed the value of older people within Sydney's Jewish community.

An additional success of the Home is the onsite Burger Day Care Center. The Center operates programs for 180 frail, aged, dementia-specific and active healthy aging nonresidents each week. Operated in partnership with JewishCare, it provides opportunity for socialization for aged clients and respite for their caregivers. The colocation at the Home for this program provides a great synergy between community and residential care. There are occasional shared activities between Day Center clients and residents of the Home, which has increased the community's familiarity with residential care at Montefiore. The Day Center clients access the Home's Allied Health services and can make use of the Home's hydrotherapy pool. This in turn provides a strong early intervention program in order to monitor client well-being and prevent crisis admissions to residential care.

Another aspect of community involvement was the design team's approach to the local neighborhood consultation phase during the design phase and prior to construction. Extensive community consultations were held. Feedback from these meetings, such as increasing the setback from the perimeter by 15 meters (approximately 49 feet) to reduce its impact on the streetscape, was incorporated into the design. The future vision for the scheme is also very inclusive of the surrounding community. Stage two design will be centered around a public plaza, with cafés and retail outlets. Design architect John Flower views the plaza as both an interface for the residents and a gift to the neighboring community aimed at reinvigorating the local corner shops adjacent to the site and further anchoring the Home within the community.

Staff and Volunteers

Human Resources

Are policies and designs in place to attract good staff and volunteers?

Montefiore says it takes a multidisciplinary or universal staffing approach with on-the-floor staff, and particularly with those who work in the dementia-specific units. For example, recreational activity officers, whose primary role is to organize activities for residents, are also expected to assist with feeding at meal times. Conversely, assistants in nursing are involved in planning outings. This reduces the number of staff who interact with residents on a daily basis and helps to build a sense of community. The Home is also supported by a very large Allied Health team and assistants for therapeutic activities such as hydrotherapy and music, art, and dance therapy.

Montefiore has a union collective agreement with its staff, allowing the organization to attract staff through increased rates of pay and to adapt classifications that reflect a multidisciplinary approach.

The 500-strong volunteer program is supported by a dedicated volunteer coordinator. Volunteers have a mandatory orientation program and regular ongoing training. They are encouraged to debrief with onsite social workers if needed. A Volunteers Recognition Day is held annually to thank them for their contribution.

- Direct care hours per day per client: Nursing = 2.82, Other (Admin/Hotel and Food Services) = 2.15

Environmental Sustainability

ALTERNATIVE ENERGY SOURCES

Australia has an abundance of natural light, and the challenge for designers is to capture and control solar energy. This scheme uses floor-to-ceiling glass panels and skylights to maximize light penetration, reducing the need for artificial illumination.

WATER CONSERVATION

Rainwater is harvested onsite in an underground retention tank and reused on the gardens to reduce demand on town water. Plumbing fittings that minimize water waste have been incorporated.

ENERGY CONSERVATION

The designers have incorporated a clever natural ventilation solution into this scheme. At the corners of the buildings, communal areas or open office space have been located. All of these open onto patios, gardens, or balconies, letting in the natural breezes from Botany Bay to the North and allowing cross-ventilation through the building. This reduces reliance on air conditioning, reducing greenhouse gas emissions, and allows the building to "breathe." Air conditioning is provided through a split decentralized system serving resident rooms, allowing individualization of temperature and comfort settings by residents. The approach to electricity use is also aimed at conservation with motion sensor-controlled lighting and low-energy light fittings. Screens over windows reduce solar glare and additional glazing reduces reliance on artificial means of cooling.

Outdoor Living

Garden

Does the garden support principles of care?

The Montefiore scheme has a mixture of courtyards and open communal gardens. The dementia-specific units have direct access to the gardens, and there are separate courtyards for the assisted living and nursing home units. Some suites for assisted living residents

FIGURE 1-10 Montefiore's Winter Courtyard is one of numerous courtyards and gardens across the site. *Brett Boardman Photography; Courtesy of Calder Flower Architects*

open directly onto a winter courtyard. However, like many multistoried schemes, the conundrum here is that there is no access to gardens for residents on the fourth and fifth floors without taking an elevator to reach them. To some extent this is alleviated by communal areas at most corners of the building that let the outside in with floor-to-ceiling windows and, at some locations, being open to the floor above.

The design team describes the courtyards as barrier free, that is, they allow free and safe movement and optimize the functional ability of residents regardless of impairment. To this end, garden paths are wide and flat, rails and seating are ergonomically designed, garden bed walls double as seats or rest stops, there are few dead ends, and the design is simple and easy to understand. All these support the philosophy of autonomy, security, functional competence, and enjoyment. However, one of the awkward aspects of the design is the five-meter-high (approximately 16 feet) steel wall that separates the assisted and skilled nursing dementia unit gardens. In some respects it is a clever solution as it gives the nursing care unit, which is actually a story above the assisted living unit, access to a garden. However, residents of the assisted living unit are confronted by the overbearing wall. Although there is climbing planting that softens this wall, the height, combined with the four levels of building surrounding the courtyard, compromise the sense of freedom. The courtyards also offer little privacy from the overlooking stories and there is a sense as one walks through them that one is being spied upon from above. The planting selection and design are formal and even subtropical with appropriate plant materials, which, while making the garden beds vibrant, are more ornamental than inviting.

In the Australian context, the temperate weather and low population density has meant most older Australians have a strong affinity to "the backyard" as a relaxed garden space. The incorporation of the Home's gardens really looks ahead to the next generation of older Australians, who have lived in higher-density housing with less access to the outdoors. The ultimate impact of this change is the loss of domesticity in outdoor areas. While other Australian schemes have defined their outdoor spaces as places of work with clothes lines and herb gardens, the Montefiore approach to the outside is more resort-like than utilitarian, for the use of residents as a place for relaxation, recreation, and contemplation.

Project Data

Design Team

ARCHITECT

Flower and Samios Pty Ltd
Level 1, 181A Glebe Point Road
Glebe NWS 2037
Australia
www.flowersandsamios.com.au

INTERIOR DESIGNER

Gilmore Interior Design
www.gilmoreid.com.au

LANDSCAPE ARCHITECT

Oculus
http://oculuslandscape.tumblr.com

SITE SIZE

- Site area: 29,350 square meters (315,921 square feet; 7.25 acres)
- Building footprint: 9,330 square meters (100,427 square feet)
- Total building area: 31,882 square meters (343,175 square feet)
- Total area per resident: 106.3 square meters (1,144.20 square feet)

PARKING

133 parking spaces

COSTS (NOVEMBER 2006)

- Total building cost: $112,000,000AUD ($118,309,900 USD)
- Cost per square meter: $3,513 AUD ($3,766 USD)
- Cost per square foot: $354 AUD ($374 USD)
- Investment per resident: $405,797 AUD ($433,093 USD)

RESIDENT AGE

Average age at facility opening date: 85 years

RESIDENT PAYER MIX

All admissions are asset or means tested and it is expected that admissions into the lower levels of care will pay an accommodation bond. All high-care places are extra service. Ten percent of residents at the Home are financially disadvantaged.

Chapter 2

A Study of Southwood Nursing Home

REASONS FOR INCLUSION OF THIS SCHEME

- This scheme is a domestic environment entirely for people with advanced dementia.
- A Special Care Unit for people with severe and challenging behaviors related to dementia has been incorporated into the design.
- This scheme is a successful "culture change" project.

Building Description

Name of Scheme: Southwood Nursing Home
Owner: HammondCare, a not-for-profit organization
Address:
Southwood Nursing Home
Hammondville, New South Wales
Australia
Occupied since: 2007

FIGURE 2-1 The Hammondville campus with Southwood at the center identifiable by its silver metal roofs and pond. The Meadows is at the top of the photo. *Courtesy of HammondCare*

FIGURE 2-2 Scheme location. *Courtesy of Pozzoni LLP*

FIGURE 2-3 Site plan. *Courtesy of Pozzoni LLP*

Description of the Type of Community, Including Number of Residents

Southwood Nursing Home has 83 residents who have moderate to very severe dementia and who reside in six distinctive cottages. It is the latest of three dementia-specific homes that have been developed at the Hammond Village campus, located in the southwest of Sydney, over the last few decades. HammondCare has attempted to learn from and improve upon each previous scheme. To fully understand Southwood, therefore, one needs to examine, at least minimally, the progression of dementia care and dementia-care environments at HammondCare campuses.

Founded in 1932, HammondCare developed one of the first integrated aged-care service programs in Australia by the 1950s. Since the 1990s, the organization has focused on providing innovative service models for people affected by dementia. Their first purpose-built scheme for people with dementia was opened in January 1995 and is known as "The Meadows." The design of the Meadows provided small "households" for 40 assisted-living residents, divided into three separate cottages. At the time of its inception, its design consisted of three cottages, each with fully functioning domestic preparation and serving kitchens and full laundries. Parlors had been designed to take the place of nursing stations, and carpet rather than vinyl was used in all areas except those that may be "wet" areas. The fundamental design approach to the Meadows was residential and completely noninstitutional. It was the organization's first scheme that focused on a social rather than medical model of care and as such was the "'original experiment" which provided the foundation for Southwood's design.

This original Meadows design was premised on eight simple principles: Households should be small, their aesthetic should be domestic and familiar, there should be good resident visual access to social and communal spaces, there should be appropriate resident cueing to enhance their independence, unwanted stimulation should be reduced, there should be an overriding feeling of safety and security by the resident, outdoor access by the resident should be easy and minimally supervised, and the household should be located close to the surrounding community. The organization has since built a total of six facilities for 411 residents in eastern Australia based on these principles, focusing on improvement and innovation with each new project, but springing from the lessons learned at the Meadows.

Southwood is the fifth design and care program iteration using these principles and is the first that is entirely for older people with severe dementia needing continual nursing care. This case study discusses the Southwood scheme, but by necessity, must point to the influence of the Meadows. By approaching Southwood in this manner, this reflective look back also intends to bring to light the impact of the changing needs of Australia's population on the design of residential aged-care facilities.

FIGURE 2-4 Southwood Home supports 83 people with dementia in six stand-alone cottages, each with their own front door. *Courtesy of HammondCare*

Geographics

Vernacular Design

How does the scheme/environment respond to the locality?

Southwood Home is in the Sydney suburb of Hammondville, which has a mix of new project homes and original pioneer homes built in the Great Depression as a land settlement scheme. One of the design principles used is "close to community." The Meadows design addresses this by blending into the streetscape with a suburban vernacular design. While Southwood is similar, with its metal roofs, gable ends, verandas, and domestic gardens, it also picks up on a more modern interpretation of the Australian federation era with bold colors and the higher pitch of the roof over the administration area. The Home is nestled into the back of the Hammond Village site and thus, unfortunately, has limited outlook into the surrounding community. Although this means it has little impact on the suburb, it limits the potential for residents to benefit, at least visually, from a sense of continuing to reside in the local community.

The Meadows' cottages were designed in a "Y" or boomerang shape, with two corridors of bedrooms as the top and the foot being the kitchen, living, and dining room. This design is very effective in reducing the institutional look and feel of the building, but it requires considerable land use. Southwood had to accommodate 83 residents, twice as many as the Meadows. The "Y" was thus flattened into a rectangle and the cottages lined up so as to fit onto the narrow site. While this still meets the original internal design criteria, it also means that externally it is not as domestic looking as the Meadows. It also illustrates that the rising cost and availability of land calls for new solutions that are land-use effective but do not compromise on domesticity.

Care

Philosophy of Care

What is the operators' philosophy, and how does the building match this philosophy?

HammondCare states that its mission is to improve the quality of life for people in need. Its philosophy emphasizes the intrinsic value and right to respect and dignity for each person. On the basis of this, its design brief for Southwood was, therefore, to design an environment for people with dementia that promoted independence and compensated for both physical and cognitive disability. The Meadows' design principles were translated afresh into the Southwood scheme. The result is six single-level cottages that are residential and domestic in design and operation.

Land availability in this part of the world has traditionally led to single-story domestic dwellings, often on quarter-acre blocks. This tradition lends itself to the requirements of good, understandable homey design when approaching a development that will provide for older people with dementia. In this instance, interestingly, the site available had to accommodate all of the six households to function financially. The resultant layout successfully manages this conflict between single-story solution and a necessary density. The juxtaposition of buildings and the design of the external spaces are at once domestic, friendly, and welcoming.

Each of the six cottages is small; five are home for 15 residents each and the sixth is a Special Care Unit for eight people whose Behavioral and Psychological Symptoms of Dementia (BPSD) are so severe that they cannot be supported in other nursing homes. The organization would ideally have liked these cottages to be even smaller, but it has an overriding commitment to providing services to all regardless of ability to pay. This meant that for financial viability, five of the cottages must accommodate 15 residents. The cottages are normalized environments; that is, they are designed to look and operate as ordinary suburban homes, albeit with a larger number of occupants. It could be argued that, possibly because of site constraints, there is more success in achieving the desired outcome of emulating normal suburban homes in the first scheme, the Meadows, than there is in this later incarnation. Certainly the Meadows is surrounded by well manicured gardens as you approach, reminiscent of your own home. There is an external arrival point for the six cottages that attempts to provide a subdued central focal entrance, particularly for visitors. However, arguably, it struggles with the dichotomy of the other six separate main entrances for the six separate cottages and feels lonely.

Staff, together with residents when they wish to participate, prepare all meals in a domestic kitchen in each cottage. Residents use a domestic laundry located in each cottage and hang the wet clothing on the garden clothesline to dry in the sun. The floor plan is straightforward with the kitchen and open dining and living rooms located at the center of the cottage. A corridor of bedrooms emanates from this central social space to either side. The cottages are carpeted throughout, and each living room contains a fireplace and opens onto landscaped gardens. Each cottage has a

FIGURE 2-5 Each cottage has a kitchen where all meals are prepared by care staff and residents. *Courtesy of HammondCare*

FIGURE 2-6 Memory boxes, artwork, and paintwork are used to assist with wayfinding in the short corridors. *Courtesy of HammondCare*

front doorbell that must be used by all visitors and there are no coded entry key pads or swipe cards at these entries.

The design intent is to follow the intuitive language and typology of a single-family residence. As such, the design is only partially successful. An additional design intent is to passively orient, guide, and compensate for the disabilities of residents affected by dementia. However, once an individual is in the central social spaces, that is, the "public" space within the language of "home," that individual has the confusing choice of two nearly identical bedroom corridors. Each, however, leads to a sunroom, which allows external access to sitting areas and ultimately leads back to the living areas. When a resident is leaving their private bedroom, it is clear in what direction they need to travel to the hub of activities, and the distance is not overwhelming.

In an effort to minimize staff intrusions and outside stimuli, the design provides a series of service corridors linking the ends of the cottages. These corridors also serve to successfully enclose the gardens, and have direct access to each cottage at either end.

The floor plan is based on the principles of easy wayfinding and good visual access. A resident who is in the cottage can see where they need or want to go giving them each the choice of interaction with others or privacy. From the kitchen, staff members have visual access down both corridors, across the living spaces, and outdoors to maximize indirect supervision. The design attempts to reduce the sense of sameness in order to assist residents with wayfinding. Each corridor is painted a different color, and each side has a variety of bedroom door handles and light fixtures. Memory boxes beside bedroom doors display photographs and memorabilia that aid residents in recognizing their own rooms. Bedroom doors are never directly opposite each other to prevent residents from walking out of their room and into another across the corridor. Common fixtures have been modified to compensate for the deficits of the least able resident, with electrical switches being large plate rocker switches and lavatory taps being colored red for hot and blue for cold. There is a night light over each resident toilet to guide residents at night. Flooring in the en-suite resident bathrooms is a nonslip vinyl for safety. Other safety features include windows with restricted openings, locked cupboards for chemicals under the kitchen and laundry sinks, as well as locked drawers where sharp kitchen utensils are stored. In addition, there is a master shutoff switch for the electricity and gas. Every area of the cottage is designed with resident safety in mind, but also to be as minimally restrictive as possible.

Southwood's design hides institutional processes. This design solution was pioneered in the Meadows (and originally inspired by California Disneyland's underground service corridors or "utilidors"). Staff corridors are located at each end of the cottage behind a disguised door opened by a security card device. These corridors give unobtrusive egress and access to clean and dirty utility rooms, building management systems, equipment storage, and the administration area. Roof spaces are accessed through stairwells in the staff corridors, negating the need to go through cottages. There is distinct physical and psychological separation between the residents' home and facility processes. As one staff member

FIGURE 2-7 Residents can personalize their rooms with furniture and furnishings. *Courtesy of HammondCare*

FIGURE 2-8 Each cottage has a living room and a television room. *Courtesy of HammondCare*

said, "When I am in the cottage my focus is on the resident, but when I am back of house I can walk quickly, and my attention is on the task at hand."

Community and Belonging

How does the scheme design and operation support this ideal?

Southwood is an interesting case study in that it was part of a resident relocation project. In 2007, HammondCare closed a nursing home constructed in 1972 on the same campus called Sinclair, which provided skilled nursing support to older people with dementia. Originally a mainstream nursing home, in the 1990s, the increasing demand for specialized residential care for people with dementia saw Sinclair converted into a dementia-specific service facility. With its multibed wards, communal bathrooms, "racetrack" design, and limited access to the outdoors, Sinclair was not the ideal environment for people with dementia. At Sinclair's closure, 55 remaining residents were transferred to Southwood. During this period, a research study was conducted to capture the impact of the transition on the residents.[1] The transition was significant as residents were moving from an institutional building design, medical approach, and hierarchical staffing model to domestic-styled cottages with a social model of care and multiskilled, or modified universal staffing. The research study measured the level of resident engagement in Sinclair and, after the move, in Southwood. Engagement was defined as a resident being involved positively in visible activity including use of any aspect of his or her environment. The study found that in Sinclair, 20 percent of residents were engaged. Four months after the opening of Southwood, the level of engagement had risen to 58 percent. The easily accessible gardens with pergolas, birdbaths, and walking paths gave many opportunities for positive interactions. The back-of-house solution had eliminated many distracting stimuli, and Southwood's lighting was a great improvement on Sinclair, with floor-to-ceiling windows in the living and dining rooms at the center of each cottage. The gardens, kitchen, and laundry allowed residents to engage in more meaningful activities than those offered in Sinclair.

The built environment, however, was just one contributing factor. Sinclair had a traditional and hierarchical model of staffing with sharply delineated roles for assistants in nursing, cleaners, kitchen staff, recreational activity officers, and registered nurses. When the Meadows opened in 1995, the organization recognized that the distinctly different building needed a distinctly different staffing approach. A multiskilled, or universal, staffing model was developed and has since been implemented in all of the organization's dementia-specific services. Careworkers, known as Specialized Dementia Carers, assist residents with personal care, prepare cottage meals (often with the assistance of residents), clean the cottage, administer most medications, develop care plans, and lead case reviews. Registered Nurses act as Specialized Dementia Advisors, providing clinical expertise and input on management of behaviors of concern. This team approach requires that staff shift their attention from tasks to holistically caring for people. The study identified that in Sinclair, staff were engaged in work-related tasks 73 percent of the time. In Southwood, this

[1] Ronald Smith, R. Mark Mathews, and Meredith Gresham, "Pre- and Postoccupancy Evaluation of New Dementia Care Cottages," *American Journal of Alzheimer's Disease and other Dementias*, February 2010.

decreased to 59 percent. In Sinclair, staff members were engaged in resident-interactive tasks 16 percent of their time, and in Southwood, this increased to 41 percent.

The most dramatic change between the Meadows and Southwood is the care profile of residents. While the Meadows was designed for people with early- to moderate-stage dementia who were ambulant and able to participate in activities of daily living, the average Southwood resident has moderate to severe dementia, is incontinent, has severely impaired speech, and has either limited or no mobility. Engaging these residents in the social model of care is challenging. While the cottage is designed for resident participation in activities such as peeling potatoes, washing dishes, hanging out clothing to dry, and cleaning the home, activities often need to be modified. This has impacted the environment, to the extent that each design solution was measured against the needs and abilities of the least able resident. For example, the kitchen floor space was increased in Southwood to accommodate an immobile resident in a large Floatation chair. While residents might not be able to make scones with a staff member in the kitchen, they can be in the midst of the activity and appreciate the scents of homemade baking.

Innovation

If the operator pursues a policy of innovation and pursuit of excellence, how is this demonstrated?

The Home is innovative in that it can support older people with dementia to the end of their lives in an environment that is domestic and familiar. Southwood shows that people with high care needs function better in settings that are normalized, where they can feel a sense of control over their lives and are provided with choices as they move through the day's activities. For example, Southwood has a strict restraint-free policy. Families and even some staff initially found this approach very challenging. The organization has taken the position that there are greater risks in using restraints such as risks to dignity, freedom, and even personal safety. The impact of the policy in Southwood was startling. Residents who had come from other nursing homes where they had been restrained and had needed assistance to transfer from bed or chair, began to walk without mobility aids and grew in confidence. Residents who had sat in chairs all day began to water the gardens, mow the lawn, and lie on the grass. The subsequent evaluation found that mortality rates decreased in the new environment, and this finding continues to be supported by the data.[2] One flaw of the cottage design is the sunrooms at the ends of the cottage, which are less visible from the kitchen and central living areas, and it is in these sunrooms where most resident falls have occurred.

Southwood shows innovation in providing services for people whose BPSD means that they are not able to be supported in the other nursing homes, particularly when compared with the "state of the art" in care provision for this aged population segment in the Sydney area.

It must be noted, however, that Southwood represents simply a step forward in the care provision process and cannot be viewed as the "ultimate" solution, particularly as compared with other aged care facilities throughout the world. Southwood operates a Special Care Program that focuses on people who are at risk of having their cognitive conditions addressed by overmedication, physical restraints, or who are at risk of simply being homeless, or at least inappropriately accommodated because their BPSDs are challenging to support. The program at Southwood has two components with the first being a Special Care Unit, Linden Cottage, one of the six cottages on campus. Linden is similar in design to the other cottages except that it is an eight-resident household. Weekly resident case conferencing between the cottage staff, specialist mental health team and family generate and evaluate care strategies. When successful medical, psychiatric, and psychosocial strategies have been utilized and a robust care plan is in place, the resident may move internally to other Southwood Cottages but still be supported as part of the Special Care Program. This phase supports the resident to access permanent mainstream residential aged care in a service model that best meets their needs. A ninth bed in Linden cottage, which remains free, means the resident can immediately return to the cottage should the relocation prove to be unsuccessful. A tenth bedroom is used as a quiet room and is located at the opposite end of the cottage from the other bedrooms. It is designed and located to minimize disturbance to other residents should one resident be significantly distressed.

The organization also demonstrates a commitment to excellence through what it will *not* do. In Australia since the late 1990s, there has been a growing focus on rules and regulations that push aged-care operators to design buildings in a more medical- and staff-efficient model, which is akin to hospital design. These regulations are made with good intentions, but they result in buildings that tend to be hostile to people with dementia. For example, safety regulations required that Southwood has fire extinguishers lining the corridors outside resident bedrooms. Such regulation assumed people with full cognition live in the Home and thus could fully understand

[2] Smith, Mathews, Gresham, p. 272.

FIGURE 2-9 The backyard of Linden Cottage, Southwood's Special Care Unit, where residents hang out the washing and mow the lawn. *Courtesy of HammondCare*

the use and location of these devices. At other sites, it has been the experience of care providers that fire extinguishers are being used for less constructive purposes than putting out fires. The design team borrowed from the Meadows and concealed the extinguishers behind visually unobtrusive cupboards in the hallways, and fire hose reels were included in the outdoor areas to comply with regulations.

Neighborhood Integration

Community Involvement

Is the scheme and service designed to integrate successfully with the local community?

Southwood has a philosophy of "Life Engagement." The care staff learn residents' life history, identify activities meaningful to them, and work creatively with the whole team to make those activities happen. Thus, although the Home has a weekly art class, a music therapist, regular bus outings, and residents may participate in wider Village activities such as the Men's Group and Choir, the emphasis is on connecting residents to their broader community and assisting them to maintain relationships within that broader community. This may mean, for example, enabling a resident to attend his or her regular church or a family event, or working with families to help them connect with the resident with dementia, or it may even be respecting a resident's right *not* to be involved in group activities.

Because of the resident profiles at Southwood, it can be very challenging to initiate and maintain a resident connection with the broader community. In the Meadows, the majority of residents have the capacity to participate in activities outside of the facility, such as going shopping, but in Southwood, a large proportion of the residents suffer from physical frailty along with advanced dementia and are unable to walk. In these circumstances, community is brought into the Home. Both the design of the cottages and model of care are intended to support this community connection. Each cottage has a parlor that can be converted into a spare room in which family members may stay overnight. Families can assist with meal preparation in the cottage and share meals with residents. All bedrooms are private occupancy with en-suite bathrooms, giving residents and families privacy. Connection with community for some Southwood residents may be as simple as enjoying the sunlight pouring through the windows of the living rooms, or having a family member sit in the garden with them. The Special Care Unit is not a restricted or secure cottage. Relatives are encouraged to take residents on outings outside the Southwood campus. However, a critical key element of the cottage model is the emphasis on participation in the daily ebb and flow of the household. This is fundamental to maintaining a meaningful routine as well as a connection to a sense of community, even if it is only participation in the rhythms of the cottage.

Staff and Volunteers

Human Resources

Are policies and designs in place to attract good staff and volunteers?

It is the intention that Southwood's distinct care philosophy, its household design, and universal staffing approach to attract and retain staff who are passionate about working in a noninstitutional care environment. The move from Sinclair to Southwood was an important culture change operation for staff. Staff who had worked in Sinclair were not automatically eligible to work in Southwood because the new model of care was so different. The new model needed staff willing to rethink their entire approach to care and to take on expanded duties such as case management, care planning, cooking, and medication administration. Fifty-eight Sinclair staff completed the recruitment process, and 37 were ultimately successful. The remainder were redeployed to other services elsewhere in the organization or sought work outside the organization.

The new Southwood team embarked on an intensive retraining and culture change program. Care staff received two weeks formal orientation to the new model of care. In the five weeks following the opening of Southwood, workplace trainers gave intensive "on the floor" support

FIGURE 2-10 Walking paths are accessed from the living rooms or sunrooms. Path edges contrast to the path to give definition and guidance, while raised garden beds or bench seats are "destinations." *Courtesy of HammondCare*

to staff in putting it into action. An evaluation phase followed, and the trainers spent three consecutive days in each cottage to scrutinize workplace practices. On the fourth day, they reported back issues, strengths, and areas needing improvement to the care team and manager. Four weeks later, the trainers returned for another three days to evaluate the overall implementation and to trouble-shoot issues still outstanding from the initial visit. This process laid the foundation for an ongoing allegiance among staff to the new model of care. One of the marks of its success is that, 18 months after opening, Southwood maintained a 95 percent retention rate of Sinclair staff who had transitioned to the new service. One caregiver commented: "The institutional style of care in Sinclair gave us a kind of security blanket. You could defer to someone higher up. In Southwood, each cottage is like a family, we have to support one another and everyone has to pull their own weight." A registered nurse said, "It was so hard at first to get used to, but now I wouldn't go back to the old way. This model is so much more stimulating."

Southwood also has a comprehensive ongoing education program in place. Staff regularly attend theme days on topics such as Boundaries and Self-Care, Engaging Residents, and Behavior Management. Staff can complete accredited aged-care training certificates through the organization. Southwood will benefit from a "Positive Aging" Clinical Training Centre, which opened in early 2011 on the Hammondville campus. This school will train 200 nursing, allied health, and medical students each year and give them opportunities to experience the distinctly different model of aged care. There is an expectation that this will inspire interest and career moves toward the aged-care sector and even to taking up roles within the organization's own workforce in its aged-care or subacute services.

Southwood also benefits from the Hammond Village Volunteer Program. Over 100 volunteers provide a range of services for residents including transport, pastoral care, and one-to-one life engagement.

- Direct care hours per resident, per day in Linden Cottage: 7
- Direct care hours per resident per day in other cottages: 4

Environmental Sustainability

ALTERNATIVE ENERGY SOURCES

There is little need for artificial lighting in Southwood's cottages during daylight hours, as the large windows in the communal living spaces and skylights in bedroom hallways provide an abundance of natural light. The glare from the harsh Australian sun is reduced by covered veranda areas and the extensive use of soft, nonglare floor coverings.

WATER CONSERVATION

Rainwater is collected from the cottage roofs, piped to a nearby pond, and then used for garden irrigation.

Southwood has seasonal planting and mostly deciduous trees to allow winter sun in and keep the summer sun out. The vast majority of planting is drought resistant, and irrigation is through a drip system, essentially halving irrigation water use. Laundry wastewater is linked to a graywater recycling program. Ozone technologies are used to sanitize linen in the onsite commercial laundry, significantly reducing chemical, water, gas, and electricity use.

ENERGY CONSERVATION

The cottages have been designed for cross ventilation, minimizing the reliance on air conditioning. Electricity and gas use is metered individually for each cottage, enabling accurate detection of efficiencies and waste.

Outdoor Living

Garden

Does the garden support principles of care?

Each of the Southwood's cottages has a back veranda and landscaped garden. As with the cottage interiors, there is significant attention to detail in the garden. The design is dominated by a walking path, accessed from the living rooms or sunrooms. The path is simple, and leads back into the cottage or to a destination such as a garden bench. Paths are wide enough to accommodate a resident in a wheelchair or two people walking side by side. The path edges contrast with the path itself to give definition and guidance. Raised herb garden beds are tended by residents, and the produce is used in the cottage kitchens. The verandas, with their outdoor settings and barbecues, reflect the value that has been placed on social relationships.

Unfortunately, due to the constraints of the site, the cottage gardens are not large and thus limit usability as well as being somewhat less visually inviting. In the Meadows, the "Y-"shaped design of the cottages give the gardens much greater depth and more faithfully represent the concept of "the quarter-acre block," which is engrained in the psyche of older Australians. This scheme also raises the issue of appropriate fencing for large-scale developments. An open style of fencing has been used to enclose the cottage gardens. This gives transparency both inside and outside the cottages and emphasizes that these are homes, not locked wards.

Security for people with dementia is important, but it is often intrusive and provokes feelings of containment and restraint. Innovative security measures at Linden Cottage, the special care unit, were included in the design. Like all Southwood cottages, the Linden Cottage living and dining spaces open directly onto a patio and fenced landscaped garden of some 120 square meters (1,292 square feet). However, the garden fence has an unlocked gate, leading to a very large, open area including a fenced pond, which adds thousands of square meters to Linden's breakout space. Agitated residents can also walk in this larger fenced area at any time of day or night. The organization's approach to care here is that if a resident wants to get out of any cottage in Southwood, you open the door and let them go. You may walk with them; you may follow, but they have the right not to be restrained.

FIGURE 2-11 All cottages have a private backyard with terrace, barbecue, walking paths, and landscaped gardens. *Courtesy of HammondCare*

Project Data

DESIGN FIRM

Allen, Jack and Cottier Architects
79 Myrtle Street, Chippendale
New South Wales, Australia
www.architectsajc.com

AREAS/SIZES

- Site area: 20,850.0 square meters (224,427.53 square feet)
- Building footprint: 5,116.0 square meters (55,068.17 square feet)
- Total building area: 5,116.0 square meters (55,068.17 square feet)
- Total area per resident: 61.64 square meters (663.47 square feet)

PARKING

As part of Southwood's development, the central campus laundry was relocated, which provided an extra 50 parking spaces between Southwood, the Meadows, and the older facility, Bond House. Fifteen of these open-surface spaces are adjacent to the public entrance to Southwood, while the others are closer to the service entry used by many staff.

COSTS (NOVEMBER 2007)*

- Total building cost: $13,298,499 AUD ($13,145,555 USD)
- Cost per square meter: $2,600 AUD ($2,787 USD)
- Cost per square foot: $241 AUD ($258 USD)
- Investment per resident: $160,223 AUD ($168,573 USD)

RESIDENT AGE

Average age of residents: 84.5 years

RESIDENT PAYER MIX

The Home is available to all, regardless of their ability to pay. All residents pay a monthly fee, which is 85 percent of Australia's age pension. Those who have significantly higher income pay an additional income or asset-tested fee that is remitted to the Australian government. Those who are able to pay a refundable entry loan—known as an "accommodation bond"—do so, but more than 40 percent of the Home's residents are financially disadvantaged and only pay the standard monthly fee.

* Note this was based on 83 residents: There are 84 bedrooms.

Chapter 3

A Study of Wintringham Port Melbourne Hostel

REASONS FOR INCLUSION OF THIS SCHEME

- This scheme is a small hostel for older people who were previously homeless or at risk of homelessness.
- Wintringham's underlying design concept is one of housing rather than aged care, challenging preconceived ideas about "care protection" as opposed to individuality, choice, and freedom.
- While defiantly noninstitutional, this scheme reflects its client group, and emphasizes the familiar rather than the family and is perhaps even deliberately "hostile" to visitors.
- This scheme provides an unconventional approach to residential aged-care design in Australia.

Building Description

Name of Scheme: Wintringham Port Melbourne Hostel
Owner: Wintringham, an independent not-for-profit organization
Address:
Wintringham Port Melbourne Hostel
Swallow Street
Port Melbourne
Melbourne, Australia
Occupied since: July 1996

FIGURE 3-1 The Wintringham community hall or "shed" has a pool table and kitchen and opens onto a garden barbecue area. *Martin Saunders Photography*

FIGURE 3-2 Scheme location. *Courtesy of Pozzoni LLP*

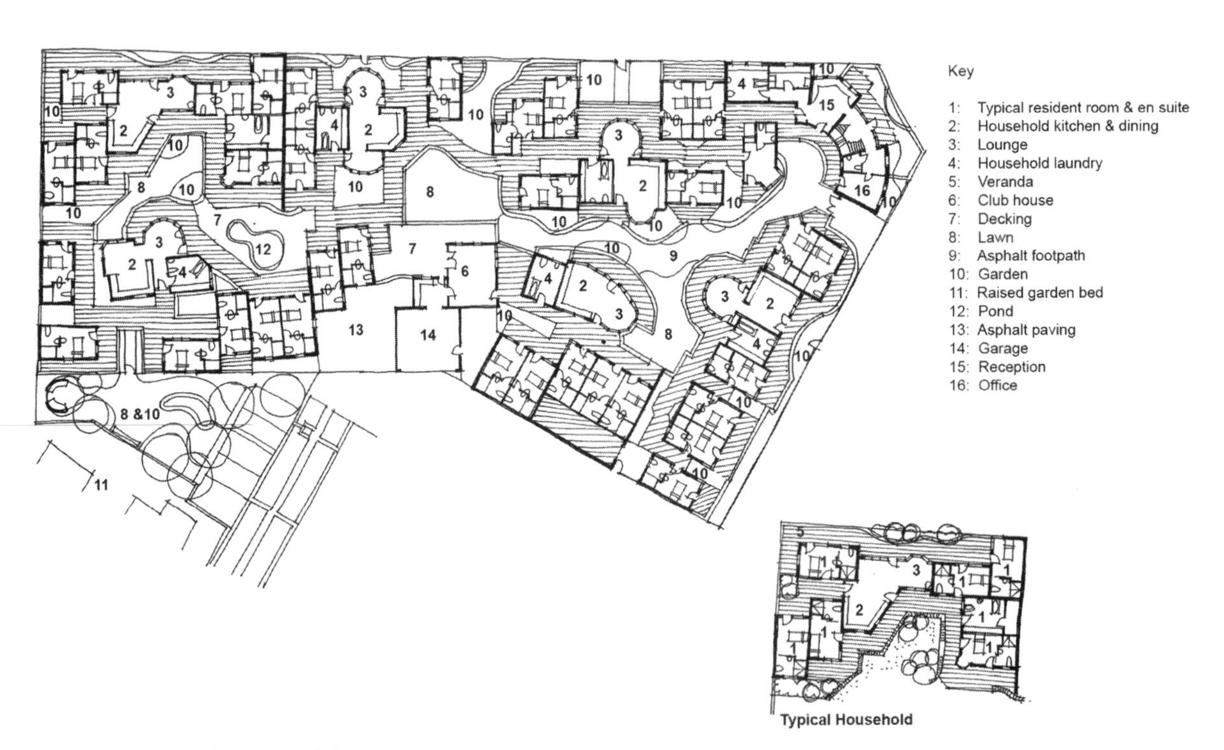

FIGURE 3-3 Site plan. *Courtesy of Pozzoni LLP*

Description of the Type of Community, Including Number of Residents

Wintringham Port Melbourne is a 35-bed hostel for older men and women who were previously homeless or at risk of homelessness through living in inappropriate accommodation. Approximately 85 percent of residents are male, and there is a high incidence of psychological illness, acquired brain injury, social and behavioral issues, and premature aging. In addition, some residents have early-stage dementia. This unique resident profile influences the Hostel's design.

Wintringham Port Melbourne Hostel received a World Habitat Award in 1998. The World Habitat Awards were established in 1985 by the Building and Social Housing Foundation as part of its contribution to the United Nations International Year of Shelter for the Homeless. Two awards are given annually to projects that provide practical and innovative solutions to current housing needs and problems, from the global South as well as the global North.

FIGURE 3-4 The Hostel's winding paths were designed to give the visitor the clear sense of being in someone else's property and to increase resident feeling of control. *Martin Saunders Photography*

Geographics

Vernacular Design

How does the scheme/environment respond to the locality?

The Hostel is located in Port Melbourne, a bayside suburb with a working-class history and strong link to the waterside and seamen's unions. The Hostel was built on disused railway land.

Aesthetically, the Hostel is nearly synonymous with the surrounding streetscape. On approach, it is difficult to distinguish the Hostel from the neighboring single-level Late Victorian terraces. The Hostel has no signage or high fencing, which normalizes its presence. It incorporates surrounding textures such as sandstock brick (an inexpensively made common brick using local materials) and timber verandas, and reflects the scale of nearby houses. Some resident rooms have small verandas fronting onto the street. This provides a space for watching the day pass by and, more importantly, subtly integrates residents into the local community.

Few aged-care homes age gracefully, as commercial construction materials often used are hard and aggressive, and date rather than gain character with the passing of time. In contrast, over the past 15 years, the Hostel's cedar timbers have silvered, lending the building character and settling it into the streetscape.

FIGURE 3-5 Port Melbourne Hostel supports 35 older people who were previously homeless or at risk of homelessness. *Martin Saunders Photography*

Care

Philosophy of Care

What is the operators' philosophy, and how does the building match this philosophy?

Wintringham's mission is to provide dignified, affordable, high-quality care and accommodation to frail men and women who are homeless or at risk of homelessness. To accomplish this mission, in the early 1990s, Wintringham received capital funding assistance from the Australian government to build three hostels specifically for long-term residential support for elderly, frail, homeless men and women. Port Melbourne is the third of these hostels and incorporates what Wintringham learned from the two previous hostel developments. The design brief was to support Wintringham's philosophical ideals of Options, Rights, and Dignity. The physical environment was to be noninstitutional and safe, was to be designed to support residents in order that they could retain control over their lives, to be conducive to individualized care, and to be aesthetically attractive.

The design team first and foremost conceptualized the Hostel as housing, rather than as an aged-care residence. The design team believed that this was an important starting point that unshackled them from preconceived ideas and approaches that tended to embed in the built environment "care protection" rather than the concepts of individuality, freedom, and choice.

The resulting design scheme is a cluster-style accommodation. Each cluster, or "household," is made up of five to seven resident rooms with veranda access to a communal area that has a fully equipped domestic kitchen, combination dining area and television room, and a laundry. Each resident has his or her own fully furnished bungalow-style room with a personal shower and toilet. All rooms have a small veranda or porch, easily accessible by the resident. In addition, there is a community hall or "shed" that has a pool table and a community kitchen that opens out to a garden barbecue area.

While Wintringham Hostel's design could be defined as defiantly noninstitutional, it does not necessarily suggest an atmosphere of some archetypal family environment. Rather, its design is intended to be familiar rather than familial. This distinction was important as many of Wintringham's clients had not experienced a traditional home setting, a fact that became a key concept in the design of the series of Wintringham care facilities. For example, timber has been used extensively. This material is indicative of a familiar and low-key environment and immediately signals a departure from institutionalism. Security is deliberately understated with the low picket fence around the perimeter providing a spatial rather than physical barrier. Resident rooms and communal areas are linked by covered verandas rather than internal corridors, providing simultaneously a sense of separateness and connectivity. The development also sits easily in its streetscape as it reflects the scale and key building elements of the neighboring late Victorian houses that surround the site.

The approach to care in the Hostel reflects a commitment to supporting older people rather than being paternalistic or limiting their choices. Residents have complete freedom to leave the Hostel at any time of day. For this reason, the Hostel is unable to support people with dementia that has progressed beyond a mild level or those whose level of disorientation to time and place presents too great a risk in the open environment. One of the challenges in supporting this group of people is that many have evidence of long-term, well-entrenched patterns of drinking and varying degrees of alcohol-related brain injury. Behavior-modification strategies are, therefore, an important aspect of care planning. The Hostel

FIGURE 3-6 The Hostel is so noninstitutional in design that it is difficult to distinguish it from the surrounding late Victorian terrace houses. *Martin Saunders Photography*

FIGURE 3-7 The Hostel is divided into small households with circulation within and between the households by external paths or covered verandas. *Martin Saunders Photography*

does not aim for "recovery" but rather management of levels of consumption within the parameters of safety, while maintaining the individual's freedom of choice. Alcohol and smoking management strategies are developed and monitored by the household care providers.

Community and Belonging

How does the scheme design and operation support this ideal?

The clustering of households, use of building materials such as cedar and soft sandstock bricks, household kitchens, and communal areas all contribute to the idea of community and belonging by appealing to a domestic aesthetic. However, the distinct resident profile of Wintringham Port Melbourne Hostel impacts on the expression of these ideals. The majority of residents are male, very mobile, and have few clinical care needs. Most have a high level of independence. Some residents use the Hostel as a base and leave in the day or night to spend time in the surrounding community. Others, due to long periods of homelessness or acquired brain injury or psychiatric illness, find it difficult to engage and participate in communal activities. It is, therefore, crucial that

FIGURE 3-8 Each household has five to seven resident bedrooms and a communal area with kitchen, dining room, television room, and laundry room. *Martin Saunders Photography*

residents are given the option to choose their level of interaction with the Hostel community. This is addressed by the way spaces were designed within the Hostel. The Hostel has four, deliberately designed layers of space:

- Space for private, intimate use (bedroom)
- Areas for personal, social contact (bedroom front door and veranda)
- Neighborhood meeting places (lounge room and kitchen dining room)
- Community meeting places (people from different households meeting in the communal shed)

These layers give residents control of their level of engagement and give the possibility for privacy and security. Verandas connect each of the 35 resident bedrooms to one of the six households. These verandas are particularly important as they mark an invisible threshold between the public and private. Residents sitting on the veranda can be aware of what is happening around them, even have a sense of belonging to that activity, without having to be in the midst of the action.

Interestingly, the design brief also included a charge to make the Hostel "hostile" to visitors. Wintringham CEO Bryan Lipmann writes: "We were not trying to discourage residents from having visitors. It was more that we wanted to create an atmosphere which gave the residents power over their area and which clearly stated to everyone else that they were in someone else's home. You can't walk down the internal laneway without feeling that you are on someone else's property, that you are in fact 'running the gauntlet' as you pass by."[1]

[1] "Wintringham: Providing Housing and Care to Elderly Homeless Men and Women in Australia," *The Journal of Long-Term Home Health Care*, 2003.

Innovation

If the operator pursues a policy of innovation and pursuit of excellence, how is this demonstrated?

The operator of the Hostel, Wintringham, is a leading innovator in the provision of services to older people who are homeless. Like all large cities, Melbourne has a significant population of homeless people. Housing options for the homeless have traditionally been limited to rooming houses, cheap hotels, or night shelters. In the 1980s, shelters became de facto homes for the aged homeless unable to access mainstream aged-care services. These shelters were often places of violence, and the shelter operators were unable to provide the specialized care needed.

Wintringham was formed as a charitable organization to advocate for permanent solutions to this issue. A founding principle of Wintringham's advocacy activities and service provision is the belief that this client group is made up of older people who are homeless, rather than homeless who are older. This is more than a semantic distinction; it is intentionally asserting the right of older people who are homeless to access the same standard of care services as any other Australian citizen.

The Port Melbourne Hostel is operated using the same aged-care subsidies that are received by all other Australian aged-care providers from the Australian government, but provides a distinctively different model of care to mainstream services.

Two innovations are particularly important in the Hostel's built environment. First, the design explores the relationship between indoor and outdoor space. The brief requested that there was to be no internal circulation and that the circulation was to be by veranda. The design architect was informed by his previous work in the Antarctic in responding to this challenge. One of the Australian Antarctic Division's main buildings, Casey Base, was originally designed with nearly 200 meters (656.17 feet) of internal walkway linking all parts of the buildings so as to remove the expeditioners from stressful contact with the extreme outdoor climate. The base was closed soon after it was built for a number of reasons, including the psychological effect of the design on the expeditioners. Their disconnection from the external environment led to a "fear of the outside" and heightened sense of isolation and confinement. The forced enclosure was a debilitating experience and diminished their desire to go outside even when the weather was good.[2] The new Casey Base was designed with separate, unconnected buildings that force expeditioners to traverse the external conditions regularly, leading ultimately to improved psychological health.[3]

Port Melbourne Hostel's covered verandas provide essential circulation between spaces and require residents to regularly experience the external environment. The external circulation creates an important social environment and a more natural way for a group of people to live communally and interact socially. The Casey Base example was used by the design team to convince regulatory authorities of the validity of having no internal corridors in the facility.

Second, the Hostel's design is informed by the belief that environments shape behavior and self-image. The finishes of the Hostel are of a high standard, and Wintringham believes that an attractive and dignified space enhances residents' sense of ownership of the Hostel and is positively supportive of their self-image, well-being, and how they view the world. After 15 years of operations, the buildings remain well-maintained and in good order.

Neighborhood Integration

Community Involvement

Is the scheme and service designed to integrate successfully with the local community?

About half of the residents have no contact or support from family and friends and no recorded next of kin. Wintringham estimated that only 15 percent of residents have regular contact with support networks from outside the Hostel. As it is challenging to bring community into the Hostel, the focus is on supporting residents to engage in the broader local community. Residents from homeless backgrounds have not often had the opportunity to access or develop lifelong recreational pursuits due to financial and health constraints. A recreational officer builds a relationship with each resident in order to help the resident identify recreational interests or lifestyle choices and strategies to help the resident overcome barriers to participation in these interests. Residents have been supported to travel both overseas and domestically, go charter boat fishing, attend art exhibitions, attend live blues band concerts, and do simple activities such as going to the pub for a beer. Residents are able to access electric scooters at the Hostel, making it possible for them to participate in community activities independently.

Staff and Volunteers

Human Resources

Are policies and designs in place to attract good staff and volunteers?

Port Melbourne Hostel is staffed by part-time house care providers who are responsible for providing personal care, medication management, emotional and social support, and for preparing meals in the domestic kitchen of each household. The Hostel is staffed around the clock. During the day, the staff/resident ratio is generally one staff member per seven residents, in the evening, one staffer per 15 residents; and at night, two care providers onsite, one of whom is asleep but on call. The Hostel is also supported by a manager and full-time recreational worker.

Wintringham's objective is to recruit staff members who share its values of Options, Rights, and Dignity for older people who are homeless. Staff members need to be not simply competent, but also need to be nonjudgmental and willing to work with clients who may have mental health or behavioral issues. New staff receive a two-day orientation and are teamed with experienced staff for their first shifts. Initiatives such as paid parental leave for men and women, a five-year service award that includes a cash bonus, opportunities for working across other sites and programs, a health and well-being program, access to professional counseling, and flexible leave arrangements are in place to attract and retain staff. The organization has a high retention of staff with many employees receiving 5- and 10-year milestone awards.

[2] *A Psycho-Environmental Evaluation of Australia's Antarctic Rebuilding Program,* Clarke, Wellington & Kong, Melbourne University Programme in Antarctic Studies, Department of Architecture, 1981.

[3] *Redevelopment of Australian Antarctic Station: Australian National Antarctic Research Expeditions Club Statement of Evidence to Parliamentary Standing Committee on Public Works,* Saxton and Sadler, 1987, pp. 305–313.

Volunteers work primarily in the Wintringham recreation program, assisting residents to access the computer and Internet, for example. Volunteers can also assist with maintenance, case management, and supporting the household care providers.

- Direct care hours per day per client: 6 hours/resident/day

Environmental Sustainability

ALTERNATIVE ENERGY SOURCES

The Hostel is designed to maximize natural lighting and reduce reliance on artificial sources. Living areas have a northern aspect, and windows are oriented for maximum solar gain wherever possible. The circulation verandas serve as light shelves by reflecting light into resident bedrooms through their windows.

WATER CONSERVATION

The scheme was designed with low-flow shower heads and dual-flush toilets. Built in 1996 prior to their widely accepted use, there were no other measures such as graywater recycling and water retention tanks, and these are now difficult to retrofit on the site.

ENERGY CONSERVATION

The design uses passive cooling and heating techniques. Windows are not large, thereby reducing solar gain or loss. High ceilings in combination with ceiling fans and substantial insulation accommodate for seasonal weather changes and moderate temperature.

The scheme was designed to have minimum environmental impact. Renewable construction materials that can be recycled at the end of their life cycle have been used. These include such things as plantation timbers for the structure and cladding and lining, cedar for door and window frames, window sills and nosing, and pine for architraves, skirting and flooring. Finger jointed timber was preferred as it makes useable lengths of timber from pieces that would otherwise be discarded. Carpet and particle board were avoided to reduce pollutants and to give greater indoor air quality.

Outdoor Living

Garden

Does the garden support principles of care?

While the buildings are separated by the circulation verandas, the gardens continuously wind through the site, giving a variety of spaces and heightening their prominence. Complying with the design brief, the garden design subtly supports resident independence. For example, retaining walls encircling the courtyards double as garden seating and the balustrades subtly provide continuous handrails to assist passage.

FIGURE 3-9 Verandas, rather than internal corridors, are used for circulation. *Martin Saunders Photography*

FIGURE 3-10 The Hostel has many small gardens and courtyards. The retaining wall around the water feature is also used as garden seating. *Martin Saunders Photography*

Each courtyard has a distinct landscaping theme using plants commonly found in Australian gardens such as tree ferns, banksias, lemon trees, and Japanese maples. The inclusion of a large water feature lends a calming element to the site. A courtyard with a barbecue for resident gatherings facilitates a sense of community. These features also provide cueing for orientation. As with the buildings, the gardens are well maintained to reflect the philosophy of valuing residents and encouraging self-esteem.

Project Data

DESIGN FIRM

Allen Kong Architect Pty Ltd
First Floor, 464 Victoria Street
North Melbourne, Victoria 3051
www.allenkongarchitect.com.au

AREAS/SIZES

- Site area: 3,156.55 square meters (33,976.82 square feet, 0.78 acres)
- Building footprint: 1,295 square meters (13,939.26 square feet)
- Total building area: 1,438 square meters (15,478.50 square feet)

PARKING

3 automobile spaces in surface parking; 2 spaces in a garage

COSTS (1996)

- Total building cost: $2,325,522 AUD ($2,440,868 USD)
- Cost per square meter: $1,617 AUD ($1,697 USD)
- Cost per square foot: $147 AUD ($158 USD)
- Investment per resident: $66,443.49 AUD ($69,739.08 USD)

RESIDENT AGE

Average age of residents: 69 years

RESIDENT PAYER MIX

All residents are financially disadvantaged, having been homeless or at risk of homelessness. They pay a daily fee of 79 percent of the aged pension (lower than the 85 percent of the aged pension which is the maximum standard fee set by the Australian government).

Chapter 4
A Study of Tjilpi Pampaku Ngura

REASONS FOR INCLUSION OF THIS SCHEME

- This scheme is a respite home for Aboriginal Australians that has operated successfully for over a decade in a very remote part of Australia.
- This scheme shows that effective and meaningful consultation with the local community is imperative to achieving appropriate design solutions.
- This scheme addresses the challenges of designing, constructing, and operating health-care services in remote locations, and has applicable lessons for remote services internationally.

Building Description

Name of Scheme: Tjilpi Pampaku Ngura Aged Care Facility

Owner: Nganampa Health Council, an Aboriginal owned and controlled health organization on the A<u>n</u>angu Pitjantjatjara Yankunytjatjara Lands in the far northwest of South Australia

Address:
Pukatja
Ernabella Community
Ernabella
South Australia

Occupied since: October 2000

FIGURE 4-1 Tjilpi Pampaku Ngura Aged Care Facility is a 16-place respite facility for older A<u>n</u>angu in the very remote A<u>n</u>angu Pitjantjatjara Yankunytjatjara Lands. *Courtesy of Kirsty Bennett*

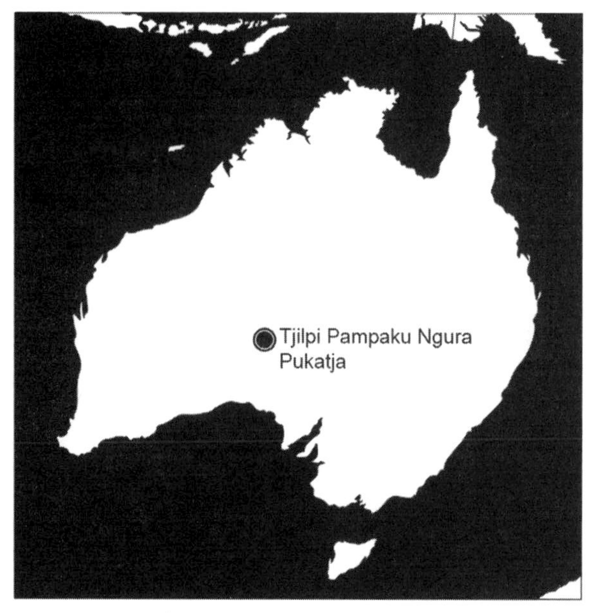

FIGURE 4-2 Scheme location. *Courtesy of Pozzoni LLP*

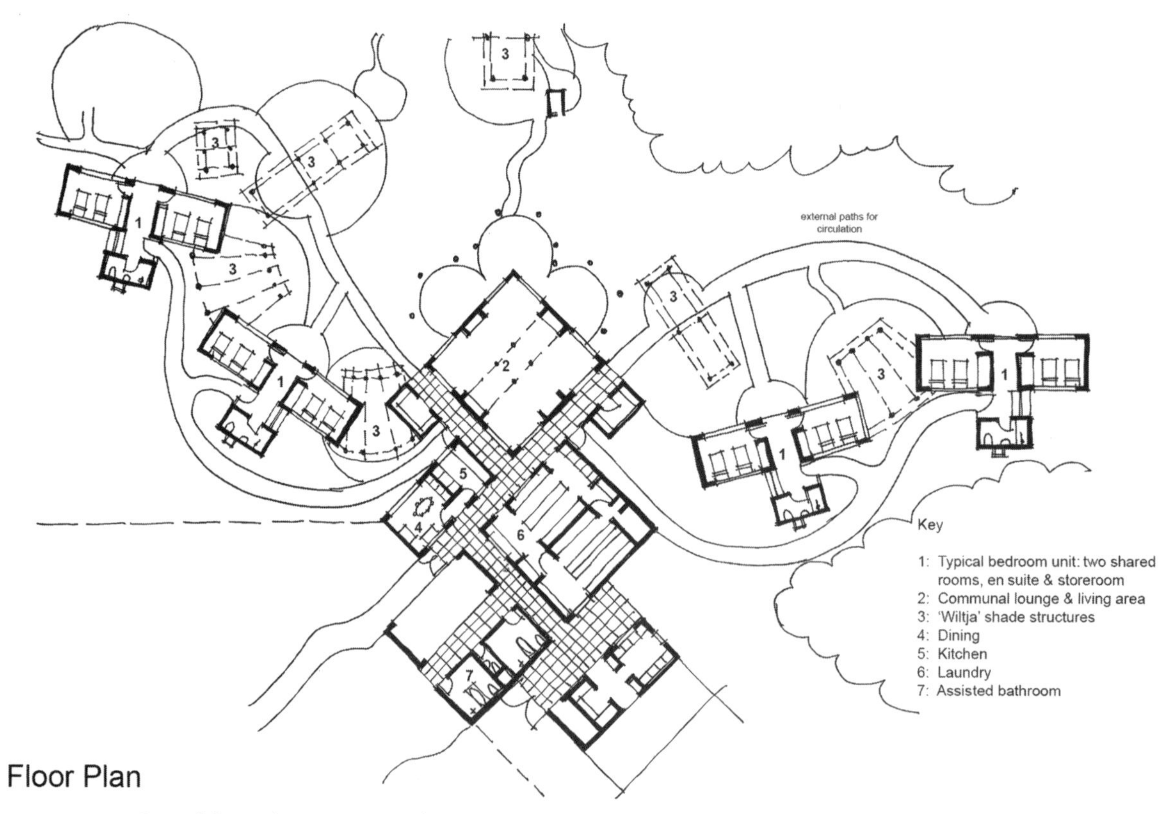

FIGURE 4-3 Ground-floor plan. *Courtesy of Pozzoni LLP*

Description of the Type of Community, Including Number of Residents

In 1981, the South Australian Parliament passed the A<u>n</u>angu Pitjantjatjara Yankunytjatjara Land Rights Act, which recognized the Pitjantjatjara, Yankunytjatjara and Ngaanyatjarra people as the owners of 103,000 square kilometers (39,768.52 square miles) of land in the far northwest of South Australia. This area of land is now known as the A<u>n</u>angu Pitjantjatjara Yankunytjatjara Lands or simply, "the Lands." To provide perspective to the size of the Lands, they account for one-tenth of the total area of the State of South Australia, about the same size as the state of Kentucky in the United States, or three times the size of the Netherlands in Europe. It is an arid environment with low rainfall where the summer average temperature is around 37 degrees Celsius (98 degrees Fahrenheit), but overnight temperatures drop, on average, to 5 degrees Celsius (41 degrees Fahrenheit) during the winter months. The Lands are very remote and entry for non-A<u>n</u>angu is only with the permission of the A<u>n</u>angu and following the issuance of a permit. There are six main communities of A<u>n</u>angu, giving the Lands a total population of approximately 2,500 people. The owners of the Lands generally call themselves A<u>n</u>angu, which means "people."

The Nganampa Health Council provides a range of health-care services across the communities such as child health, women's and men's health, dental programs, patient support services, aged-care services, and health-worker training. The Tjilpi Pampaku Ngura, meaning "old man, old woman," Aged Care Facility is the only aged-care facility in the Lands. It is located in the Pukatja (Ernabella) community, which is in the Musgrave Ranges in South Australia, about 30 kilometers (18.64 miles) south of the Northern Territory border and a 450-kilometer (279.62 miles) drive from Alice

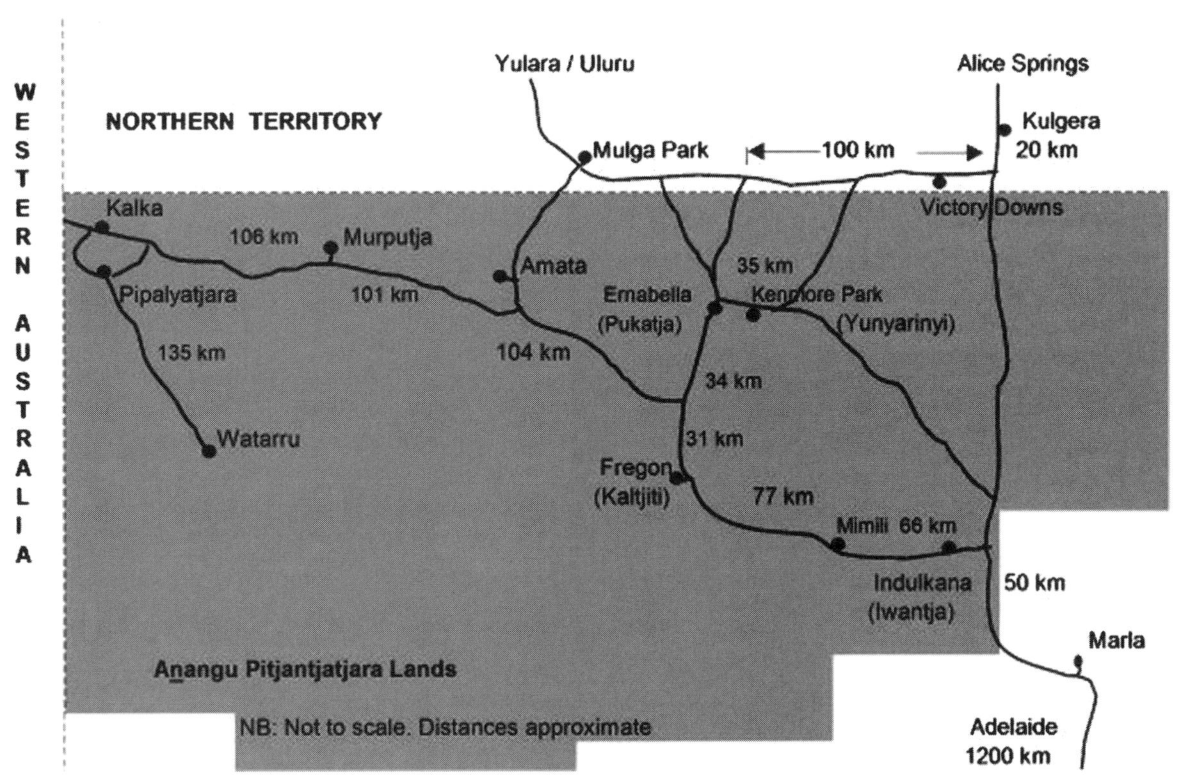

FIGURE 4-4 The A<u>n</u>angu Pitjantjatjara Yankunytjatjara Lands are 103,000 square kilometers (40,000 square miles) in size. They are located in the remote center of Australia.

Springs, the nearest major regional center. Pukatja's population ranges between 600 and 700 people including a number of "Piranpa," or non-Aboriginal people.

Tjilpi Pampaku Ngura provides 16 short-stay beds for older A<u>n</u>angu in need of respite, rehabilitation, and convalescence. Most respite residents come for two to three weeks at a time. Some stay for periods of between six and eight weeks while others may only come for a day or a few nights. Recently, some older A<u>n</u>angu have become permanent residents.

The facility is made up of five separate buildings. There are four small bedroom units and a larger building with some accommodation, a kitchen, laundry, living spaces, and administration. The community also constructed shade structures, called "wiltja," in numerous locations around the site.

Geographics

Vernacular Design

How does the scheme/environment respond to the locality?

In this area of Australia, because of the harshness of the environment and poor water quality, suitable housing is measured by the availability of running potable water, a functioning toilet, and a place to cook. The design of Tjilpi Pampaku Ngura, therefore, has an emphasis on toughness and durability. It has a lightweight steel structure on reinforced concrete slabs. The buildings are encircled by low, compressed-fiber cement sheets for rodent protection. Corrugated iron, an iconic and resilient Australian building material, has been used for roofing. While the facility appears somewhat "box-like" from the exterior, this impression has been reduced on the interior by the use of skylights. Large artworks from the Lands are hung on exterior walls. Much attention was also given to ensuring the buildings were easy to maintain. Fittings are simple, as it is extremely difficult to get equipment serviced and parts can take weeks or months to arrive.

FIGURE 4-5 The facility consists of four small bedroom units and a larger building. Works of Aboriginal art are hung in external corridors. *Courtesy of Kirsty Bennett*

For the community, however, the building itself was not nearly as important as its location and the cultural and spiritual significance that the location holds. While for most non-Aboriginal people home is a structure made of bricks and mortar, for many Aboriginal people, the land itself is considered home. It is viewed as a source of cultural and spiritual nourishment. It shapes life, law, and culture and is the foundation for identity and a sense of belonging. The location and orientation of Tjilpi Pampaku Ngura Aged Care Facility was, therefore, carefully chosen and has magnificent views toward the mountain ranges.

Care

Philosophy of Care

What is the operator's philosophy, and how does the building match this philosophy?

The objective of Tjilpi Pampaku Ngura Aged Care Facility is to enable aged, frail A<u>n</u>angu to remain on the Lands for as long as possible, rather than being hospitalized or admitted to residential care in the regional centers, the nearest of which is at least 450 kilometers (279.62 miles) distance from the Lands. Some older A<u>n</u>angu live with or close to their families, though most live in very basic conditions and with limited access to transport.[1] Tjilpi Pampaku Ngura's respite model is very appropriate for this context, as it allows older A<u>n</u>angu to stay in the Lands by providing essential services and also by giving families respite in order that they have the capacity to continue caring for older people in the community for as long as possible. Older A<u>n</u>angu have central roles in the cultural and spiritual life of the community and are seen as the keepers of culture and

[1] M. Arch, M. Paddy, et al., "Care for Frail Older People on the A<u>n</u>angu Pitjantjatjara Lands," *Issues Facing Australian Families: Human Services Respond,* 3d ed. Edited by W. Weeks and M. Quinn, Longman, Australia, 2000, p. 194.

FIGURE 4-6 The simple bedroom units are linked by covered walkways. For the indigenous residents, the building is not nearly as important as the cultural and spiritual significance of the location on which it stands. *Courtesy of Kirsty Bennett*

knowledge. An enforced move out of the Lands is an enormous loss and sadness to the community as a whole, not just for the individual or family concerned.

Also central to the Nganampa Health Council's philosophy of care is an inclusive, consultative approach. In the eyes of the Aṉangu people and those who assisted in its development, the single most significant reason the facility is a success is the intensive consultation process conducted prior to the construction of the building. For many years, the people on the Lands had been concerned by the inadequacy of services for older people, and there was no formal support available which would allow them to remain on the Lands. That necessary formal support was in Alice Springs, approximately 460 kilometers (285.8 miles) away, meaning that it would be extremely difficult to see their families and land. In response to this void, Nganampa Health Council developed an Aged and Disability Care Program, with the first step being consultation with all the communities on the Lands to establish what kinds of services were needed and where they should be located. An Aged Care Steering Committee was established and met five times during a six-month consultancy period to discuss the outcomes. The older people voiced their opinion strongly that they did not want to live permanently in a nursing home, but would visit it for a while when needed rather than go to Alice Springs. People traveled hundreds of kilometers from all parts of the Lands to participate in these meetings.[2] After it was agreed that a respite model would be established, an architectural model of the building was developed and taken to all the communities for review, and suggestions from these reviews were incorporated into the final design. These reviews and consultations were carried out by a senior member of the Aṉangu community and a non-Aṉangu health professional experienced in aged-care service development so that meaningful answers and correct information could be gathered.

During the consultation process, communities were asked what was important to older Aṉangu. The responses were that older Aṉangu desire the outside, no matter how sick they might be, to lie near fires, be close or near to the ground, take part in singing and dancing and storytelling. They want to travel between the communities on the Lands to maintain family and cultural links or to socialize. They want to go hunting and gathering (even if they can no longer physically hunt), teach young Aṉangu their traditions, have visitors and care for older people, disabled people, and grandchildren. In terms of a physical environment, the Aṉangu want to have shelter from the elements and shady places to sit that have a view of the countryside, a place where they can feel safe and have good food and bush tucker (foods gathered from the land), and a place where they can practice traditional arts. In short, the Aṉangu indicated that any aged-care environment must be designed in a manner that maintains and respects their Lands.

The design process was a collaboration between three architects, each specializing in either Indigenous housing, construction in remote communities, or design for aged care. The resulting scheme responds to the design criteria set out by the communities. The facility consists of four bedroom units spread out across the landscape. They are not connected to each other, but stand alone to give separation that respects the relationships between the Aṉangu and their cultural sensitivities. Each unit has two bedrooms

[2] *Ibid*, p. 195.

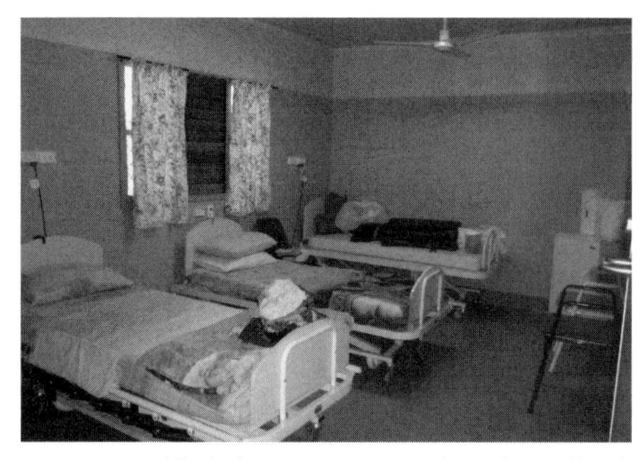

FIGURE 4-7 The bedroom units are simple, with two shared bedrooms, a large en-suite bathroom, and a store. Older A̲nangu value the opportunity to be outside, no matter how sick or frail they may be. *Courtesy of Kirsty Bennett*

FIGURE 4-8 The lounge room is a multipurpose space. Residents are encouraged to continue their involvement in cultural activities, such as painting. Beds are often moved into the lounge room so residents who are very frail or unwell can be in the company of others. *Courtesy of Kirsty Bennett*

and a large en-suite bathroom as well as a store. A path connects the households to a central area, which has social spaces, a shared bathroom and toilets, commercial kitchen, laundry, and administration offices. A separate pathway system links the bedroom units with the service and support areas in order that services and deliveries can be provided discreetly.

Community and Belonging

How does the scheme support these ideals?

It took three years before a location for the facility was chosen on the outskirts of Pukatja. All the A̲nangu communities were in agreement that the chosen location was the best place for the facility. This was the most critical aspect of the scheme's development because the location is fundamental to giving residents a sense of belonging. The location is culturally appropriate and meaningful, particularly as it has views toward a mountain range that is sacred to the A̲nangu. Most of the older A̲nangu live outside most of the time, and buildings are only used for sleeping, for protection during bad weather, to store belongings, or when a person has particularly bad health. Thus the building itself is not as important as the building's location, and it is the land and the country that matter.

The design of the facility enables older A̲nangu to continue to live their preferred way of life and participate in their traditions. For example, fires are very important socially and culturally for the A̲nangu, At Tjilpi Pampaku Ngura, different types of fires are made for specific traditional purposes and are moved during the day to suit the sun and the wind. The fires are enclosed in fire pits to prevent risk of injury.

Innovation

If the operator pursues a policy of innovation and excellence, how is this demonstrated?

Tjilpi Pampaku Ngura shows innovation in meeting the needs of older A̲nangu and in its cultural sensitivity. For example, many older A̲nangu are chronically ill, many have diabetes, and many suffer from vision impairment and diseases associated with eyes, kidneys, and the heart. (Australian Aboriginal health has been one of the vexed challenges for Australian governments for decades: On average, their life expectancy is significantly lower than non-Aboriginal Australians.) At Tjilpi Pampaku Ngura, some clients have extremely limited mobility. The facility was designed to allow beds to be moved outside so that residents would have maximum opportunity to be outside. Paths are wide, and surfaces were selected to allow for mobility aids. En-suite bathrooms are quite large and allow for a high level of assistance if required.

The design team was told that the A̲nangu did not want to bring the outside into the building and that if older A̲nangu wanted to experience the outdoors, they would simply go outside. The purpose of the building then really became a retreat from the outside. Window openings are, therefore, small, and natural light is more limited. Each household has a windbreak nearby so that residents do not have far to go to reach a sheltered space.

The design team was also challenged to reinterpret the principles of aged-care design. A "domestic," or "familiar," environment in this context was one which has easy access to the outdoors taking precedent over home-style furnishings and noninstitutional building design. The need for visual access had to be balanced

FIGURE 4-9 A "wiltja" or shade structure constructed by the community. *Courtesy of Kirsty Bennett*

with the privacy desired by the older Anangu. Circulation between buildings was more important than circulation within the buildings.

While this scheme is notable for its approach to meeting aged-care needs in an Indigenous context, it is just as important to acknowledge its success in meeting the design challenges posed by its remote location. Buildings previously built on the Lands had been built onsite, with constructors living for weeks or months at a time in the community. This was not the ideal solution as Nganampa Health Council had difficulty attracting quality builders, and onsite inspections are costly. Tjilpi Pampaku Ngura was therefore designed as a modular transportable system that could be built in a major center under controlled factory conditions to allow for a very short construction period on the Lands. This was one of the first ventures using this delivery method and the installation process. The scheme was eventually constructed onsite, with a building company spending many months in the community. Although the construction method changed, it was still felt that the modular design was appropriate, and modular transportable systems have become the norm for building in remote areas such as Pukatja and indeed, across remote Australia.

Neighborhood Integration

Community Involvement

Is the scheme and service designed to integrate successfully with the local community?

The respite facility's inclusion supports the strong Anangu value of relationships and family by enabling residents to remain for as long as possible on the Lands. It also provides a means for the passing of knowledge

FIGURE 4-10 Different views of the landscape, rather than furniture or color, are used for wayfinding. *Courtesy of Kirsty Bennett*

held by seniors to another generation and maintains traditional family roles. Aside from providing respite, the facility also offers bathing and laundry, meals, firewood collection for residents, and clinical services that help sustain older Anangu on the Lands.

Families are welcome to visit the facility and, as some camp, access to basic services such as water, toilets, and areas for lighting fires is provided. Families are not permitted to enter bedrooms as they are considered to be the private and secure place for residents. To ensure it is a place of rest for the residents, the service is distanced from the community and is located on the outskirts of Pukatja separated with a high fence from the site. This is seen by the Anangu as a positive aspect of the design as it keeps other people from moving into the older Anangu's place rather than a device for keeping the older Anangu in. Appropriate fencing has also increasingly been an important issue due to the high care needs of residents, including dementia care and support needs.

Staffing and Volunteers

Human Resources

Are policies and designs in place to attract good staff and volunteers?

FIGURE 4-11 Circulation around the facility is by covered walkways. Paths are wide to allow for mobility aids and relocation of beds. *Courtesy of Kirsty Bennett*

Tjilpi Pampaku Ngura has 15 staff members, 10 of whom are Aṉangu. It is staffed 24 hours a day and provides an average of 3.5 staffing hours/client/day. The Aṉangu staff play an important role in the care of respite residents as they understand the language and cultural sensitivities around gender, authority, and relationship. They are encouraged to spend time with residents, to hear their stories, and develop relationships so that the older Aṉangu know they are valued. Non-Aṉangu staff receive training in Aṉangu history, the various Aṉangu organizations and their roles, good Aṉangu manners, basic Pitjantjatjara vocabulary, and an introduction to bush foods and Aṉangu traditional lifestyles.

It is exceptionally difficult to attract, train, and retain staff in such a remote location. One of the benefits the facility has brought to the community is the opportunity for training. During startup and over the past decade, programs have been developed in partnership with South Australian tertiary colleges to develop skilled workers within the community. Despite challenges such as illiteracy, staff have received nationally recognized qualifications in aged care. However, there are many barriers to retaining staff and maintaining a consistent team. The Aṉangu culture is highly mobile, and people often move between the communities to attend to family issues, making it difficult to sustain staff continuity. The remote location also poses challenges, with the availability and quality of housing often being poor and the lack of educational opportunities.

In recent years, the facility has increasingly focused on equipping itself to provide palliative care to older Aṉangu to prevent transfers to hospitals off the Lands. A Program of Experience in the Palliative Approach was delivered to all staff. Some members of the team have visited palliative care centers elsewhere to learn best practice methods in caring for terminally ill residents.

Environmental Sustainability

For this scheme, environmental sustainability takes on a whole new meaning compared to an urban service. The challenges posed by the arid environment and remote location also meant it was difficult to include features for environmental sustainability. Design solutions can have implications on the wider community. For example, to reduce reliance on air conditioning in the clinics, an evaporative cooling system using rainwater runoff was trialed at one of Nganampa Health Council's clinics. While it worked as a cooling system, there were issues with ensuring children did not swim in the runoff tanks and the Council had to return to using traditional methods of air conditioning.

Because of the desert setting and the extreme temperatures, the design team had a greater focus on making the building operationally sustainable in the long term. A good deal of attention was given to ensuring that there were durable solutions for water supply, sewage disposal, and power supply. Hot water fixtures and fittings are of industrial quality to prevent corrosion as there is a high level of dissolved salts in the water. Some areas continue to be challenges such as reliable electrical supply. While an emergency generator would seem a logical solution, the likelihood that the generator would work in the event of power failure is low due to the difficulty of maintaining it in this remote location. The fact that the building still stands and is fully operational 10 years from its opening in such a challenging environment is an achievement in sustainability.

Outdoor Living

Garden

Does the garden support principles of care?

Despite the challenge of planting and maintaining a garden in the desert, the facility has large eucalyptus trees for shade, and a water irrigation system was developed for low-level planting around the households.

Project Data

DESIGN FIRMS

Adrian Welke, Troppo Architects
6 Stack Street
Fremantle, WA 6060
Australia
www.troppoarchitects.com.au
Kirsty Bennett, KLCK Architects
68 Oxford Street
P.O. Box 1092 Collingwood
Melbourne Victoria, 03066
Australia
Paul Pholeros, Architect
Australia

AREAS/SIZES

- Site area: This facility is situated within a remote desert environment of some 40,000 square miles (103,600 square kilometers). While the location is vital to the Indigenous community, the site size is not available.
- Building footprint: 552 square meters (5,942 square feet)
- Total building area: 552 square meters (5,942 square feet)

PARKING

In a desert environment 40,000 square miles in size, parking spaces are innumerable.

COSTS (AS OF 2000)

- Total building cost: $2,000,000 AUD ($2,129,282 USD)
- Cost per square meters: $3,623 AUD ($3,884 USD)
- Cost per square foot: $337 AUD ($361 USD)
- Investment per resident: $250,000 AUD ($266,160 USD)

RESIDENT AGE

The majority of residents are between the ages of 60 and 80 years old. There are occasionally older residents, the oldest being 99 years.

RESIDENT PAYER MIX

Tjilpi Pampaku Ngura is funded by the Australian government and South Australian state government through a special funding scheme for health services in rural and remote communities.

Chapter 5

A Study of Brightwater Onslow Gardens

REASON FOR INCLUSION OF THIS SCHEME

- Onslow Gardens is an expression of the philosophy of valued roles for people who are at risk of being devalued in society.
- The scheme uses universal design principles to create an enabling environment.
- The scheme shows the challenges faced to meet very specific care needs that may later change.
- The facility is a case study in the challenge of culture change.

Building Description

Name of scheme: Onslow Gardens

Owner: Brightwater Care Group, a large charitable provider on the west coast of Australia, offering residential, in-home, and advocacy services for people of all ages. It specializes in providing dementia-specific care, and supporting people with special needs such as acquired brain injury, Huntington's disease, and young people with a range of disabilities.

Address:
Hamersley Road
Subiaco
Western Australia

Occupied since: 2001

FIGURE 5-1 Heritage features of the surrounding neighborhood such as bay windows, gables, and shingle cladding have been incorporated into the Onslow Garden's design.
Courtesy of Brian Kidd

FIGURE 5-2 Scheme location. *Courtesy of Pozzoni LLP*

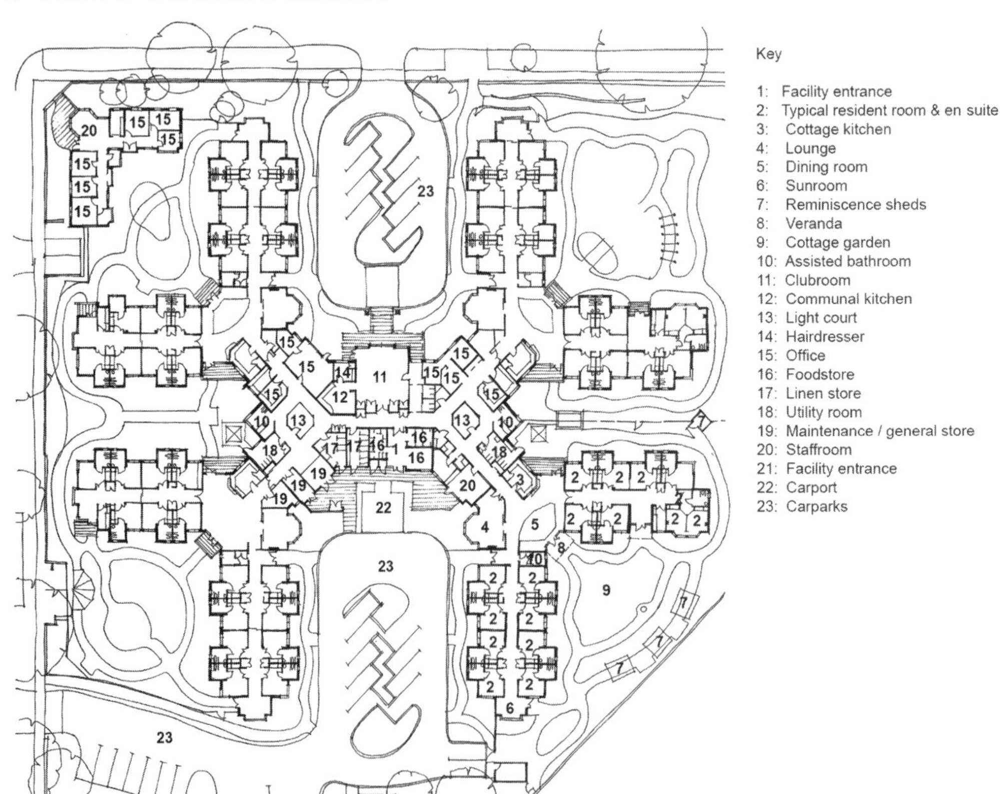

FIGURE 5-3 Site groundfloor plan. *Courtesy of Pozzoni LLP*

Description of the Type of Community, Including Number of Residents

Onslow Gardens accommodates 60 nursing home residents across four houses. The intent of the home is to support people with both high and extremely diverse care needs who have difficulty accessing residential aged care due to the complexity of care required. The scheme comprises four houses or "cottages" with shared social areas. All the cottages support people with a variety of care needs. Some residents are young with acquired brain injuries or disabilities, others have very high care needs due to dementia, Parkinson's disease, psychiatric issues, or physical conditions such as amputations or bariatric care. Some residents are frail and aged. Ninety-three percent of residents have a physical condition and 38 percent cognitive decline (including dementia, disorientation, and memory loss). Sixty-one percent of residents require wheelchair and hoist assistance.

Geographics

Vernacular Design

How does the scheme/environment respond to the locality?

Onslow Gardens is situated in a heritage precinct. The intention of the scheme is to blend into the local residential context, thereby ensuring that residents are not "set apart" as being different. Although the four cottages are large, the single-story modular design, bays, and roofscape minimizes their visual impact and reduces the overall scale. Car parking is distributed around the site to reduce the institutional overtone. The architecture of the surrounding heritage houses has been incorporated into Onslow Gardens with details such as bay windows, gables, clay roofing tiles, and shingle cladding. The exterior brick face of the houses is varied, as are the roof tiles and gable details, to increase visual interest and reduce scale. Each cottage has its own front door, a street address, a street number on its letter box, and unobtrusive signage. The public telephone box, postal box, and bus stop located on the footpath outside the home add to its domestic character.

Care

Philosophy of Care

What is the operators' philosophy, and how does the building match this philosophy?

The design of Onslow Gardens was strongly influenced by the philosophy of "social role valorization," formulated by Wolf Wolfensberger in the 1980s. The

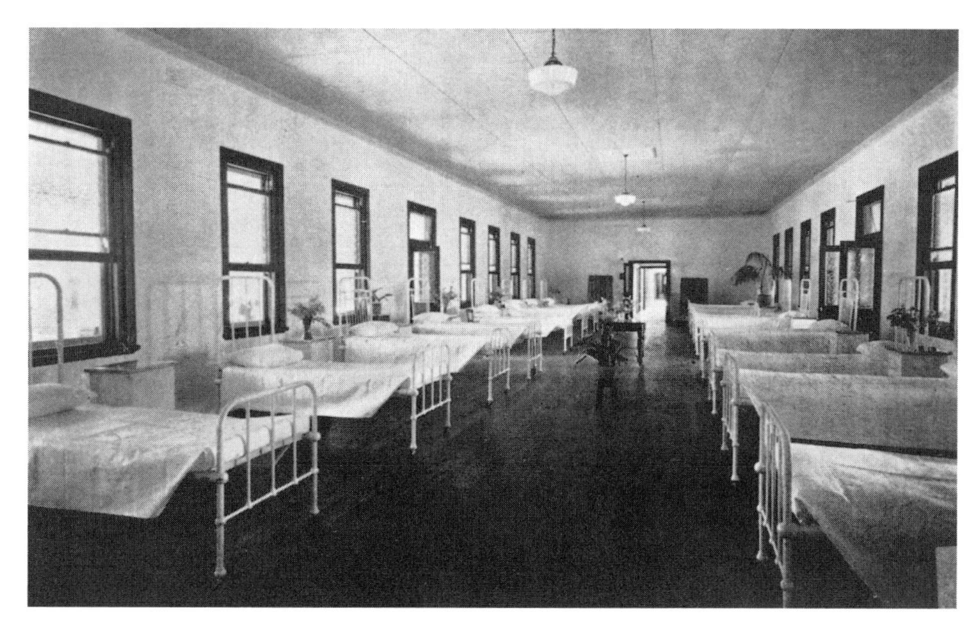

FIGURE 5-4 Onslow Gardens replaced "The Homes of Peace for the Incurable and Dying" which had long, barrack-like wards. *Used with permission of Brightwater*

goal of social role valorization is to create, support, or recognize socially valued roles for people who are devalued or at risk of being devalued in society. Wolfensberger argues that people who are devalued in a society are more likely to be subjected to systematic patterns of rejection by the community, be cast into negative social roles, or be kept at a social or physical distance. Older people who are frail, disabled, or have cognitive impairments and young people with disabilities are at risk of falling into this category. Social role valorization emphasizes the importance of enhancing people's social image in the eyes of others and enabling their access to good things such as home, family, dignity, respect, a sense of belonging, a voice in the community, opportunity to participate, work and self-support, and a normative place to live.

The Onslow Gardens site has been occupied by the Brightwater organization (originally known as "Homes of Peace") since 1901. The original building on the site, known as "The Homes of Peace for the Incurable and Dying," supported people in need of hospice and palliative care. In its later years, it also supported younger people with disabilities, the frail aged, and people of all ages with high care needs; at one point the youngest resident was three years old.

After World War II, the Homes expanded rapidly and eventually accommodated up to 270 residents in a complex of barrack-like wards, with up to six residents per room. Social spaces were limited to wide verandas. The facility was fully serviced onsite, with its own commercial kitchen, laundry, engineering workshops, staff quarters, and an administration wing. The model of care was a decidedly medical one; for example, there was a strongly hierarchical staffing model and residents were referred to as patients. It was an imposing complex in the streetscape and its institutional character was reflected in both the built form and in the delivery of care.

FIGURE 5-5 A 1960s aerial view of the original home, which was demolished at the end of the 1990s to make way for Onslow Gardens. *Used with permission of Brightwater*

When the Homes of Peace was demolished in the 1990s, the organization's intention was to continue caring for people with similar high care needs, but to reflect a more contemporary approach of engaging in a social, rather than institutional, model of care and thus an ideal opportunity to experiment with the philosophy of social role valorization.

The client brief to the architect instructed him to transform the site into a scheme that integrated residents into the local community to improve their self-esteem and enhance positive perceptions by the wider community of people with disabilities and impairments.

The scheme resulted in four cottages designed as domestic homes. Each home accommodates 15 residents and is self-sufficient with its own front door, kitchen, laundry, and large garden. The majority of rooms are single occupancy with an en-suite bath. The cottages are linked by central, shared social areas such as a club room, hair salon, and visitors kitchen. The scheme is visually integrated into the streetscape, as it mirrors the scale and design of neighboring residential homes. Located at the intersection of two streets, the potential for residents to interact with the community through two frontages is maximized.

In more recent years, Brightwater has emphasized the philosophy of Person Centered Care, a philosophy developed by Tom Kitwood[1] and later, Dawn Brooker,[2] which has been very influential in the Australian and United Kingdoms' aged-care sectors.

Person-centered care is the concept of an interpersonal relationship between the caregiver and care receiver and is designed to create a cultural shift from control and "doing *for* the person" to partnership and "doing *with* the person." In services where there has historically been a medical model, this "culture change" has universally been a challenge for staff, including the Onslow Gardens staff. The benefits of having a new physical building is sadly limited if there is no mind shift in the management of the service.

It was originally intended that each of the four cottages at Onslow Gardens would have clearly defined

[1] Tom Kitwood, "Towards a Theory of Dementia Care: The Interpersonal Process," *Aging and Society,* 13, pp. 51–67, 1993.

[2] Dawn Brooker, *Person-Centered Dementia Care: Making Services Better,* (2007). Jessica Kingsley Publishers: London.

FIGURE 5-6 The club house at Onslow Garden. *Courtesy of Brightwater*

FIGURE 5-7 The cottage dining rooms are sparsely furnished to allow for ease of movement for residents in wheelchairs. *Courtesy of Brightwater*

resident profiles: one for young people with physical disabilities or acquired brain injuries; one for people rehabilitating after surgery; one for people with dementia; and one cottage for the frail aged. Over the service's 10-year period of operations, these cottage profiles have shifted to such an extent that there is now no distinction between the four cottages. This has made design features that were originally incorporated for a specific resident group, such as those rehabilitating, redundant. Additionally, some residents may not feel comfortable with the current resident profile mix in the cottages. For example, a young person with an acquired brain injury may feel uncomfortable sharing the cottage with a frail aged person with dementia.

Community and Belonging

How does the scheme design and operation support this ideal?

The small cottages of 15 residents support the ideal of living as a community. As approximately one-third of residents have cognitive decline including dementia, memory loss, and disorientation, the small size of the cottages reduces the potential for confusion and distress. It also creates the potential for residents to develop relationships within each cottage. The design of the scheme is flexible, allowing the cottages to operate entirely self-sufficiently, or interconnected with the other cottages. Doors adjacent to the kitchen in each cottage lead into the central communal social areas and from there, residents can visit the other cottages. Two cottages are interlinked on the exterior by garden paths, allowing easy travel between them.

The attention to detail in the central communal areas also reflects a focus on creating the potential for developing a sense of community and strengthening relationships. There is a kitchen with a large table adjacent to the hair salon, providing a social space for residents and families to converse while waiting for a hair appointment. These social areas are within the building envelope for staff security at night and ease of access between cottages. While perhaps necessary and practical, it was a challenge to make these spaces pleasant and welcoming. The architectural solution was to raise the ceiling heights, creating a feeling of space, and using two light wells to flood the interior space with natural light, creating a space more conducive to socializing.

The move from the old home to Onslow Gardens did have a transformative effect on the residents' sense of belonging. Previously residents had shared bedrooms with up to five other residents. At Onslow Gardens, the majority of rooms are single occupancy, providing the opportunity for residents to personalize their own space and to have privacy when they want it. Care staff knock before entering resident rooms. This seemingly small action has affirmed resident ownership and created a culture of respect. Onslow Gardens originally had two shared rooms, one designed specifically for a younger disabled man who was so used to institutional communal living that he did not want to be alone. At the time of this writing, the management team was discussing options for converting these rooms to single occupancy, which highlights the difficulty of designing for specific individual residents and their needs. During the design phase, there was also pressure from staff who were familiar with the older building, for more shared rooms to be included in the design. The architect compromised, including eight movable walls between 16 bedrooms. These walls have never been used, as residents have preferred the privacy of their own rooms. This issue reflects the challenge of changing cultures and shifting staff perception of resident needs when redesigning the physical environment.

In this scheme, providing appropriate seating for residents is an important factor in encouraging residents to engage in social activities and communication. Brightwater offers a specialist seating and equipment clinic, and much attention has been given to Onslow Gardens residents. Brightwater senior manager, Virginia Moore, said,

FIGURE 5-8 A resident bedroom at Onslow Gardens. *Courtesy of Brightwater*

FIGURE 5-9 Each cottage has a living room. *Courtesy of Brightwater*

"inappropriate seating for people with impaired mobility is energy consuming. Their focus is constantly on balance and maintaining an upright position. When you provide appropriately tailored seating, their energy can be redirected to engaging in the community." The majority of residents use specialized wheelchairs rather than the large ambulatory care chairs often used in a typical nursing home environment. This again reflects a commitment to social role valorization, as it is normal to see someone in a wheelchair in the wider community, whereas ambulatory care chairs immediately suggest a medical environment and stigmatize the person as being "different."

Innovation

If the operator pursues a policy of innovation and pursuit of excellence, how is this demonstrated?

The design principles underlying Onslow Gardens may be commonplace today, but in 2001 they were innovative. Moreover, the fact that four cottages accommodate a very eclectic resident profile—residents with dementia, younger people with acquired brain injury, older people with very high physical or psychiatric needs—is supportive of the contention that good design is capable of supporting a broad spectrum of needs.

The built environment is prosthetic, compensating for individuals' impairments. The design uses dementia-friendly design principles. For example, the "V" shape of the cottages maximizes visual access for residents and staff. Coming out of their bedrooms, residents can see down the short length of corridor to the kitchen and, in most instances, to an alcove at the end of the corridor. A staff member in the kitchen has visual access down the bedroom corridors and out to the garden areas, creating nonobtrusive surveillance. There is a subtle language of color, texture, and use of objects to assist with orientation. Bedroom doors are different colors and have a variety of paneling on the doors themselves. The communal social areas, the two light wells, have different sculptural or furniture arrangements and act as markers to independent wayfinding. The cottages are designed as domestic homes to promote a sense of familiarity, belonging, and enjoyment. The lounges have fireplaces and large bay windows. Each cottage has a kitchen where residents can assist with meal preparation if they choose to do so.

However, one of the challenges in caring for residents with such diverse care issues is the furniture layout. As 61 percent of the residents use specialized wheelchairs, the cottages are sparsely furnished. For example, there are few if any chairs around dining tables to enable residents to use their wheelchairs during meal times. This impacts the domestic quality of the cottages and poses a challenge to rethink aesthetics in such a specialized care environment. Strongly colored vinyl flooring has been used in the central living and dining areas, which, while practical, has institutional overtones and is at odds with the design's intent to communicate a sense of home and domesticity.

Each of the cottages has essentially the same layout. However, in some circumstances specific features were built into the cottages to address perceived care needs. For instance, one cottage was originally intended to support people in need of slow rehabilitation due to illness or surgery. Steps were built into the garden path, as a balance and dexterity exercise to accommodate these residents. The originally intended resident profile never occurred in this cottage, and the steps are now a significant barrier for the current residents, the majority of whom use wheelchairs or have compromised mobility. Once again, this demonstrates the challenge of designing for specific-needs groups: A design element intended for a specific group has become a design impediment to the needs of current residents.

Neighborhood Integration

Community Involvement

Is the scheme and service designed to integrate successfully with the local community?

The site was originally fully bounded on all four sides by roads, one of which is a particularly busy main street. The original Homes of Peace was a large institutional complex spreading over 2.5 hectares (6.2 acres). In order to reduce the scale of the new home, it was decided that Onslow Gardens would support only 60 residents on a reduced site footprint of approximately 1.12 hectares (2.77 acres). Onslow Gardens was intentionally situated at the corner closest to the neighboring community to maximize opportunities for integration into the local community. The remainder of the site, approximately 1.4 hectares (3.46 acres), was sold off for private development, and is now occupied by 35 up-scale houses. Therefore, Onslow Gardens is now surrounded by residential houses, blending into the community that has sprung up around it.

The cottage, in which the majority of young people with acquired brain injury or disabilities live, known as Tinglewood, is well integrated into the local community. The cottage has a street frontage, a separate entrance, back garden, and summer house for socializing with family and friends, and the lounge bay windows look directly onto the local football oval. While only two residents in this 15-resident cottage are independently mobile, the majority regularly take advantage of the nearby cafés, shops, and library using specialized wheelchairs and wheelchair taxis.

Staff and Volunteers

Human Resources

Are policies and designs in place to attract good staff and volunteers?

Two-thirds of the current staff at Onslow Gardens originally worked in the Homes of Peace. With such a different building and model of care, the challenge was for staff members to rethink how they worked together. For example, the staff formed teams attached to each cottage in order to reduce the number of people residents would have to relate to each day. For the first 10 years of operation, Onslow Gardens had a traditional approach to staffing. However, at the time of this writing in 2011, it is moving to a multiskilled staffing model to recognize the diverse roles care staff perform and to support the focus on person-centered care.

Onslow Gardens has a large Allied Health team based on the site with a physical therapist, occupational therapist, speech pathologist, and therapy assistants. There is also a social worker available due to the complexity of resident issues.

There is a very active group of 20 volunteers at the home who assist with outings, sensory programs, and resident personal care. Allied Health supports the volunteer team, with the speech pathologist providing training in areas such as feeding residents with swallowing disorders, and the occupational therapist giving training in working and communicating with people with dementia.

- Direct care hours per day per client: 4.5

Environmental Sustainability

ALTERNATIVE ENERGY SOURCES

Onslow Gardens uses solar heating with electric booster support. A building management system is used to control and monitor all systems. Natural light has been maximized with the use of sky lights in bedroom corridors and light wells in the communal social areas creatively bring natural light into what would otherwise be very dark spaces.

WATER CONSERVATION

Water-saver shower heads and a reticulation bore for garden watering were incorporated into the design. As the home is situated in an area prone to bush fires, legislation required a 100,000 liter (26,417 gallon) water storage tank for fire fighting.

ENERGY CONSERVATION

Passive design principles such as cottage orientation to the east and west, window hood (fixed window shade structures) sun controls, and roof and ceiling insulation reduce the need for artificial heating and cooling. Low-energy lights have also been used.

FIGURE 5-10 All four cottages have a large garden or back garden with wide paths leading back into the cottage.
Courtesy of Brightwater

Outdoor Living

Garden

Does the garden support principles of care?

Each cottage has its own large garden with distinct path design. The paths always lead back to a cottage and there are no dead ends, which could lead to disorientation and frustration. The cottage for people with dementia has three sheds in the gardens and residents are encouraged to rummage through their contents for reminiscence. One shed contains objects from an old Australian country kitchen, one contains an early twentieth-century wash trough, and another contains a variety of trinkets from the same era. These items help to provoke interest, memories, and conversation. Tinglewood house has a pond with an inclined bridge, to give the garden for young people an element of delight, exploration, and stimulation. Some cottages have limited access to the outdoors in inclement weather, as they lack covered patios and walkways.

Project Data

DESIGN FIRM

Kidd and Povey Pty Ltd
7 Monger Street
Perth, WA 6000
Australia
www.kiddandpovey.com

AREA/SIZES

- Site area: 11,199 square meters (120,545 square feet, 2.77 acres)
- Building footprint: 3,543 square meters (38,136.53 square feet)
- Total building area: 3,543 square meters (38,136.53 square feet)
- Total area per resident: 59 square meters/resident (635.61 square feet)

PARKING

Open surface lot providing 30 parking spaces

COSTS (MAY 2000)

- Total building cost: $4,927,900 AUD ($5,186,163 USD)
- Cost per square meter: $1,391 AUD ($1,464 USD)
- Cost per square foot: $127 AUD ($136 USD)
- Investment per resident: $82,131 AUD ($86,086 USD)

RESIDENT AGE

Average age of residents: 72 years

RESIDENT PAYER MIX

All residents pay a monthly fee, which is 85 percent of Australia's age pension. Those who have significantly higher income pay an additional income or asset-tested fee, which is remitted to the Australian government by the service provider, which equals 95 percent of Australian aged-care services.

Part II

Japanese Schemes

Chapter 6

A Study of Akasaki-cho Day Care (Kikuta)

Authors' Note *In February 2009, four of this book's authors visited Ofunato, located in the Iwate Prefecture along the coast in northeastern Japan. We toured several aged-care facilities including Himawari and Kikuta, and following an exhausting two days, we were afforded peerless Japanese hospitality at a banquet held at Kikuta, the historic home repurposed as an elderly day care for community residents. The banquet was prepared and served by staff, working beyond their usual hours to make us feel welcome and comfortable. It was an unforgettable time of camaraderie, lively discussion, and selfless hospitality.*

On March 11, 2011, at approximately 2:00 PM local time, a magnitude 9.0 earthquake occurred with an epicenter in the Pacific Ocean not far from Ofunato. Iwate Prefecture was the hardest hit area of Japan by this record-setting temblor. While such a destructive earthquake would be damaging enough, there was a following tsunami that was even more devastating to Ofunato and the surrounding area. This tsunami completely eradicated the historic home and day care that was Kikuta, leaving only the gate posts as a reminder of the beautiful home and wonderful work that was being done in that home. No clients were in the structure, but they were nonetheless quite hurt by its destruction. That pain is felt around the world and most acutely by those of us who had the opportunity to share, at least in a small way, this now lost built environment.

REASONS FOR INCLUSION OF THIS SCHEME

- Kikuta is a century-old traditional Japanese house used as an adult day care center for people with dementia.
- The facility is a day-care center that is driven by four core philosophical concepts: community, lifestyle, cultural tradition, and memories of a former time.
- The facility's small size and traditional design challenges the inherent assumptions of many purpose-built adult day-care centers.

FIGURE 6-1 Akasaki-cho (Kikuta) Day Care serves older people in the local community with dementia. It was built as a traditional Japanese home over a century ago, and many of its original features were restored. *Courtesy of Stephen Judd*

- Design features of a traditional Japanese home have been deliberately retained to enhance familiarity for the clients.

Building Description

Name of Scheme: "Kikuta" (also known as Akasaki-cho Day Service Center) is the name of the house and the name of the local village doctor whose house it once was.

Owner: Dr Noriya Kikawada, President, Social Welfare Foundation Tenjin-kai

Address:
196 Yamamagoe,
Ofunato-cho
Ofunato-shi, Iwate
Japan 022–0002

Occupied since: April 2005

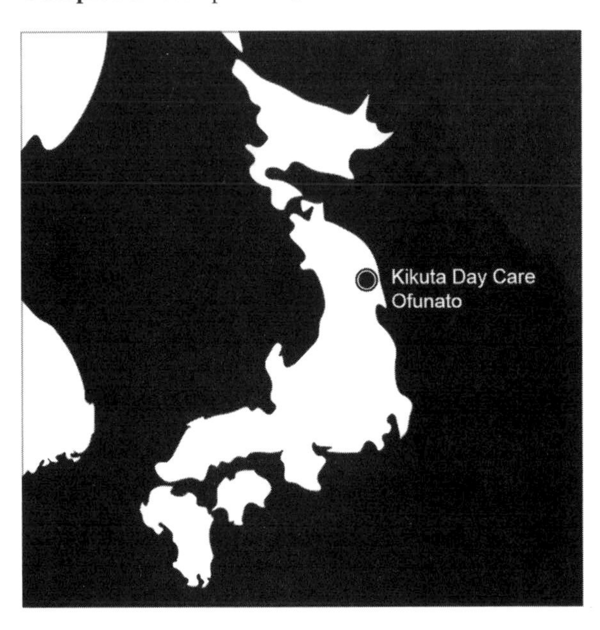

FIGURE 6-2 Scheme location. *Courtesy of Pozzoni LLP*

Kikuta Day Care: Japan

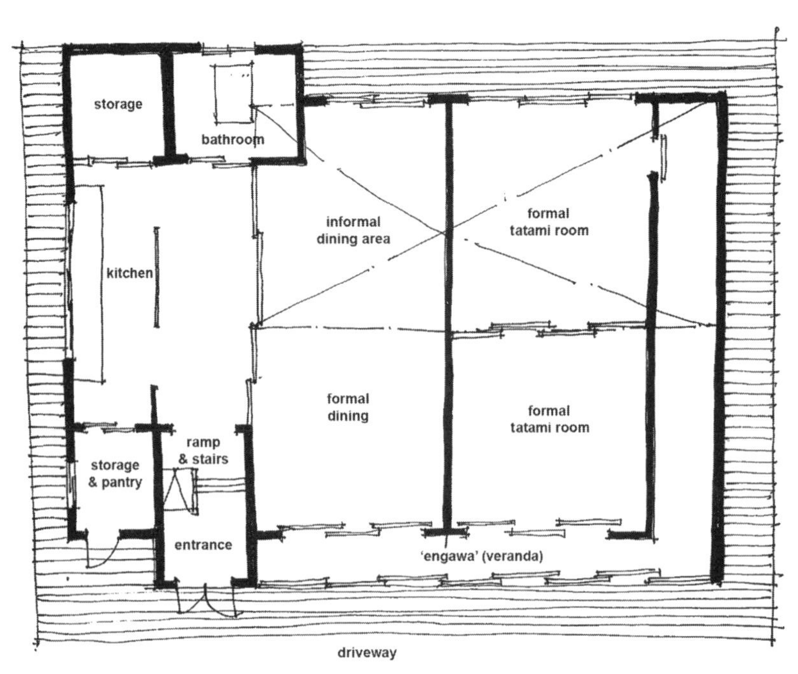

FIGURE 6-3 Floor plan.
Courtesy of Pozzoni LLP Floor Plan

Description of the Type of Community, Including Number of Residents

Located in the northeast Japanese seaport of Ofunato in the Iwate Prefecture, Kikuta is a day-care center specifically for aged people with dementia. The center is housed in a restored century-old traditional Japanese house and is located in a residential neighborhood.

Under Japan's Long-Term Care Insurance system, Kikuta is classified as a "community-oriented service" providing "dementia-specific day service." All of Kikuta's clients come from the local community and therefore know each other and share many common interests and a common social foundation. Kikuta has a distinct advantage over new purpose-built community day-care centers. As a traditional house within a residential neighborhood, the travel time in the mini-bus which picks up clients from their homes in the morning and returns them home in the afternoon is very short.

Kikuta is not a large house accommodating, at most, 12 clients each day. Clients of the day-care center have mild to moderate dementia, and generally visit, on average, four to five times each week. Many of the clients attend each day, creating a sense of familiarity and strengthening relationships.

The building is a traditional Japanese house. It is a one-story wooden structure with a floor area of 261 square meters (2,809 square feet), which is considered a suitable size for a large family in Japan. Kikuta is located in a residential area, and there is a preschool, a primary school, and a junior secondary school nearby.

FIGURE 6-4 Kikuta is at the heart of a residential neighborhood. Nearby schools facilitate an informal intergenerational program. *Courtesy of Stephen Judd*

Geographics

Vernacular Design

How does the scheme/environment respond to the locality?

The restored building was originally built as a private house in the community. By retaining the original exterior design, Kikuta is seen by the local community as completely integrated, both aesthetically and socially.

Care

Philosophy of Care

What is the operators' philosophy, and how does the building match this philosophy?

The philosophy of dementia care at Kikuta is based on the idea of "living together in the local community." This approach means that the starting point for care at Kikuta is the support and care that clients, families, staff members, and local residents living side by side can provide to each other. The focus is not on the support provided primarily by the staff.

The key words or phrases relative to Kikuta are "community," "lifestyle," "memories of a former time," and "cultural tradition." Thus for Kikuta, the selection of an old private house in which to locate the day-care center was very important. This type of traditional house was assumed to be the sort of house in which older people would have lived in the past. The building was the private home of Dr. Kikuta, who used to make house calls to the community on horseback, and for whom the house is now named. The doctor and his family lived in the structure until about 40 years ago, and the house has been known in the community as "Dr Kikuta's house" since then.

FIGURE 6-5 Clients praying at the Shinto altar in the living room. *Courtesy of Stephen Judd*

When restoring the building, care was taken in preserving its character. The traditional features of the Japanese house such as kamado (kitchen stove), kamidana (Shinto altar), and ranma (carved wooden panels above doors) were restored. A toilet and a bathroom were added and were designed to be easy for clients to locate and access. Although some of the house's features could be considered as barriers to accessibility, they were left in their original state to promote familiarity for the clients. For example, the front door threshold, an important icon in a Japanese house, was retained even though it is a step higher than the ground. A pebbled garden is located outside the main entrance, which could be interpreted as a trip hazard. These choices were made because a house with a higher front door threshold and a pebbled garden are very familiar to elderly people in Japan. A ramp for wheelchairs was installed, but done so with carefully selected material and color to blend carefully with the traditional house and to retain the domestic atmosphere.

The house has many spaces that are important for supporting the lifestyle of Kikuta's clients. There is a Shinto altar for prayers, a functional kitchen, and a vegetable garden. The cherry, maple, and other trees surrounding the house have been preserved and can be enjoyed in all seasons by the clients. The Tenjin-kai Social Welfare Association remarked that Kikuta's theme is "restoration of home and humanity."

FIGURE 6-6 The original entrance to Kikuta, with threshold steps, was retained because it was traditional and standard. A ramp was also installed for less mobile clients. *Courtesy of Stephen Judd*

Community and Belonging

How does the scheme design and operation support this ideal?

Kikuta is a place where clients can experience a "home life." It is also a place where clients can come together, recreate and relax, and where members of the surrounding community can gather. In order to promote community involvement and community belonging for Kikuta's clients, four principles have been incorporated into the care program and environmental design.

The first principle is to enable clients to continue the lifestyle and life rhythms to which they have become accustomed. Spaces have been incorporated where clients are able to continue domestic tasks such as cooking in the kitchen, sewing, washing and drying clothes, performing a variety of crafts on the engawa, the veranda-like corridor, and tending to plants in the garden. By preserving the kamidana (Shinto altar) clients can continue their custom of clapping hands in front of it each morning to begin the day. The functional kitchen enables the staff and clients to cook together, or to be more precise, for clients to teach young staff members to make traditional seasonal dishes, then sit around the table and talk over each meal.

The second principle is to create a place where clients, staff, and local residents can feel secure. Kikuta uses paper-on-wooden-frame sliding doors such as fusuma and shoji as room dividers instead of solid walls, and

FIGURE 6-7 Meals shared at a common table create a "home life" and promote a sense of belonging. *Courtesy of Stephen Judd*

floors are covered with traditional straw-and-rush tatami mats. This creates distance and privacy, but does not isolate clients from each other. Instead, it gives a sense of the presence of others in the house and the activities they may be enjoying. By using this concept of "humane distance," clients never feel alone.

FIGURE 6-8 Straw and rush tatami mats, a traditional Japanese flooring, are used extensively. *Courtesy of Stephen Judd*

The third principle is to create a calming atmosphere where clients feel settled for a long time. To accomplish this, the calming features of the traditional house have been maintained, including the traditional kitchen stove, pillars, ranma panels, Shinto altar, and tatami mats. These features create an ambience in which clients can settle in and spend time comfortably, even without verbal communication with others. Kikuta's design is an attempt to be environmentally therapeutic so that its clients—and other members of the local community—feel at peace despite their dementia.

The final principle is to create an environment that stimulates the five senses. For example, soft lighting and flowers appeal to the sense of sight, the rhythmic sound of food being chopped on a cutting board, the whispers of breezes and the twittering of birds appeal to the sense of hearing, and the softness of soil, the chilliness or warmth of winds and the warmth of a sunny spot on the engawa veranda appeal to the sense of touch.

Innovation

If the operator pursues a policy of innovation and pursuit of excellence, how is this demonstrated?

In Japan, although the concept of "families" is rapidly changing, Kikuta made a concerted effort to create a place where not only clients, but also their families, staff, and people of the local community can feel safe and comfortable. The use of the restored building and the model of care practiced have meant Kikuta is widely recognized as a home-like place throughout the local community.

Another of Kikuta's goals is to protect a significant local cultural asset and thus create a positive community perception of the day-care center. When first purchased,

FIGURE 6-9 Kikuta's clients can participate in domestic tasks such as cooking in the kitchen, sewing, washing, and gardening. *Courtesy of Stephen Judd*

the building was in disrepair. It was restored by reusing almost all of the existing materials without causing damage to the surrounding landscape. The restoration of the building, which was once the home of a prominent person of the community, was welcomed and appreciated by the local community members, who regard the restored building as a community asset.

Neighborhood Integration

Community Involvement

Is the scheme and service designed to integrate successfully with the local community?

One of the primary objectives for Kikuta was to create an inviting atmosphere so that people from the surrounding community would feel comfortable visiting at any time. This objective has been achieved in several ways. For example, the engawa was designed to offer good visual access from the gate posts to the inside of the house and thus any activities that may be taking place. Neighbors are welcome to come to the engawa and have a conversation with clients inside the house without needing to fully enter the house, which is a very traditional Japanese approach to socializing with neighbors. There are no barriers, such as a fence, around the house, making the space appear open and inviting to visitors. Neighbors frequently take their dogs for a walk and stop for a conversation with clients or help in the vegetable garden. In the summer, schoolchildren on their way home stop to join residents in a game of "split the watermelon." Clients also teach visiting children how to play traditional games like ohajiki1.

Kikuta is constantly involving the local community in activities. For example, the guest room is used by people from the local community to hold community information meetings on dementia. Visits from Kids Volunteers from the local primary and junior secondary schools are encouraged and welcomed. Local people are even asked to participate in emergency drills.

Staff and Volunteers

Human Resources

Are policies and designs in place to attract good staff and volunteers?

Staff members are qualified care workers who have passed nationally administered examinations and have experience in living with older people.

- Direct care hours per day per client: 3.4

Environmental Sustainability

ALTERNATIVE ENERGY SOURCES
None

WATER CONSERVATION
"Save Water" stickers have been posted near water taps.

ENERGY CONSERVATION
"Save Energy" stickers have been posted near power sources.

Outdoor Living

Garden

Does the garden support principles of care?

FIGURE 6-10 Kikuta has a large vegetable garden and a variety of fruit trees, including the ume (Japanese apricot). *Courtesy of Stephen Judd*

When Kikuta was a private family home, the garden was an extension of the lifestyle of the original owner and a symbol of wealth. The same is true in its current use as a day-care center. Kikuta has a vegetable garden that is about 100 tsubo, or approximately 330 square meters (3,553 square feet) in size. As many of the clients used to work in the fields, it is a place where they can use their experiences, demonstrate their talents, and teach young staff members about working in the fields.

There are various trees in the garden including ume (Japanese apricot), cherry, maple, chestnut, and walnut trees, all of which show the changes of season. At Kikuta, there is a belief that it is very important to engage people with the power of nature to refresh, provide healing, and ultimately give richness to life experiences.

Project Data

DESIGN FIRM

This project is the refurbishment of a century-old doctor's house, around which has grown the community and additional buildings. There was almost certainly no design firm involved in the original structure as it derived its form and function from Japanese tradition. The design of the refurbishment was done primarily by staff and contractors involved in the construction, and it was the intention of these individuals to retain the look and feel of the original, traditional Japanese home.

AREAS/SIZES

Building footprint and total building area: 261 square meters (2,809 square feet)

PARKING

There are two or three automobile parking spaces that have been "assumed" from the layout of the property. However, there are no "intentional" or marked parking spaces on this property. There is ample drive and automobile space to accommodate delivery of clients to the day-care facility and for the maneuvering of small transport buses for client activities.

COSTS

Unavailable

RESIDENT AGE (AT OPENING)

Unavailable

RESIDENT PAYER MIX

Fully funded by Japan's Long-Term Care Insurance system

Chapter 7

A Study of Himawari Group Home

REASONS FOR INCLUSION OF THIS SCHEME

- This scheme is an excellent early example of the group home movement in Japan.
- This scheme provides unparalleled involvement of the residents in activities of daily living, such as shopping, gardening, growing vegetables, and food preparation.
- This scheme has a typical, though unexceptional, vernacular design.
- This scheme shows an excellent example of high levels of engagement with the surrounding Ofunato community.

Building Description

Name of scheme: Group Home Himawari
Owners: Dr. Noriya Kikawada, President of Tenjin-kai Social Welfare Foundation
Address:
196 Yamamagoe
Ofunato-cho
Ofunato-shi
Iwate, 022–0002
Japan
Occupied since: December 1996

FIGURE 7-1 Himawari is located in Ofunato, a fishing and port city in rural Iwate Prefecture of Japan. *Courtesy of Jeffrey Anderzhon*

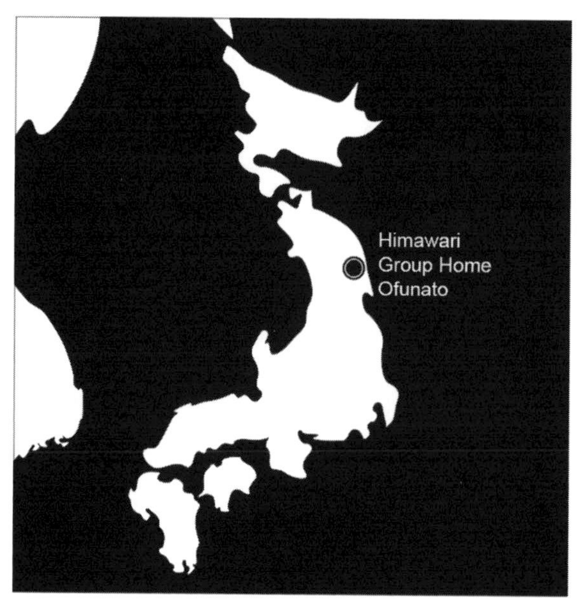

FIGURE 7-2 Scheme location. *Courtesy of Pozzoni LLP*

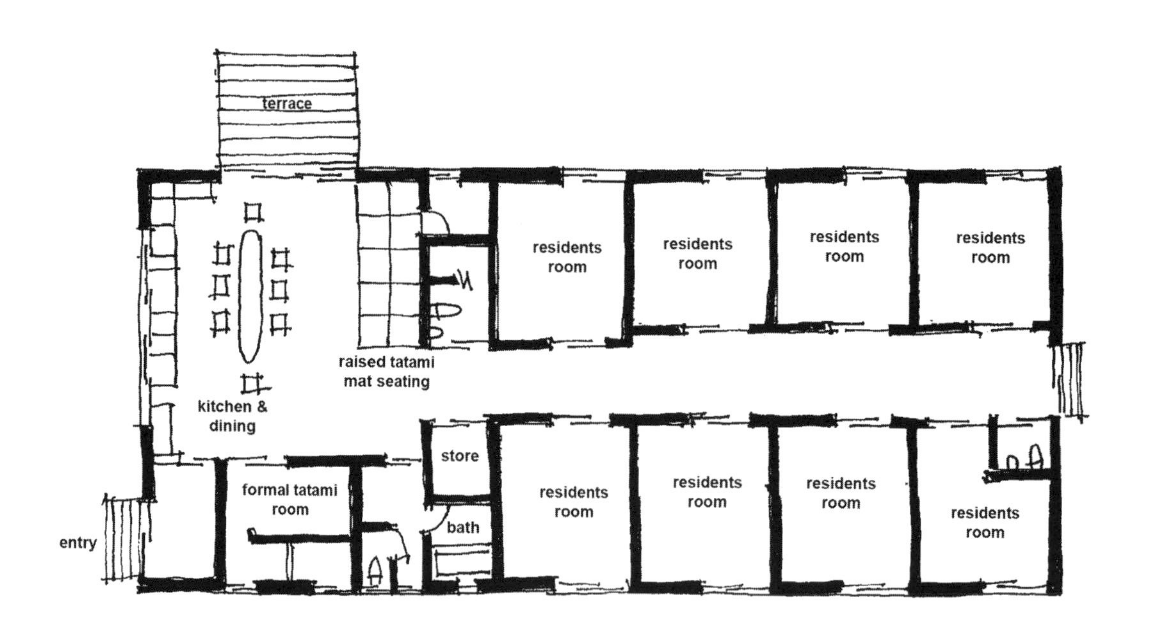

FIGURE 7-3 Ground floor plan. *Courtesy of Pozzoni LLP*

Description of the Type of Community, Including Number of Residents

Himawari was the first group home in Iwate Prefecture and the eighth group home to be opened in Japan. Group homes in Japan usually accommodate eight older people with dementia and are characterized by a far more "domestic" household style of accommodation for people with dementia with, ideally, strong participation of the residents in activities of daily living. When the Long-Term Care Insurance (LTCI) scheme was introduced in Japan in 2000, there were only 270 group homes.[1] After the scheme's introduction, the number of group homes has increased to more than 10,000 across Japan. This phenomenal growth of a particular model of care for people with dementia, spurred on by a national insurance scheme, is unprecedented. However, while all group homes have the same regulatory framework, which includes design features, not all group homes are the same. As Professor Hirokazu Murakawa of Japan College of Social Work states: "Some (group homes) are vulture-like, preying on the elderly with dementia. Others may appear impeccable from outside but poor in substance. Himawari stands out for its provision of care with emphasis placed on spirituality of each person at the grass root level."[2]

Himawari has eight long-term permanent residents with dementia. In addition, it has one respite or "short stay" place. Some older people in the community use this respite place three to four days each month to relieve stress on family care providers.

Himawari is designed as an average Japanese home and is staffed by professional care providers. All residents have symptoms of moderate to advanced dementia. At the time of writing, three residents were using wheelchairs and three needed assistance to walk and get out of bed. It is a principle of Himawari that residents can remain, if at all possible, to the end of their lives.

Himawari is located in Ofunato, a small city on the beautiful Sanriku Coastline, in Iwate Prefecture in the north of Japan's main island, Honshu.

[1] M. Nakanishi and T. Honda, "Processes of Decision-Making and End-of-Life Care for Patients with Dementia in Group Homes in Japan," *Archives of Gerontology and Geriatrics,* 48, 2009, p. 296.

[2] Professor Hirokazu Murakawa of Japan College of Social Work, Tokyo, in his Foreword, in Richard Fleming and Yukimi Uchide, *Images of Care in Australia and Japan: Emerging Common Values,* Stirling, Scotland, 2004, p. 2.

Geographics

Vernacular Design

How does the scheme/environment respond to the locality?

Situated on a hill with views to Ofunato Bay to the east and the mountains to the west, Himarwari is surrounded by market gardens that are tended by residents. It is a simple single-story building constructed using light-gauge steel frames, concrete-tiled roof, and preformed cladding. While the design is architecturally nondescript, it does fit within the same nondescript vernacular of the surrounding community. It sits comfortably among its neighbors displaying the usual characteristics of most modern housing in this relatively poor area of the country. The building almost has the appearance of being prefabricated. A lightweight single-story panel-clad structure sits simply on a concrete slab and roofed with concrete tiles finished in a gloss sheen familiar to most modern domestic buildings in the region. No stylistic influence of the one or two older traditional or historic buildings in the locality can be or, arguably, needs to be detected.

Care

Philosophy of Care

What is the operators' philosophy and how does the building match this philosophy?

As there are a preponderance of group homes in Japan, they can look very similar from the outside. However, what sets Himawari apart is the philosophy of care that the Tenjin-kai Social Welfare Association instills in its staff and how that philosophy is played out in Himawari's operations each and every day.

Himawari's philosophy of care is to support older people with dementia to live "an ordinary life," not a life in an institutional facility. This Group Home puts great emphasis on staff viewing residents as precious individuals and believing in the potential of residents to succeed in day-to-day activities. The Himawari philosophy has six principles, or what the Japanese call "keys":

1. Residents are not care receivers, but people living their own lives. Residents are seen as "the leading character in his or her own life." In other words, their right to self-determination, choice, and decision making is respected.
2. Belief in "lifelong development." No matter how old the person is or what their physical or cognitive condition, the Himawari philosophy maintains that residents always have potential to gain something new physically, intellectually, or spiritually.

FIGURE 7-4 A resident warmly welcomes guests to Himawari Group Home. *Courtesy of the Dementia Services Development Centre, Stirling University*

FIGURE 7-5 Residents take part in all the daily activities of maintaining the household. *Courtesy of the Dementia Services Development Centre, Stirling University*

3. Respect for "connections." As the person with dementia declines, interpersonal relationships are seen as increasingly important. The person with dementia is able to preserve his or her sense of identity and existence through close connections or relationships with others.
4. The "whole person" is known and accepted. Residents and staff are seen as friends living together under the same roof. In-depth understanding of each other is not simply encouraged but is an integral part of the daily life at Himawari.
5. Care staff need what the Tenjin-kai Social Welfare Association calls the ability to have "acute insight." As the cognitive ability of the residents decline, care staff have to be able to understand what the individual needs of the resident are and quickly discern factors or circumstances that each resident might find disabling.
6. Live unhurriedly and with a sense of fun. This is seen as integral to creating a joyful environment for older people. What the visitor to Himawari immediately recognizes is that its residents and staff have fun.

FIGURE 7-6 Himawari's care staff are encouraged to know the resident well and value their background. *Courtesy of the Dementia Services Development Centre, Stirling University*

FIGURE 7-7 Traditional Japanese social practices continue within Himawari. *Courtesy of the Dementia Services Development Centre, Stirling University*

Himawari is an excellent example of how that philosophy has been translated into the building design. The design objective was to create a dwelling where residents would feel safe, secure, healthy, and comfortable in all aspects of daily life. The building is the size of an ordinary private home. The entrance is free from steps for ease of access. The corridor is wide to accommodate residents with mobility aids or a wheelchair and has nonslip flooring and a handrail. The design includes 10 private bedrooms, some with traditional Japanese *tatami* mats for flooring, as used in traditional Japanese homes. Residents furnish the rooms with their own furniture. A central living and dining area is shared by all the residents and staff. Residents and staff plan the evening menu, shop locally, and prepare the meal together. The house also has a large vegetable garden, making the home completely self-sufficient, with staff and residents responsible for all the tasks of maintaining the household.

In 2010, Himawari was in its fourteenth year of operation. During that year staff at Himawari were particularly challenged to consider how to put the philosophy of "continuing to live an ordinary life" into practice through supporting a resident who needed end-of-life care. The resident had lived for many years at Himawari, and as she entered a palliative stage, staff agreed that she would continue to remain fully involved and engaged in the life and rhythms of the household. For example, staff learned the value of indirect involvement in activity, such as hearing and smelling meals being prepared, rather than actually being involved in that preparation.

The frailty of residents at Himawari is increasing and, as a result, their mobility is declining and more residents are dependent on wheelchairs. With increasing frailty, the size of resident bedrooms is becoming an issue, and Tenjin-kai is reviewing solutions to this issue in order that the home remains an easy place in which to live.

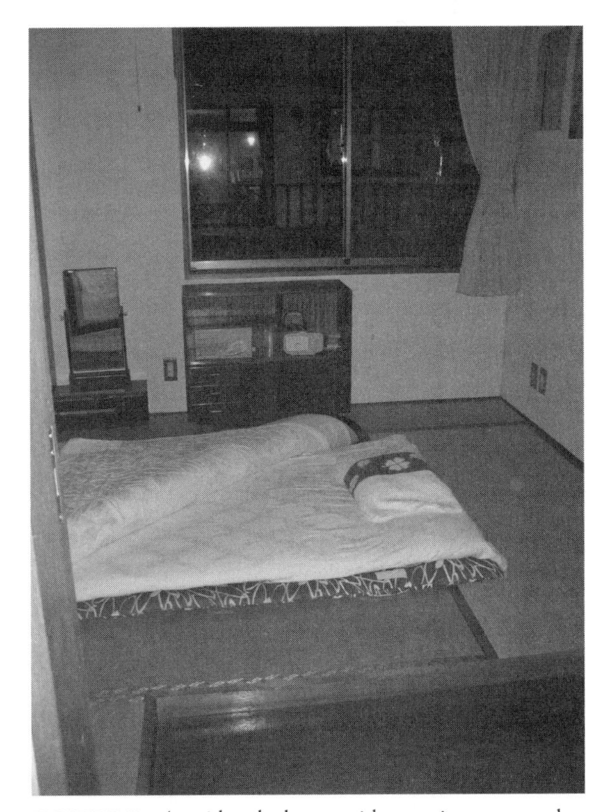

FIGURE 7-8 A resident bedroom with tatami mats as used in traditional Japanese homes. *Courtesy of the Dementia Services Development Centre, Stirling University*

Community and Belonging

How does the scheme design and operation support this ideal?

The Himawari Group Home model is very successful in creating community within the home and fostering a sense of belonging. Its domestic design and the involvement of residents in all the day-to-day activities of running the household foster a strong sense of community. Residents are able to maintain the continuum of their everyday lives. They shop at a nearby supermarket, are involved in preparing meals, washing and drying dishes, sewing, gardening, cleaning, and doing carpentry work. A central feature for all this activity is the single dining table, which is an important place for having tea and sharing conversation and stories.

Efforts have been made to make the home a relaxing and safe environment. For example, while they use fluorescent lights, these lights are covered with washi, a traditional Japanese paper that reduces the glare. There are sofas in the living room and the home is barrier-free with no steps.

Innovation

If the operator pursues a policy of innovation and pursuit of excellence, how is this demonstrated?

In 1996 when Himawari was opened, group homes were considered to be the best practice in dementia care in Japan. Unlike the existing care facilities, they were small in size, emphasized the importance of personal relationships with familiar people, and guaranteed a lifestyle similar to that which the residents would have had in their own home. At Himawari, residents also have the opportunity to feel that they are more than just a recipient of care. Rather, the Himawari model of care promotes altruism, with residents involved and useful to the household and each other.

Tenjin-kai Social Welfare Association has also integrated Himawari with other services that it operates, such as a day center for people with dementia, a dementia-specific nursing home, a geriatric health services facility, and a home-visit nurses' center. Thus, while Himawari is a small, self-contained home of people working within its community, there is a critical mass of expertise and support readily available nearby.

Neighborhood Integration

Community Involvement

Is the scheme and service designed to integrate successfully with the local community?

The location of the Himawari Group Home naturally integrates it into the wider Ofunato community. It is near a child care center, primary school, and hospital. The City Center and local shops are a short walk away, as is the nearest train and City Hall. Himawari encourages

FIGURE 7-9 Meals are prepared by both care staff and residents and shared communally. *Courtesy of Stephen Judd*

visitors, and guests are welcomed by the residents who, as this is their home, serve the visitors green tea.

Himawari is located in a newly developed residential area of Ofunato where 90 percent of residents have lived for less than 10 years. The number of young people and children in the community is declining and community festivals and traditional seasonal events such as the Bon dance rarely happen. Whereas for many care homes, the issue of neighborhood integration is a question of how the residential aged care service can integrate with neighborhood activities that are happening around them, Himawari has become a focus for how the surrounding community can become more connected. In short, Himawari is an important focus for the local community. Himawari's Administration Support Committee, made up of local government officials, community representatives, residents, and their relatives, meet bimonthly to discuss how Himawari can be used to strengthen the sense of community in the neighborhood. Strategies range from the simple, such as encouraging staff and residents to exchange greetings with locals that they meet in the street, to broader issues like involving the neighborhood in Himawari's fire drills or engagement of Himawari residents in the activities of the after-school children's club. This latter intergenerational activity sees Himawari residents being assigned the role of handing down the food culture as well as other traditions to younger generations. In the past, Japanese families were often made up of three or four generations within a single home. However, in modern Japan, most children now grow up in a nuclear family home and may have little contact with grandparents. Participation in activities with Himawari is, therefore, seen as a valuable experience. Shared activities include eating nagashi somen (noodles float down along a long bamboo gutter filled with water and are caught with chopsticks, dipped in cool broth and eaten) in summer and making mochi rice cakes in winter (pounding steamed sticky rice with large wooden pestle and mortar). In early January, nanakusa-gayu, rice porridge with seven spring herbs, is eaten to ensure health for the new year. These activities have not only helped to establish a good connection with the community but have also played a role in promoting public awareness of dementia and understanding its impacts. Himawari is also seen now as a local resource for information and advice on dementia and is visited by relatives of people with dementia.

The Himawari staff were also the major driving force in establishing an amateur theater group called Kesen Boke Ichiza in 1995. This group promotes community education in dementia through plays. In the theater group's early days, Himawari residents used to assist with setup, such as helping to tie kimonos. This now rarely occurs, but Himawari is looking to return to this, as it epitomizes the conviction that people are capable of contributing to society regardless of their dementia.

FIGURE 7-10 Residents shopping at nearby markets for food to be used at Himawari. *Courtesy of the Dementia Services Development Centre, Stirling University*

FIGURE 7-11 Himawari's vegetable garden is tended by residents and the produce is used in meals. *Courtesy of the Dementia Services Development Centre, Stirling University*

Staff and Volunteers

Human Resources

Are policies and designs in place to attract good staff and volunteers?

The majority of Himawari's staff members are qualified care workers who have passed nationally administered examinations and have experience in living with older people. The Japanese aged care system prescribes a generous staffing ratio for group homes. During the day there are three staff members to nine residents and at night there is one staff member to nine residents.

Environmental Sustainability

Environmental sustainability was not a consideration in this design.

Outdoor Living

Garden

Does the garden support principles of care?

Himawari has its own vegetable garden that is tended by residents. Some residents have worked in the fields all their lives and teach younger staff to prepare the soil, sow, fertilize, and harvest. Produce harvested is used in the home's cooking, and in the past it was also sold at a local market. This was very successful as it clearly gave residents a sense of achievement, and staff felt they had greater job satisfaction. In recent years, as resident frailty has increased, more residents grow vegetables and flowers in pots and planters. Caring for the gardens is part of the home's daily routine.

Himarwari also has a wooden terrace that is often used for meals from spring through autumn. It is an important space for meeting with the local community and holding barbecues where the quintessential autumn fish samna is grilled over a charcoal fire.

Project Data

DESIGN FIRM

Tenjin-kai Social Welfare Foundation
196 Yamamagoe
Ofunato-cho
Ofunato-shi
Iwate, 022–0002
Japan

AREAS/SIZES

- Site area: Himawari is on a health and aged care campus. The site area has not been able to be determined.
- Building footprint: 278.42 square meters (2,997 square feet)
- Total building area: 278.42 square meters (2,997 square feet)
- Total area per resident: 30.93 square meters (332.93 square feet)

PARKING

Three parking spaces with additional parking elsewhere on campus

BUILDING COSTS

Unknown

RESIDENT AGE

Average age of residents: 85.3 years

RESIDENT PAYER MIX

Service eligibility is determined by a person's condition rather than the ability to pay. Service costs are met through Japan's Long-Term Care Insurance scheme, contributions from the central government, prefectures and municipalities, and a resident out-of-pocket fee, which is capped at 10 percent of total cost of service.

Chapter 8

A Study of NPO Group Fuji

REASONS FOR INCLUSION OF THIS SCHEME

- This scheme has a unique connection to the surrounding community.
- This scheme came into existence by means of a unique set of circumstances and goals.
- The development of this scheme is unique in its approach.

Building Description

Name of scheme: NPO Group Fuji
Owner: Group Fuji, a private not-for-profit organization
Address:
1–4–2 Fujigaoka
Fujisawa, Kanagawa
Japan
Occupied since: 2007

FIGURE 8-1 NPO Fuji as viewed from the street with the café at the street corner. *Courtesy of NPO Group Fuji*

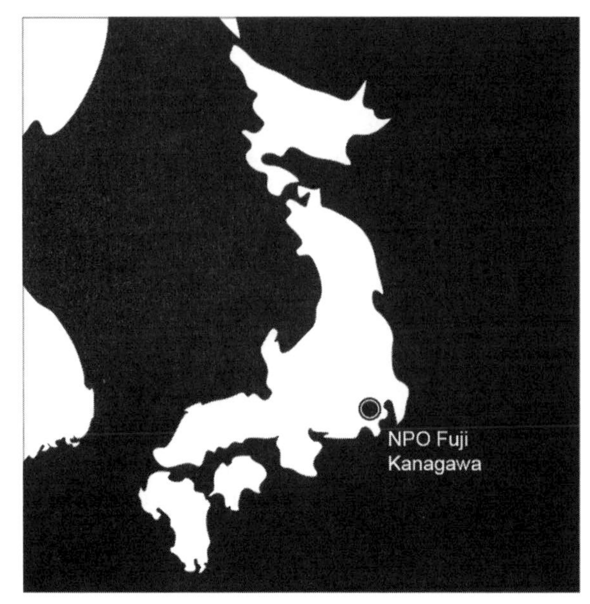

FIGURE 8-2 Scheme location. *Courtesy of Pozzoni LLP*

NPO Fuji: Japan

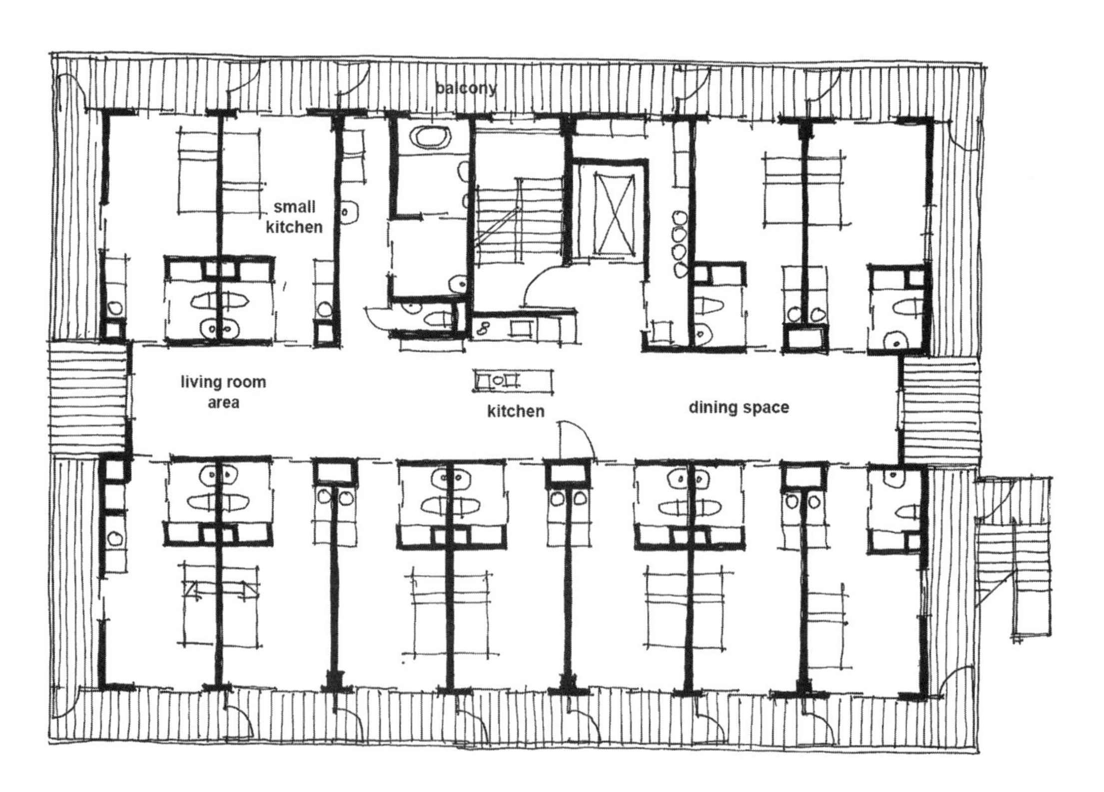

Third Floor

FIGURE 8-3 Third-floor plan. *Courtesy of Pozzoni LLP*

Description of the Type of Community, Including Number of Residents

Group Fuji provides assisted living care in suburban Tokyo for 21 elderly residents who are 65 years of age or older; multifunctional care including adult day service with short-term stay care for 25 elderly persons; and a group home for 6 youths experiencing physical and mental disabilities, all within a four-story building surrounded by a residential neighborhood. Also within this same structure, the sponsoring organization operates a restaurant and a child day-care service, both of which are open to the surrounding community.

Opportunities for multigenerational interactions within the building are offered not only through the programming but also by means of the building's organization. The multifunctional care programs for elderly persons and child day-care services are located on the first floor of the building and a group home for young persons with physical and mental disabilities is housed on the second floor. Assisted living apartments are located on both the third and fourth floors. Located on a prominent corner of the building on the street level is a small restaurant complete with its own entrance, enabling local residents from the surrounding community full access to this amenity. The restaurant is operated by the youth from the group home, providing job opportunities for them within a somewhat sheltered environment.

The assisted living residents each have a private room with small kitchen and private bathroom, maintaining and enhancing their independence. These rooms are arranged to be only a short distance from a living room and dining room shared by all residents on that floor. These social spaces provide ample opportunity for residents to congregate before, during, or after mealtime for those who would prefer eating as a group.

The NPO Group Fuji facility development originated from a very unique and interesting background. Five housewives began a cooperative support system for local community residents who needed assistance with caring for elderly parents as well as their children. The objective of these forward-thinking individuals was to develop a community support system in which local residents could participate in caring for each other as they prepared for their inevitable aging process. Their efforts developed slowly as demands for elderly care steadily increased and resulted in an initial building that housed adult day services over 19 years prior to erecting the current structure. The organization has expanded but remains operated by local residents with the mission to serve the elderly, children, and young residents with physical and mental disabilities, as well as to serve their caregivers in the surrounding community.

FIGURE 8-4 A household living room with resident rooms on either side. *Courtesy of Jeffrey Anderzhon*

Geographics

Vernacular Design

How does the scheme/environment respond to the locality?

The building is designed to fit into the surrounding residential neighborhood of single-family houses and multistory condominiums. While this building houses apartments for the elderly and a group home for youth with physical and mental disabilities, it gives the appearance of a standard modern multistory Japanese condominium building. The exterior and interior of this building exhibit some Western design influences but fits seamlessly into the Japanese suburb.

Care

Philosophy of Care

What is the operators' philosophy and how does the building match this philosophy?

The philosophy of care at NPO Group Fuji is to provide assistance and resources for caring for the elderly, children, and other vulnerable individuals within the local community, and to strengthen the local support system through providing these services in an inclusive manner. Since the inception of the organization, the objective has been to create a community where women have the opportunity to work while caring for their children and their aging parents. With limited resources from the beginning, the organization provided individualized care for elderly residents within the residents' own homes. This care was provided in a cooperative approach as a "donation" by the caregiver to serve local residents in the community. Through this initial effort, the organization identified a great community need for safe housing for elderly residents in an arrangement that allowed them to stay in the community and to live independently. The organization also quickly found that elderly residents preferred to be surrounded by other generations rather than living among a homogeneous age group. These insights led the group to develop the building that houses not only elderly residents, but young residents who have physical and mental disabilities and children within the day-care facility. The group's efforts to seek acceptance by the surrounding community is foundational to their philosophy and is manifest in their dedication to community service.

Because of their strong desire for inclusive care, local residents in the community strongly supported the development of the Group Fuji building. This community support manifested itself in the very quick sale of the building bond financing issue to primarily local residents.

FIGURE 8-5 Residents playing a game in a household living room. *Courtesy of NPO Group Fuji*

FIGURE 8-6 Intergenerational activity with local school children in a household dining room. *Courtesy of NPO Group Fuji*

The care program supports interactions between the differing age groups within the building. While staff members encourage residents to participate in a variety of activities, they also respect the desires of the residents who would prefer their privacy and time to themselves. Each resident's apartment provides a private room with kitchen and bathroom, so elderly residents are able to enjoy their independent lifestyle with only the support from staff members necessary, while additional care is available when needed. The built environment and care program at NPO Group Fuji are designed to provide care for elderly residents, which allows them to live in their apartments as long as they desire and can adequately function for themselves.

Community and Belonging

How does the scheme design and operation support this ideal?

The built environment is designed to provide opportunities for privacy and socialization as each elderly resident may choose. On the assisted living apartment floors, each group of apartments has a shared living and dining space located conveniently in the center of the floor. These shared spaces offer a large balcony where residents are able to step outside to enjoy the view to the nearby city and the mountains beyond. They can also walk down to the first floor where adult and child day services are located if they wish to meet with people from the larger community. Residents are also encouraged to use the restaurant within the building where local residents are frequently found enjoying a meal.

Innovation

If the operator pursues a policy of innovation and pursuit of excellence, how is it demonstrated?

One significant innovation made by Group Fuji is the process of the building's development. The group was established to serve the local community with cooperation from the local residents. There is a strong sense of solidarity within the organization for providing a support system for local residents who are seeking safe housing as they age and also to assist caregivers who may require outside help as they care for their children and aging parents. The group wisely utilizes government support for caring for the elderly as well as youth with physical and mental disabilities, and integrates multigenerational and functional services to create a normal living environment for them within the local community. The challenge the group faced was to integrate care for elders, youth with physical and mental disabilities, and children's day care all on the same property. This facility accomplishes the integration well, not only within the confines of the facility building, but on a larger community level.

The inclusion of a restaurant is also innovative and provides a service to the larger community. The restaurant offers healthy lunches for elderly residents, staff members, and local residents, bringing them together in a comfortable venue. This may be particularly beneficial for the elderly residents of the community who live by themselves. The staff in the restaurant come to know regular elderly customers, and they are able to keep a somewhat watchful eye on them. In addition, the restaurant hires the young residents from the facility who may have mental disabilities and trains them to cook and serve at the restaurant, skills that may be useful once they leave the facility.

The building's design fits well within the surrounding residential neighborhood. It may be argued that the building appears as noninnovative. However, the building's aesthetic is not out of place with its environs and provides the feeling of belonging to the community vernacular. The interior colors were carefully selected to provide a soothing effect for the residents, and decorations throughout the building are selected to fit into the typical lifestyle and local culture of this area.

The operation and the development of NPO Group Fuji are also quite innovative, as the organization is financially supported by local community members. The funding for the building construction was achieved by the sale of bonds to local residents. The organization hires local residents as caregivers and offers generally higher wages to them than competitors.

Neighborhood Integration

Community Involvement

Is the scheme and service designed to integrate successfully with the local community?

NPO Group Fuji is located within a suburban residential area and in a location where local residents walk past on their way to a main train station for the commute to their place of business. The restaurant, which faces the main street, provides an enhanced visibility of

FIGURE 8-7 The "Ohana" café open to the surrounding neighborhood community. *Courtesy of NPO Group Fuji*

FIGURE 8-8 Residents making cards with local high school students in a household dining room. *Courtesy of NPO Group Fuji*

this community of intergenerational care. Since the appearance of the restaurant and the building is well integrated into the surrounding aesthetic, local residents frequently patronize the restaurant. The adult and child day services are open to the surrounding community so that local residents of all ages are integrated into the care and service of this organization.

The building also houses an elderly caregiving resource center at street level where local residents can easily obtain caregiving information and professional advice. The staff of this center coordinate necessary assistance for elderly individuals who live at home and also arrange immediate help for caregivers when necessary. NPO Group Fuji has become known as a destination for community members who need or seek assistance and resources related to elderly care.

Staff and Volunteers

Human Resources

Are policies and designs in place to attract good staff and volunteers?

Group Fuji recruits staff from the surrounding community as a part of its mission to develop support systems within the local community. Most of the staff are trained to be certified caregiver professionals. Staff are compensated with competitive pay rates to encourage professionalism and dedication and to attract the highest quality of caregiver. In addition, there are numerous volunteers involved in a variety of ways with the Group Fuji organization. Staff and volunteers are trained to provide a high quality of care, as well as understanding the care philosophy of the group to encourage independence, age and social integrations, and service to the local community.

- Direct care hours per resident per day are unknown.

Environmental Sustainability

ALTERNATIVE ENERGY SOURCES

The built environmental design includes solar panels for electric generation and a "green" roof.

WATER CONSERVATION

Unknown

ENERGY CONSERVATION

Group Fuji has incorporated energy-saving lights as well as double-paned windows for energy conservation.

Outdoor Living

Garden

Does the garden support principles of care?

A small outdoor garden space is located in front of the restaurant at street level. This garden is also used as an outdoor eating area by the restaurant. Residents, children, and staff members maintain the garden space cooperatively and as an intergenerational activity. The garden space is a place where people of all ages and various backgrounds meet one another and it has become a vibrant social space. Because this space is visible from the street, the effort of the residents who maintain the area is a clear statement of their pride for their home.

FIGURE 8-9 Residents attend a music class with a volunteer musician. *Courtesy of NPO Group Fuji*

FIGURE 8-10 Plants greet visitors at the main entrance to NPO Fuji. *Courtesy of Jeffrey Anderzhon*

Project Data

DESIGN FIRM

Landbrain LLC1–2–10 Hirakawa cho
Chiyoda, Tokyo
Japan

AREAS/SIZES

- Site area: 886 square meters (9,537 square feet)
- Building footprint: 459 square meters (4,930 square feet)
- Total building area: 1,455 square meters (15,661 square feet)
- Total area per resident: 18 square meters (194 square feet)
- Individual room space for assisted living: 14 square meters (151 square feet)

PARKING

Surface parking for six automobiles

COSTS (2007)

- Total building cost: ¥320,000,000 ($3,936.647 USD)
- Cost per square meter: ¥210,999 ($858 USD)
- Cost per square foot: ¥10,321,930 ($127,020 USD)
- Investment per resident: ¥10,321,930 ($127,020 USD)

RESIDENT AGE

Average age of residents: 82 years

RESIDENT PAYER MIX

Ninety percent of the care is provided by national Long-Term Care Insurance, and residents pay 10 percent of all the care. In the unit care facilities that nonprofit organizations like NPO FUJI operate, residents are responsible for meals and a room charge, which are very affordably priced.

Chapter 9

A Study of Gojikara Village

REASONS FOR INCLUSION OF THIS SCHEME

- This scheme offers a unique approach to create a sense of community.
- There is a multigenerational approach to care provision in this scheme.
- In this scheme there is neighborhood outreach.
- This scheme embraces the "sense of imperfection."

Building Description

Name of scheme: Gojikara Mura
Owner: Taiyo no mori, a not-for-profit organization
Address:
29–4 Nagakute
Aichi, Aichi
Japan
Occupied since: 1987

FIGURE 9-1 An internal street in the main campus of Gojikara Mura. *Courtesy of Emi Kiyota*

FIGURE 9-2 Scheme location. *Courtesy of Pozzoni LLP*

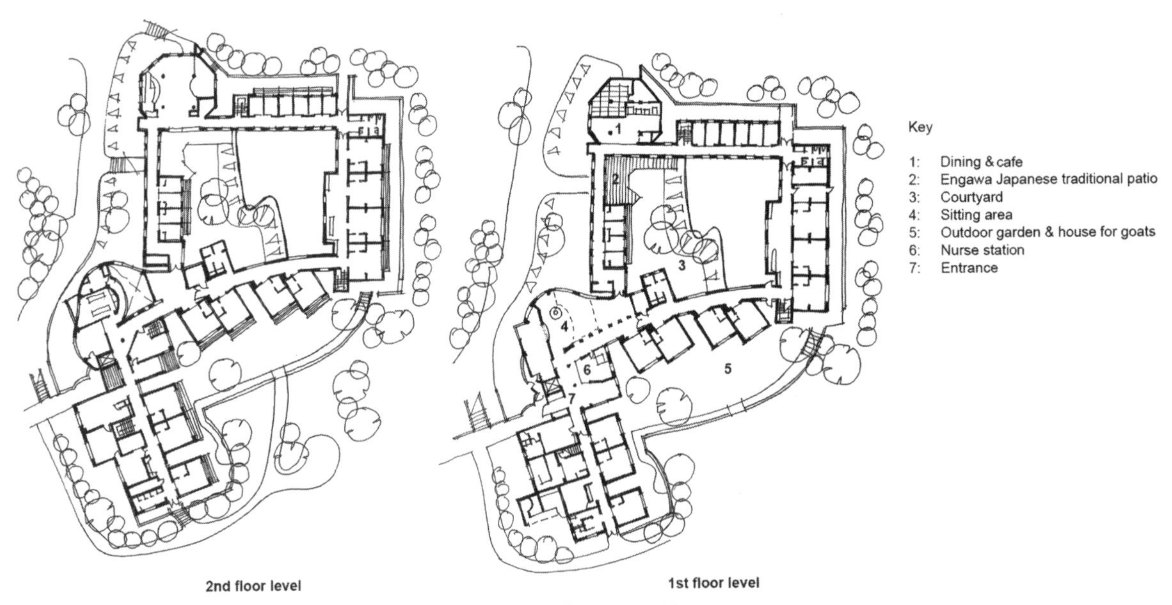

FIGURE 9-3 Nursing care building floor plans. *Courtesy of Pozzoni LLP*

Description of the Type of Community, Including Number of Residents

Gojikara Mura is located in Nagakute City in Aichi Prefecture on the Honshu island of Japan. This organization began with a child day care in 1981. Providing the service for children, the owner believed it would be beneficial for both children and elderly people to have continuous interactions. In 1987, a skilled nursing home for elderly residents was opened, and other elderly-care services were established over time to serve the elderly who required different types of support within the community.

One of this community's goals was to preserve the natural habitat and local culture from the housing development to provide a familiar living environment for the larger community's elderly population. In addition, another of the Gojikara Mura goals was to re-create a multigenerational community where elderly residents are able to experience the lifestyle they enjoyed prior to residency. To achieve these objectives, Gojikara Mura offers a variety of services, not only for elderly residents, but also their family members and visitors, allowing them to be a part of an authentic community that values their elders. The Gojikara Mura community offers 13 types of services for elderly and younger generations on the main campus, including skilled nursing care, assisted living, visiting nurses, home care, and adult day care for elderly residents. To encourage multigenerational interactions—child day care and a nursing school—two old farmhouses, serving as community centers, are also open to local residents from the larger surrounding community. Over the years, Gojikara Mura expanded its services in three additional multigenerational communities remote from the main campus but within 10 minutes' driving distance, for local residents who would prefer to receive care in their neighborhood. These remote locations provide services that include group homes for dementia, multigenerational cohousing, adult day care, child day care, respite hotel, and an organic restaurant.

On the main campus, there are 80 elderly residents served in skilled nursing care, 50 elderly residents served in assisted living, 35 elderly clients served in adult day care, 190 children enrolled in the preschool, and 300 students enrolled in the nursing school. Housed at the three remote sites, there are 13 elderly residents with dementia in cohousing along with four young female professionals and one family with children, 40 residents in three group homes, and 20 elderly clients in an adult day care. To support family caregivers, a respite care hotel offers 10 rooms in order for them to safely stay near their loved ones, and also for short-term respite for caregivers of elders living at home.

All the buildings, both on the main campus and offsite campuses, are built with a residential scale that includes timbers to maintain the appearances of each building naturally integrated into the heavily wooded surroundings. The buildings on the main campus are embedded into the preserved wooded area and are designed to minimize the disturbance of the surrounding nature. Off-campus buildings are arranged as a small community with a short connecting street that fits well into the surrounding environs.

Geographics

Vernacular Design

How does the scheme/environment respond to the locality?

The scale and materials of the buildings in Gojikara Mura are similar to typical houses in the surrounding community and familiar to residents. All of these buildings are scattered throughout the wooded area. In order to re-create a sense of community from the time familiar to the elderly residents, vehicular traffic is restricted, which in turn encourages visitors to walk through the community. As a result, the campus "streetscape" and the proximity of houses to one another resemble a typical, walkable Japanese neighborhood. Consequently, the appearance and feeling of the community is comfortable to the residents and provides a sense of "normal" community.

Care

Philosophy of Care

What is the operators' philosophy, and how does the building match this philosophy?

It is the Gojikara Mura philosophy that elderly residents need opportunities to establish meaningful relationships with people inside and outside the Gojikara Mura campus, no matter what physical and cognitive conditions they are experiencing. To accommodate this vision, the Gojikara Mura design attempts to re-create an authentic community where elderly residents are able to live in an environment and lifestyle replicating the one they had prior to relocating from their home. Both the care and building design are structured to foster a sense of community by embracing diversity, multigenerational interactions, and a slow-paced lifestyle, as opposed to the typical institutional care settings that focus on efficiency, convenience, and hygiene within a task-oriented environment. Gojikara Mura embraces the concept of imperfection, which is, for this campus, the key for creating a living environment in which elders experience a normal lifestyle.

To enhance the sense of community while embracing imperfection, various unique efforts are implemented on the campus. One of these effective approaches is to restrict vehicular traffic on the campus internal roads. Visitors and staff members are required to park their vehicles at the periphery of the property and walk to the various buildings from this outlying parking. The paths in this community are not paved, forcing people using them to walk at a slower pace. This is also an encouragement for individuals from outside the organization to slow down their pace and adjust to the rhythm of the village and its older residents. By experiencing this reduction in the pace of walking, and of life, a younger generation may form better relationships, and certainly better understanding, with their elders.

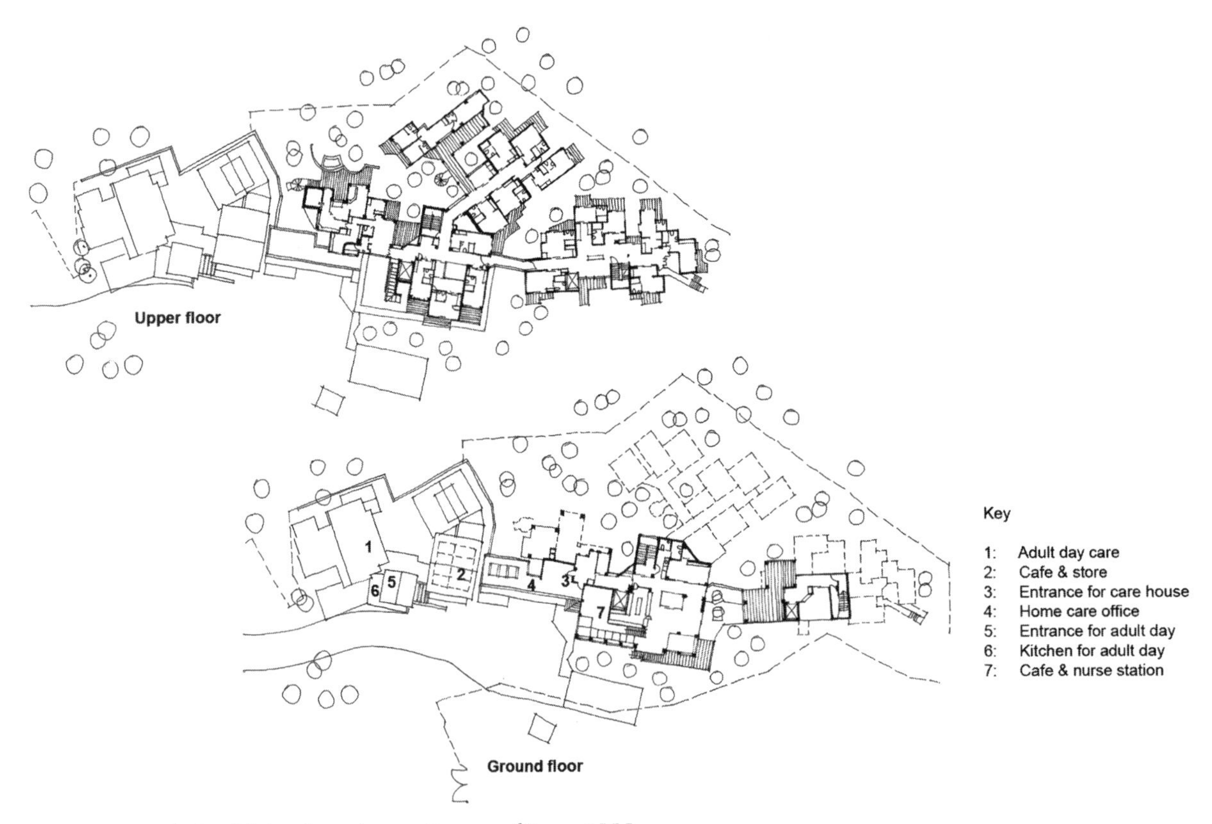

FIGURE 9-4 Assisted-living floor plans. *Courtesy of Pozzoni LLP*

When a visitor walks onto the Gojikara Mura campus, children's voices from the preschool are one of the first sounds heard. This sound fosters an innate sense of what is normal within a community. The buildings are purposefully designed on a domestic Japanese scale. Exposed timbers provide elderly residents with a sense of authenticity and familiarity, resonating with the character and style of their former houses. To embrace this concept of a "normal" community, staff members are encouraged to approach their work in a relaxed manner in order to reduce stress for both staff and residents.

Gojikara Mura also interprets the concept of safety differently from what you would typically find in long-term care settings for the elderly. Living in a typical Japanese house does not offer complete accessibility: Residents are used to negotiating and adapting their built environment to be as accessible as possible based on their needs. To foster a sense of authenticity in their everyday life, some noncritical areas of Gojikara Mura are intentionally designed as inaccessible and inconvenient. In the resulting environment, residents, staff, and volunteers are thrust into situations that require them to help each other. This approach requires and encourages residents to ask for help and facilitates socialization. Moreover, elderly residents and staff members are given opportunities to initiate discussions, which result in the modification of their living environments into their homes. In addition, this approach enhances a sense of human interdependency, and promotes a nonunified, "homelike" environment as opposed to a more unified and institutional environment.

Innovation

If the operator pursues a policy of innovation and pursuit of excellence, how is this demonstrated?

The Japanese long-term care system strives to provide elderly residents individualized care in a "normal" living environment. For this reason, small household living environments in the form of group homes and households have been adapted nationally in Japan over the last few years. However, this environmental approach has a tendency to socially isolate residents from the surrounding community, providing little or no social interaction with anyone other than staff members. With this situation in mind, Gojikara Mura gradually added multigenerational functions, such as the nursing school and the children's preschool, and located them in close proximity to elderly residences to emulate the larger community. Students, children, and visitors are not obligated to interact with elderly residents, but simply coexist and share spaces in the same village. Embracing diversity in this manner, this community has naturally grown as a multigenerational campus where elderly residents are not isolated but are an integral part of the community.

The founder and developer of Gojikara Mura purchased a unique property for the campus and has preserved a heavily wooded area from encroachment by an adjacent housing development. The site was the place where the founder used to play as a child, and he wanted to protect the nature, culture, and lifestyle that the local community associated with the site. To preserve as many of the large trees as possible, the Gojikara Mura design

FIGURE 9-5 The campus preschool serves children from the surrounding communities. *Courtesy of Emi Kiyota*

FIGURE 9-6 The café at the assisted-living building is open to the public. *Courtesy of Emi Kiyota*

philosophy has included the practice of "cutting roofs instead of cutting trees." As a result, the design provides for numerous holes in the roofs that accommodate trees growing through them.

Some areas of the built environment are designed to be purposefully inconvenient for elderly residents. These inconveniences facilitate the creation of opportunities for staff members and elderly residents to communicate and socialize with each other. Because Gojikara Mura strongly focuses on developing relationships among the people in the community, this concept has been an important part of its philosophy in both care provision and building design.

FIGURE 9-7 A preserved traditional Japanese farmhouse on the campus. *Courtesy of Emi Kiyota*

Neighborhood Integration

Community Involvement

Is the scheme and service designed to integrate successfully with the local community?

To bring people from the surrounding community into Gojikara Mura, the buildings have been designed and built in such a way that volunteers can participate in maintaining portions of the exterior and interior of the buildings as well as the grounds of the campus. Because the buildings are not designed "perfectly," volunteers are able to address the minor repairs without feeling nervous about doing a perfect job or having special skills.

Gojikara Mura not only attempts to preserve nature but also the locally significant building tradition and design vernacular. When two old farmhouses from the neighborhood were about to be demolished, Gojikara Mura bought and relocated the buildings to the campus for elderly residents and children to use as gathering places. These buildings also function as community centers to bring people from outside the campus to engage with elderly residents. These houses are frequently used for local events, such as seminars, children's education programs, or weddings.

The Gojikara Mura philosophy is that elders should be integrated into a normal lifestyle within a multigenerational community. At the adult day care, meals are prepared by the mothers of the children who attend the preschool. This arrangement allows mothers to reduce the trips between their home and the preschool and enables them to work part time. This, of course, has a mutual benefit for both the organization and the preschool mothers and is also an effective way to increase multigenerational interactions between mothers and children and elderly residents.

Another effort to create a normal lifestyle for elderly residents on the campus has been to promote a design that emphasizes small community rather than caring for the elderly in a large, institutional building. This feeling of community is reinforced by inclusion of cohousing, adult and child day care, and group homes for those with dementia, all set in the middle of a residential area apart from the main campus, but fully accessible to the main campus amenities. On this site, a respite spa and organic restaurant offer opportunities for family members to enjoy a respite with loved ones from the Gojikara Mura main campus. This remote portion of Gojikara Mura provides a destination for the main campus elderly residents for an "outing" in order to contribute to the sense of normalcy in their lives.

Staff and Volunteers

Human Resources

Are policies and designs in place to attract good staff and volunteers?

Gojikara Mura has an interesting philosophy toward staff education and training. Staff members are reminded that they should "not work too hard, and relax." The reason for this approach is that elders deserve to receive kind and genuine care from staff members who are not stressed due to their workload or pressures of the job. When staff members are stressed

FIGURE 9-8 Gojikara Mura cohousing in the nearby residential area. *Courtesy of Emi Kiyota*

because of completing multiple tasks, they might overlook what is important to the elderly residents and what might improve their quality of life. Staff members are encouraged to foster a meaningful relationship with elderly residents rather than focus only on completing tasks.

Since the organization's approach is to develop real relationships between elderly residents and staff members, staff are encouraged to reduce their pace of work and to sit beside elderly residents simply to provide social interaction. Because of the limitation of staff to pay full or appropriate attention to elderly residents, volunteers play an important part within the organization. Mothers of preschool children, nursing students, and retired people from the surrounding community all participate in nonclinical care for elderly residents such as walking with the elderly resident around the campus or simply sitting and talking.

- Direct care hours per day per client are unknown.

Environmental Sustainability

ALTERNATIVE ENERGY SOURCES

In various locations on the Gojikara Mura campus, the built environmental design includes solar panels for electric generation and energy-saving lighting fixtures.

WATER CONSERVATION

The campus uses collected rainwater for gardening purposes.

ENERGY CONSERVATION

The Gojikara Mura buildings are designed to maximize natural ventilation, and the maintaining of as many shade trees as possible has minimized the need for artificial air conditioning in the buildings.

FIGURE 9-9 Campus volunteers enjoying their break with staff members. *Courtesy of Emi Kiyota*

Outdoor Living

Garden

Does the garden support principles of care?

Because all of the buildings on the main campus are built within the heavily wooded property, people in the community are always surrounded by nature. Every resident has a view of nature, and each is able to hear the voices of children playing outside his or her windows. Local plants are placed around the buildings so that residents have access to local flowers and vegetation. Residents are provided with locations where a few vegetable gardens can be grown, and these are tended by both elderly residents and the children on campus. These vegetables are harvested and served in the resident and children dining venues. The exterior spaces are kept as natural as possible so a sense of familiarity can be provided for the elderly residents as well as local residents from the surrounding community.

FIGURE 9-10 Gojikara Mura is committed to the preservation of the campus trees. *Courtesy of Emi Kiyota*

Data Points

DESIGN FIRM
Takatsugu Oi
Japan

AREAS/SIZES
- Site area: 50,000 square meters (12.36 acres)
- Building footprint: Not available
- Total building area: Not available
- Total area per resident: Not available

PARKING
Surface parking for 50 automobiles

COSTS
Not available

RESIDENT AGE
Average age of residents: 87 years

RESIDENT PAYER MIX

Residents pay for their housing and meals, which are affordably priced, plus 10 percent of their care. The other 90 percent of care costs is subsidized by government universal long-term care insurance.

Chapter 10

A Study of Tenjin no Mori

REASONS FOR INCLUSION OF THIS SCHEME

- The extensive predesign process engaged residents, staff members, and local community members to create a culturally appropriate living environment.
- The design works to facilitate and encourage people from the local community to be a part of the care for the residents.
- The initiative of staff members to personalize each household in order to enhance the sense of home and develop a sense of ownership.
- The design utilizes symbolic meanings to promote a sense of familiarity for elderly residents with cognitive impairment.

Building Description

Name of scheme: Tenjin no Mori
Owner: Nagaokakyo Seisin Kai, a not-for-profit organization
Address:
19 Takenoshita okumiin tera
Nagaoka, Kyoto
Japan
Occupied since: 2009

FIGURE 10-1 Tenjin no Mori as viewed from the street.
Courtesy of Emi Kiyota

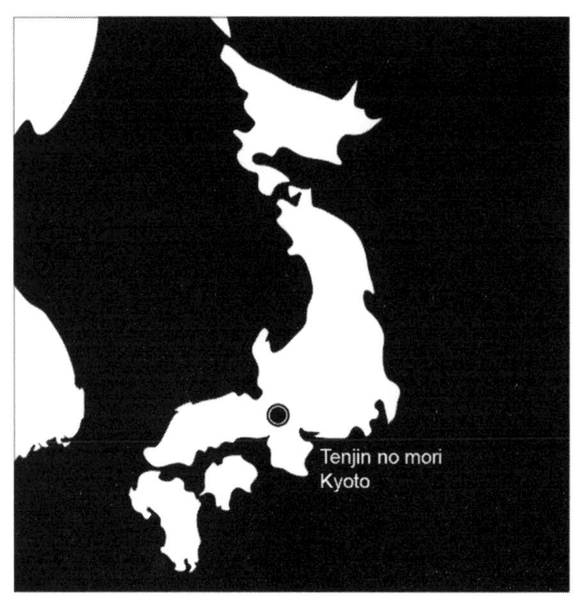

FIGURE 10-2 Scheme location. *Courtesy of Pozzoni LLP*

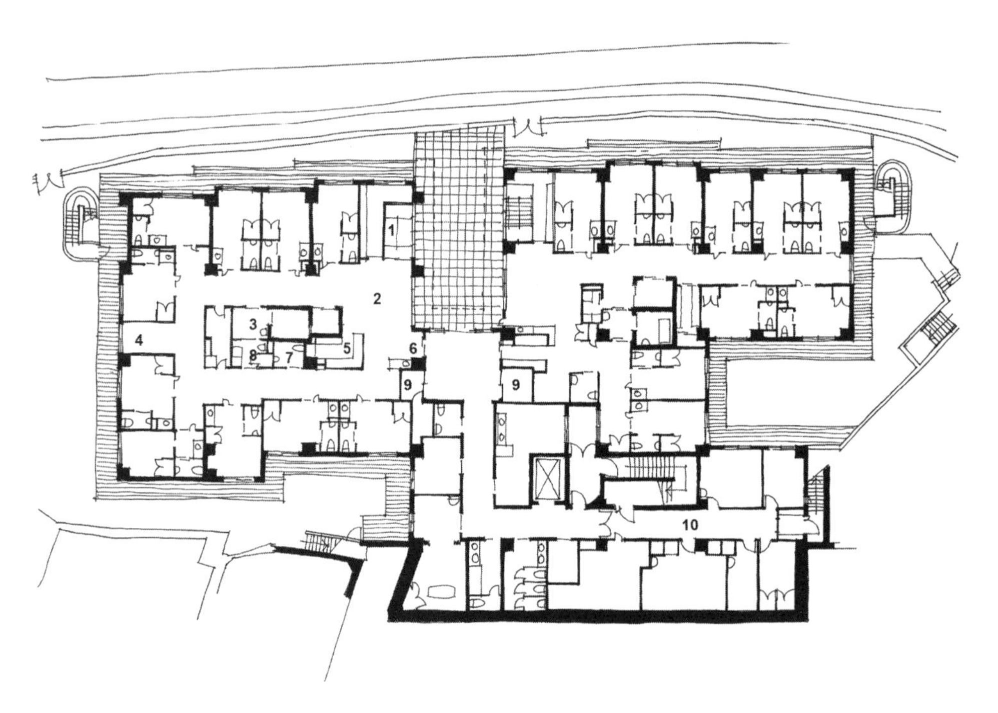

FIGURE 10-3 Ground floor plan. *Courtesy of Pozzoni LLP*

Description of the Type of Community, Including Number of Residents

Tenjin no Mori is a skilled nursing home located in Nagaokakyo, a residential suburb of Kyoto on the main Honshu island of Japan. This building supports 60 skilled nursing residents, all of whom have dementia or another cognitive impairment or have high levels of physical frailty. In addition, Tenjin no Mori provides an adult day-care service within the building for 25 elderly clients.

The building is composed of three stories containing a total of six households, with each story having two households for 10 residents each. Each household consists of single-resident bedrooms with en-suite bathrooms all within close proximity to the shared living room and kitchen. Tenjin no Mori provides each resident a bed and basic furniture, but the residents individualize their own room with their belongings. The residents themselves furnish and decorate the living room and kitchen area with the help of staff. The result is that each household takes on its own character and appearance that is a reflection of its residents.

One interesting feature of Tenjin no Mori is that rather than having a separate space for the day-care service, the clients who come to the adult day care spend their time in any one of the six households, choosing which unit they would prefer.

Geographics

Vernacular Design

How does the scheme/environment respond to the locality?

Unlike many Japanese urban environments, this neighborhood consists of low-rise Japanese-style houses. By comparison, Tenjin no Mori, at four stories, is quite conspicuous. This is only mitigated by the fact that, once inside, each household is small and domestic in scale, particularly the social spaces and the kitchen. In addition, the internal materials and finishes are quite familiar to the residents, thus providing a reassuring feeling of "home" to the residents.

FIGURE 10-4 Japanese tatami room in a unit. *Courtesy of Tenjin no Mori*

Care

Philosophy of Care

What is the operators' philosophy, and how does the building match this philosophy?

Tenjin no Mori's philosophy of care is based on three values: respect, compassion, and trust. This organization strives to accomplish these values through providing support that enhances a harmonious living environment, enables the concept of interdependence, ensures a normalized lifestyle, and encourages social interactions.

In order to achieve its mission, the organization has engaged both the local community and the residents

FIGURE 10-5 A female resident taking a nap in the living room. *Courtesy of Tenjin no Mori*

throughout the planning, development, commissioning, and implementation of the service. For example, in the planning stage, there were community meetings and one-on-one interviews with local residents in order to shape the nature of Tenjin no Mori's physical and social environment. Also, current residents and relatives of existing aged-care facilities within the region were asked how their social and care environments could be improved to serve residents with both physical and cognitive impairment.

Rather than being "task-focused," staff members are trained to ensure that the daily rhythms of each household are dictated by the preferences of its residents and their social, physical, and emotional needs rather than in accordance with a predetermined list. This approach is also extended to the support provided for family members of residents, for residents in hospice care, and for family members following the death of a resident.

Each household operates independently of the other five and is self-supporting. All meals are prepared and cooked within each household, and all activities within the household are determined by the preferences of the residents in that household.

Such a social environment can only be achieved with strong support from the management, which empowers staff members in each household to promote, as much as possible, a normal daily life among residents. One way this is achieved is through the building's design, which encourages social gatherings. For example, within the building, there is both a community space and a café that are frequently used by local community residents of all ages. Both these spaces are run by volunteers from the surrounding community.

Community and Belonging

How does the scheme's design and operation support this ideal?

The small, domestic scale and the independent operation of each household are key elements in developing a sense of community and belonging among the residents in each household. The living room spaces in each household were deliberately designed to be smaller than the typical "group homes" in Japan in an attempt to reinforce a sense of home. Each household has its own budget for the decoration of the social spaces. A household leader is assigned in each household, and the leader coordinates the care and environment that suits the needs of residents in that household. The management team provides approximately ¥102,500 (approximately $1,300 USD) annually that is divided into ¥71,000 ($900 USD) for activities and ¥31,500 ($400 USD) for physical environmental changes to encourage the staff's sense of ownership and responsibility in their work and their environment. This system allows each household to create its own unique culture and interior space.

To enhance the connection with the other households, small separate conversation spaces have been designed and are located between the households. These spaces allow residents, relatives, and staff the opportunity to naturally meet each other when they leave their household and to sit and have conversations in a comfortable and inviting space.

The interior spaces of Tenjin no Mori also provide opportunities for residents to be a part of the community. For example, the kitchen counter and sink within the households are faced toward the dining room space so that residents are able to help in the preparation, serving, and cleaning associated with each meal. Hallway design accommodates small areas for residents to personalize their own space just outside their rooms, and there is a traditional Japanese tatami flooring area next to the living room in order to encourage residents to participate in daily household activities within a familiar environment.

The neighborhood surrounding Tenjin no Mori is a close-knit community where neighbors have known each another for a considerable amount of time. These relationships have continued even as residents have entered care within Tenjin no Mori, and as a result,

FIGURE 10-6 A typical resident's room. *Courtesy of Tenjin no Mori*

local residents are frequent visitors to the facility. Community integration occurs naturally by means of the community center, which is freely available to the community for meetings. In the same way, the café offers opportunities for residents, staff members, and family visitors a place to socialize outside of their home and work places. Operated by volunteers from the surrounding community, the café facilitates interaction between those who live in the community and those who live in the building.

It would have been easy to design the community center and café on the ground floor. However, these two services are quite deliberately located on the top floor of the building, the purpose being that this location requires people from the surrounding community to go through the building to reach these facilities. This promotes familiarity with both the building's layout and the care that is provided within the building as well as increasing unplanned encounters with the residents in the building.

Tenjin no Mori also has convenient access to public transport, which means that taking residents to the shopping center and train station is easily achieved as well as making it easy for relatives and friends to visit.

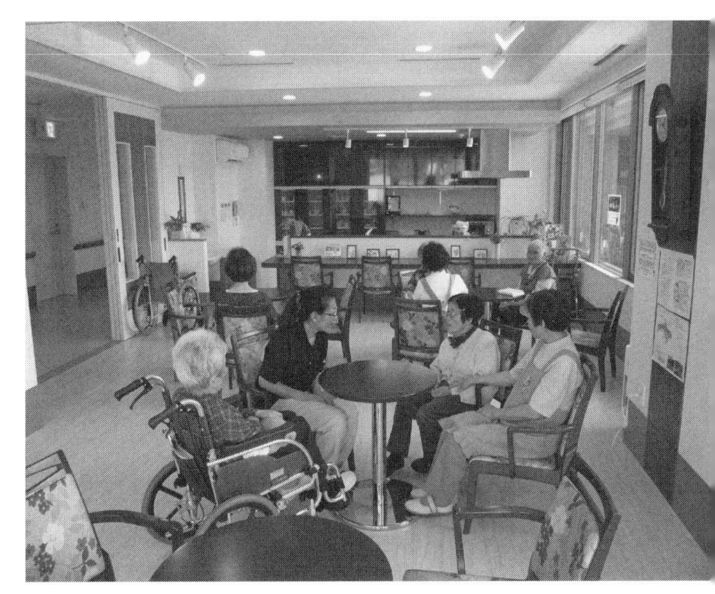

FIGURE 10-7 The café, which is operated by volunteers. *Courtesy of Tenjin no Mori*

Innovation

If the operator pursues a policy of innovation and excellence, how is it demonstrated?

There is a Japanese saying, "write the play before you build the stage," and Nagaokakyo Seisin Kai, the not-for-profit owner of Tenjin no Mori, undertook extensive predesign and programming in order to comply with this concept. Before designing the service, the owner formed an interdisciplinary project team, the goal of which was to work out how to design an environment that supported maximum independence for older people regardless of their physical and cognitive functions.

This collaboration even resulted in the building of "mock" rooms, including bedrooms and bathrooms, in a nearby existing long-term care facility. Then the team solicited the opinions of residents, staff members, and designers as to the utility and function of these spaces. The exercise resulted in a refinement and modification of the building design. This participatory design process had the additional powerful effect of educating staff members in the care approach to which Tenjin no Mori was aspiring and thus had substantive educational and design outcomes.

The collaborative process did not end once the building was completed, and staff involvement in the building's design functions is an ongoing feature of Tenjin no Mori. Staff members and residents choose all the furniture and decorations in the living room spaces in their households and thus every unit has a different and recognizable look and feel. The objective of this approach is to generate a strong sense of home, and to encourage the sense of ownership among residents and staff members of the households as their own home. This also provides an opportunity for staff to understand individual residents better and provide more effective care for them.

The goal of Tenjin no Mori is a "normal" lifestyle for its residents. In part, this is achieved by care practices that are focused on each individual resident working together with a physical environment that enables and encourages that normal lifestyle. Residents' rooms are fully personalized, and staff members and residents personalize the social spaces such as the living area and kitchen as well as the daily menu. Residents participate in daily house activities, such as preparing meals, laundry, and cleaning, while the domestic scale of the social spaces and the furniture and equipment in those spaces emphasizes the familiar and the normal.

The physical environment of the building, including uniquely designed hallways, bathroom, kitchen, and

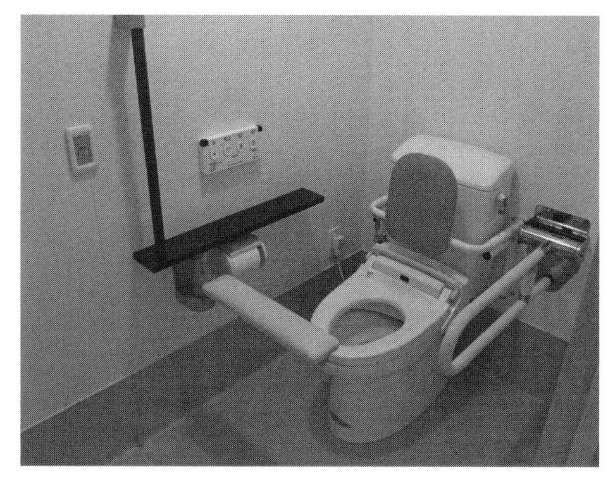

FIGURE 10-8 The bathroom arrangement was developed by staff members. *Courtesy of Tenjin no Mori*

FIGURE 10-9 Residents and staff members in a living room. *Courtesy of Tenjin no Mori*

activity spaces, is designed in such a way that residents are able to gain the benefits of rehabilitation through participating in activities throughout the day.

Staff and Volunteers

Human Resources

Are policies and designs in place to attract good staff and volunteers?

Tenjin no Mori encourages the hiring of staff members from the local neighborhood in this facility, which contributes to the maintenance of local culture and local connections. In addition to providing work locally, Tenjin no Mori provides attractive flexible work shifts, which means that staff are able to balance their work and family life. The effectiveness of these policies is evidenced by very high levels of staff retention over a long period of time. In turn, this supports consistency of care for residents as well as increasing staff satisfaction with their work.

The staffing ratio is one care staff for each three residents, and the caregivers are trained as universal workers. This means that they look after all the household work—from meal preparation to cleanup to care provision. In this staff ratio, each resident receives 3.3 hours a day of direct care from staff members.

- Direct care hours per day per resident are unknown.

Environmental Sustainability

ALTERNATIVE ENERGY SOURCES

None

WATER CONSERVATION

At Tenjin no Mori, the rainwater is collected and used for watering plants in the exterior spaces.

ENERGY CONSERVATION

A "green" roof has been incorporated into the design of the building to reduce the heating effect on the concrete roof structure and to help reduce CO_2 emissions. The building design uses insulated glazing throughout, and in living room spaces high ceilings are incorporated allowing a maximization of natural lighting in these rooms.

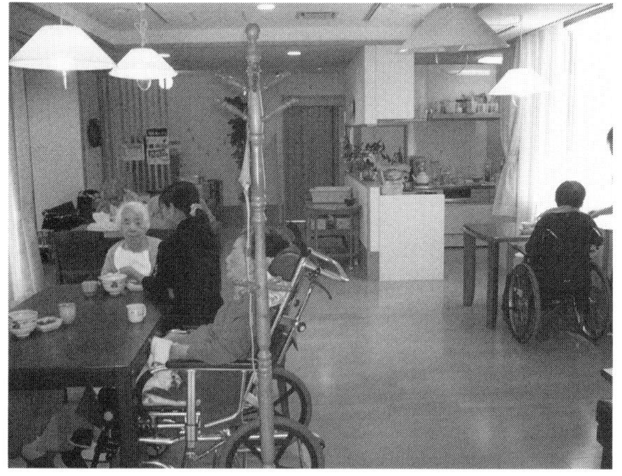

FIGURE 10-10 Mealtime in a dining area. *Courtesy of Tenjin no Mori*

Outdoor Living

Garden

Does the garden support principles of care?

The grounds of Tenjin no Mori are used as places where both residents and visitors from the surrounding community can meet informally. Seasonal festivals are also held in these outdoor spaces. Additionally, there is a large vegetable garden here where residents can grow vegetables with the help of staff participation, providing produce used in meal preparation.

On the upper floors of the building, there are patios just off of each household where residents are able to grow potted plants and enjoy the sun. This also provides a place where family members can sit privately with residents. The "green" rooftop is also a garden where residents and staff can tend to decorative plants and vegetables.

FIGURE 10-11 Outdoor open space looking towards a mountain. *Courtesy of Tenjin no Mori*

Project Data

DESIGN FIRM

Yu Architect
Japan

AREAS/SIZES

- Site area: 2,751.94 square meters (39,622 square feet)
- Building footprint: 1,231.02 square meters (13,251 square feet)
- Total building area: 3,336.8 square meters (35,917 square feet)
- Total area per resident: 46.92 square meters (505 square feet)

PARKING

Spaces for 19 automobiles

COSTS

- Total building cost: ¥650,000,000 ($8,007,820 USD)
- Cost per square meter: ¥194,494 ($2,397 USD)
- Cost per square foot: ¥$18,097 ($223 USD)
- Investment per resident: ¥1,083,333 ($133,268 USD)

RESIDENT AGE

Average age of residents: 87 years

RESIDENT PAYER MIX

Residents pay for their housing and meals, which are affordably priced, plus 10 percent of their care. The other 90 percent of care costs are subsidized by government universal long-term care insurance.

Part III

Swedish Schemes

Chapter 11
A Study of Neptuna

REASONS FOR INCLUSION OF THIS SCHEME

- The affordable apartments are located on premium and prominent real estate, thus providing an insight to the importance of elderly schemes in the planning stages of projects.
- The concept supports the sustainability of the community and neighborhood.
- Residents may not have to move from their apartment or their chosen lifestyle to a segregated older persons' care model.
- Neptuna does not take on the stereotypical appearance of an older persons' residence and as such supports its integration into the surrounding community.
- The scheme makes the powerful statement that older people have the right to reside in a positive environment that aesthetically expresses their individuality.
- This scheme provides attention to detail in the design, promoting the ability of residents to remain in their apartments and age in place.

Building Description

Name of Scheme: Neptuna
Owner: Stiftelsen Södertorpsgården, a not-for-profit trust
Address:
BoO1
Scaniaplatsen 2A
SE21117
Malmö
Sweden
Occupied since: 2005

FIGURE 11-1 The sea-side promenade viewed from the Neptuna spa pool. *Photograph by David Hughes*

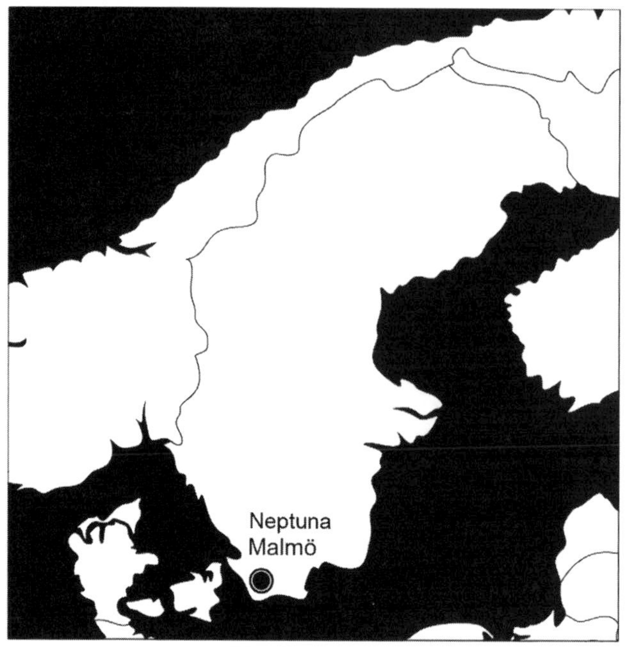

FIGURE 11-2 Scheme location. *Courtesy of Pozzoni LLP*

Neptuna: Sweden

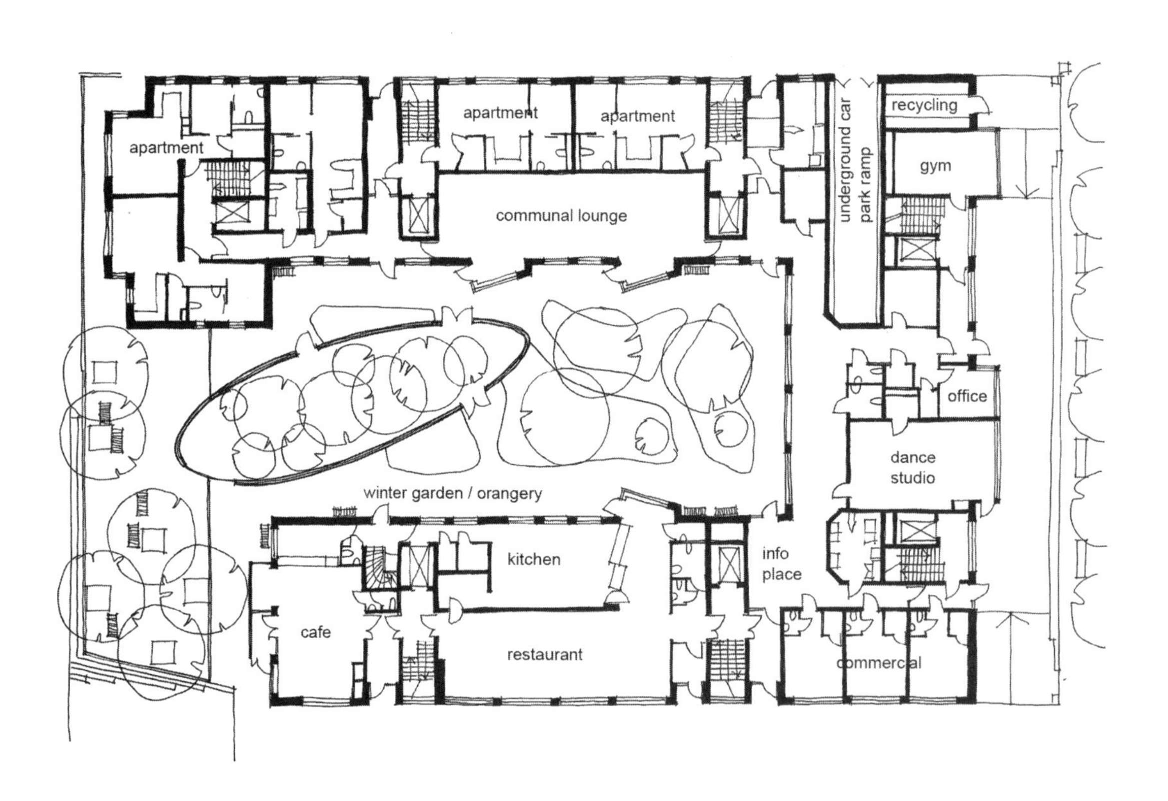

Ground Floor

FIGURE 11-3 Ground floor plan. *Courtesy of Pozzoni LLP*

Description of the Type of Community, Including Number of Residents

The Neptuna building is an affordable housing development for individuals who are over 55 years of age. It is situated within an ambitious, pioneering, and internationally recognized ecological redevelopment of the original Malmö Western Harbour area of Sweden, which aims to deliver a large-scale ecological community based on a sustainable energy culture. There are 95 one- and two-bedroom apartments included in this scheme. Also included are a wide range of health, lifestyle, and community facilities within a four-story building that is designed in a "U" shape with central courtyard and winter garden.

The BoO1 project regeneration area is part of the postindustrial waterfront region in Malmö, which has been labeled the "City of Tomorrow" in reference to its ambitious integrated solutions for sustainability. When complete, the area will house around 10,000 residents, employ about 20,000 workers, and include educational facilities for students within a 62-acre project.

The scheme is owned by Stiftelsen Södertorpsgården, a not-for-profit trust, which provides accommodation within an affordable social support model, as well as within a building and locality that would attract the highest private sector market rental and sales values. The popularity of the scheme reflects its appeal to many older people within the city who wish to trade in the family home for a sustainable urban environment.

Due to its popularity and associated waiting lists of between five to seven years, the majority of present tenants are about 75 years of age and older. Occupants are required to be over 55 years, retired from work, receiving a pension, and registered as a resident of Malmö. Applications are coordinated and reviewed by the municipality, but the Trust owners retain final tenancy control and approval.

What sets Neptuna apart from traditional supported or retirement housing schemes is that the development places older people at the heart of a new and prestigious high-quality seafront community which is part of an acknowledged exemplary "Lifetime Neighborhood." This may be a reference to the fact that Neptuna was included within the original redevelopment strategy to provide a positive local and integrated retirement facility, which would mean that at a point in the future, today's local younger residents could remain and retire within the area without having to move out of the community.

Neptuna compliments both the design and environmental ambitions of the wider redevelopment program by delivering an innovative living space and building that promotes a wide community inclusion and involvement.

Geographics

Vernacular Design

How does the scheme/environment respond to the locality?

The Neptuna scheme provides no immediate visual prompt that it is a housing complex for older people, or indeed that its occupants are elderly. In this respect, it responds positively to its presence within this high-quality, high-profile neighborhood that has become a very desirable place to live as a result of the good design of the housing throughout the development. The contemporary, cubist-based design of Neptuna compliments neighboring buildings, whose color schemes are offset against the more neutral-based materials used by Neptuna. The balconies, unique winter atrium, and contemporary ground-floor café, bar, restaurant, health suite, and other amenities located on the promenade seamlessly present as one of the numerous seafront apartment developments providing private accommodation.

The scale of the four-story building is in keeping with the overall redevelopment design master plan, which purposely placed larger buildings on the exposed seafront to provide shelter to the inner spaces where more domestic-scale properties, such as family apartments and homes, are located.

The architects intended a contemporary version of the nearby medieval town of Lund and, in many ways, have succeeded. Behind Neptuna an intricate network of alleyway connecting spaces, focused on the pedestrian, make it distinctly uncomfortable to use motorized transport. The buildings, whether the taller ones on the perimeter or the two-story dwellings within the town,

FIGURE 11-4 A glimpse beyond Neptuna's buildings into the neighborhood center. *Photograph by David Hughes*

tend to form the spaces by often being built to the roadside, thus making the overall effect quite unique. In this respect, there are no high-density tower blocks with the singular exception of the high-profile "Turning Torso," a dramatic landmark skyscraper designed by the renowned architect Santiago Calatrava.

Care

Philosophy of Care

What is the operators' philosophy, and how does the building match this philosophy?

This is an affordable elderly housing community rather than a traditional supported housing model that would include a care component. There is no formal care operator and thus no related philosophy of care. However, the facility manager provides a certain level of care advice and support during weekday times for the residents. Care in both the personal health and practical domestic sense can easily be purchased privately from a choice of local care and support operators. There is presently no collective support agreement or centralized contract. This reflects somewhat, within certain areas of Sweden, the move away from the Nordic translation of total federal government responsibility for the welfare of the elderly.

In the absence of a formal operator care philosophy, it is realistic to consider the building as providing a deliberate culture of promoting tenant independence and an associated level of support through its design, environment, and facilities, at both individual apartment and common social space levels. Within each apartment, the level of attention to the prospective and future needs of the older tenants anticipates future physical support requirements and negates the need for additional practical aids that can fundamentally alter the appearance of many older people's dwellings from a domestic to a medical environment.

Large window areas, high ceilings, the provision of a well-proportioned external balcony area at each apartment and associated panoramic views deliver high levels of natural light and easy access to the outside environment. These are factors that have been proven to contribute to general well-being for older people and those with dementia support needs.

The design and scale of the apartments, which are between 43 square meters and 54 square meters (462.85 square feet and 581.25 square feet) facilitates a variety of furniture arrangements, which in turn supports tenants

FIGURE 11-5 A typical apartment living room. *Photograph by David Hughes*

FIGURE 11-6 Common spaces for all residents include a communal lounge. *Photograph by David Hughes*

with physical support needs such as the need for wheelchairs or ambulation assistive devices. In addition, the provision of adaptable kitchens and high-quality wet-room bathroom suites, which include toilet, shower, and lavatory, all fully adjustable and flexible, is further enhanced by adjustable integrated cabinets and storage areas, all of which provide sensitive, practical support on a domestic scale.

The larger development scheme amenities and services, which are provided within the overall rental fee, include a café, restaurant, laundry, small fitness suite, spa, solarium, sauna, library, large external glass atrium, and activity area. Together, these amenities and the Neptuna structure combine to promote a socially sustainable environment that supports the tenants' well-being, fitness, independence, and social interaction.

FIGURE 11-7 The spa at Neptuna overlooks the promenade. *Photograph by David Hughes*

Community and Belonging

How does the scheme design and operation support this ideal?

The building offers three, or potentially four, distinct levels of privacy, community, and belonging. These are offered first by the individual apartments themselves, followed by the various floor levels, then the Neptuna building as a whole with its associated central facilities, and finally its position and integration within the wider waterfront community and neighborhood.

The "promenade" in front of the building along the seafront has an abundance of relaxing sitting areas. Once among the buildings, one will discover a delightful series of interconnecting spaces offering tantalizing and inviting glimpses beyond.

Discussions with the design architects and a number of established apartment tenants determined that while a normal neighborhood culture was present, a strong sense of a building-wide collective community within Neptuna does not presently exist. It was evident that tenants established closer relationships with their immediate apartment neighbors and people who share activities, a situation reflective of the wider general community.

A range of events are organized, but the level of retained ability and independence of the present tenant profile suggests that the retired occupants relate to the wider community more than the actual building community. This may well change as the age profile changes with tenants becoming older. This could be a reflection of the well-being of the occupants and their relationship to the building with the building's support and promotion of good health.

The scheme design provides limited opportunity for "occasional and informal" apartment neighbor socialization as the building is served by seven elevators and associated stairs. These effectively service four apartments per floor, with no linked corridors between them. While this model maximizes the available space for the apartments, delivers positive levels of privacy and a domestic scale often ignored in more traditional supported housing schemes and retirement villages, it severely restricts casual interaction between residents. Informal support networks have developed, however, and anecdotal evidence points to the feeling that older tenants believe they would be able to call upon the support of fellow occupants should their health fail in older age.

Postoccupancy evaluations have determined that usage by residents of the scheme's central facilities has not been as high as was originally anticipated within the design and building function. There is evidence, however, that the practical areas, such as laundry, library, and activity areas, are well utilized, and the exciting top-floor sauna, spa, and sun room are quite popular with a core group of users, whereas the café, restaurant, and original licensed bar have yet to become a meaningful venue for Neptuna or people from the neighboring community. This may have something to do with competition from "real" bars in the surrounding neighborhood, or that the overall neighborhood has still to establish itself in terms of social activity or patterns. The high-profile external ground-floor glass atrium is also a facility that has been underused by residents.

Innovation

If the operator pursues a policy of innovation and pursuit of excellence, how is it demonstrated?

While there is no traditional care operator policy of innovation to share as this scheme provides no registered or formal care, the building demonstrates innovation and excellence at a number of levels. Most obviously, this is demonstrated in its ability to deliver a high-quality affordable housing environment to older people within such a high-profile, prestigious redevelopment region and emergent community. It is important to consider the scheme and its contribution to the wider regeneration project and its objective to deliver a mixed community profile.

Within the design of the individual apartments, the attention to detail and level of investment provide an environment that supports occupants as they age, representing a level of innovation that is often absent from many supported housing models.

Neighborhood Integration

Community Involvement

Is the scheme and service designed to integrate successfully with the local community?

The scheme is designed to respond positively to the wider design and environmental ambitions of the regeneration project by providing a community that can contribute to the neighborhood economy by using and accessing local community facilities via foot, bicycle, or public transport.

The overall building design reflects and compliments its waterfront neighbors by delivering high-quality accommodation that supports a contemporary urban look and lifestyle including the positive application of balconies, courtyards, and pedestrian areas. The location of the library, activity suite, and gym on the ground floor with high-profile street frontage provides strong visual prompts to the wider community as to the function of the building, its presence within the locality, and the associated positive image of older people as active citizens and integrated members of the local neighborhood.

In the larger community just outside Neptuna, facilities include a suite of commercial health and beauty shops, hairdressers, a podiatrist, and massage therapy along the street frontage, all of which are open to and well used by the local community, further promoting intergenerational activity and involvement. In addition, the scheme has a licensed bar, café, and larger restaurant on the ground floor with high-profile street and waterfront locations. As these amenities are open to the public they provide positive opportunities for community integration, socialization, and the development of greater intergenerational activity.

The ground-floor central courtyard and garden also reflect the design ambitions of the wider neighborhood. With its open access to the area and the waterfront, it presents a welcoming and inclusive culture in both physical and human terms that is so often absent in supported communities for the elderly, which focus upon security and therefore give the feeling of isolation rather than integration.

It will be interesting to observe over time whether it is the "real" facilities in the wider neighborhood that are of more value than the prescribed facilities within. This is an interesting observation for older people's facilities everywhere: that in fact older people just want access to

FIGURE 11-8 Neptuna's café is open to the surrounding neighborhood. *Photograph by David Hughes*

mainstream community participation and involvement, rather than be segregated. Interestingly, the atrium or winter garden greenhouse is not open to the public.

Staff and Volunteers

Human Resources

Are policies and designs in place to attract good staff and volunteers?

A single scheme manager provides a level of advice and support during weekday working hours for the residents. However, there is not a dedicated care program or staff as this is a development intended for independent elderly residents. The manager is financed through the resident service charges. The manager's role combines some administration, practical tasks, and signposting on advice. The restaurant is run on a commercial basis with no tenant subsidy. There is no staff in the sauna or gym. The residents are required to access these facilities themselves.

Environmental Sustainability

Neptuna is part of a wider pioneering housing and mixed-use development that has strong environmental credentials and ambitions without compromising the overall master plan design objectives and associated quality ambitions. The building is situated within an area that is predominantly designed for pedestrian access by way of shared-space planning, and prioritizing pedestrians and cyclists over motorized vehicles. The local integrated bus service that links the community to wider Malmö uses vehicles that run on a natural gas and biogas mixture.

A low-carbon urban regeneration agenda drives the redevelopment ambition, with the former industrial docks being transformed into a green residential and mixed-use community based on a 100 percent locally produced renewable energy platform. The area has been designed using a green planning tool called the "Green Space Factor" and has also utilized a local stormwater management system. The building, in line with the wider region, supports an integrated waste management system with recycle "chutes" for various waste being positioned in each foyer. The appropriate waste is recycled to produce renewable energy.

ALTERNATIVE ENERGY SOURCES

No alternative energy sources have been incorporated into the design, but there has been an energy conservation system incorporated into the ventilation system. Under enacted regulations, all new resident energy consumption must be below 110 kWh/m/year.

WATER CONSERVATION

All water conservation measures required by regulation have been incorporated into the design.

ENERGY CONSERVATION

Neptuna was originally chosen to study because of its purported sustainability and environmental credentials, but the research, meetings, and follow-up discussion with the design architects did not provide any information in this regard that was particularly useful or unique.

Outdoor Living

Garden

Does the garden support principles of care?

Despite the obvious challenges imposed by the Scandinavian climate, outdoor living is an important part of Swedish society and culture. Therefore, retaining and promoting accessible garden resources was an integral part of the building design and ambition. The building responds positively to its unique location and dramatic outlook by ensuring that all apartments benefit directly from their clear relationship to the sea and horizon.

Traditional garden areas are limited, in line with the wider waterfront and community model, but outside living is provided by means of the individual apartment balconies, a central courtyard hard-landscaped area with seating that links to the main entrance and the scheme

FIGURE 11-9 Inside the winter garden on a summer's day. *Photograph by David Hughes*

frontage. In addition, garden space at Neptuna is enhanced by a large dramatic glass atrium and winter garden facility that was added to the original concept and designed separately by a landscape architect after the original commission for the building.

The apartment balconies are positioned so that each one has, at a minimum, a partial seafront view. Several apartments have full uninterrupted seafront vistas that would command the highest property values within a commercial context. The relatively close proximity to the neighboring buildings, their balconies, and open-plan living concept is accepted as the cultural and wider community norm and not viewed as a negative issue. The balconies are individualized and well used by residents, providing a flexible and stimulating external garden space for each resident. In addition, the common room and the top-floor spa with its large-scale terraces have strong and direct visual connections to the outside and neighboring community.

The landscaped garden is deliberately an open plan, as the scheme has no requirements to promote tenant safety or supervision. This space provides a sheltered environment in winter and a shaded area in summer. Unfortunately, the impact and original planned functionality of this garden area, and arguably the building itself, has been compromised by the addition of the large

FIGURE 11-10 The winter garden pushing into the courtyard. *Photograph by David Hughes*

glazed atrium or winter garden at the front of the scheme. This atrium has partly obscured the designed views from some of the apartments and balcony areas, and reduces the impact and relationship of the building to the open seafront area. Informal evidence suggests that this visually dramatic facility, which in many ways defines the building's frontage, has proved expensive to maintain from a glass and plant perspective and of limited practical benefit as tenants do not tend to spend valued time within the area due to the winter temperatures. Unfortunately, the greenhouse proves to be too cold for use in winter and too hot for use in summer and as a result of this lack of use, is appearing somewhat in need of maintenance.

Project Data

DESIGN FIRM

Arkitektgruppen i Malmö AB
Niklas Olsson and Lars Karud
Angelholmsgatan 1a
214 22 Malmö
Sweden
www.arkitektgruppen.nu

AREAS/SIZES

- Site area (Neptuna not BoO1): 2,560 square meters (27,556 square feet; .63 acres)
- Building footprint: 1,360 square meters (14,639 square feet)
- Total building area: 8,605 square meters (93,623 square feet)
- Total area per resident: This information is unavailable. The scheme is composed of affordable apartments, and the number of residents in each apartment varies.
- The one- and two-bedroom apartments range from 43 to 65 square meters (462.85 to 699.65 square feet).

PARKING

There are 32 parking spaces in the building's basement. The low car space to overall apartment ratio reflects the developer's ambition to support the wider region's environmental objectives by promoting local community use and integrated public transport.

COSTS (2005)

- Total building cost: 136,000,000 SEK ($21,707,313 USD)
- Cost per square meter: 16,000 SEK ($2,554 USD)
- Cost per square foot: 1,434 SEK ($234 USD)
- Investment per resident: This information is unavailable. The scheme is composed of affordable apartments, and the number of residents in each apartment varies.

RESIDENT AGE

Residents are required to be a minimum of 55 years old, retired from work, receiving pension, and registered as a resident in Malmö. However, due to its popularity and the five- to seven-year waiting list, most people do not move into Neptuna until they are significantly older than 55. The present average resident age is about 75 years.

RESIDENT PAYER MIX

The original funding profile was based on rental levels that were linked to tenant income and pension entitlements. The cost of renting an apartment is about 5,266 SEK ($835.340 USD) a month.

Part IV

Danish Schemes

Chapter 12

A Study of Salem Nursing Home

REASONS FOR INCLUSION OF THIS SCHEME

- A building that supports very dependent older people within the constraints of a new building built on the original footprint of a previous building.
- The design brought a sense of collective identity to a building that supports four households over two floors.
- Salem delivers a balance between the individuality, privacy, and identity of each household without the feeling of isolation.
- The building is well respected by the staff that work within it.
- The scheme delivers a very focused environment that makes best use of space, light levels, and sensitive staff support layout.

Building Description

Name of Scheme: Salem AELdreboliger Nursing Home

Owner: The building is owned by a private fund, which is administered by Diakonissestiftelsen, a private not-for-profit company. The care is provided by the local Gentofte Council–supported community organization, and is overseen and managed in line with the wider Danish care model by a local community group that includes Council, nursing home staff, and community representatives.

Address:
Mitchellsstraede 5
2820 Gentofte
Denmark

Occupied since: 2005

FIGURE 12-1 The winter garden and balcony serving social groups C and D from the lawn. *Photograph by David Hughes*

FIGURE 12-2 Scheme location. *Courtesy of Pozzoni LLP*

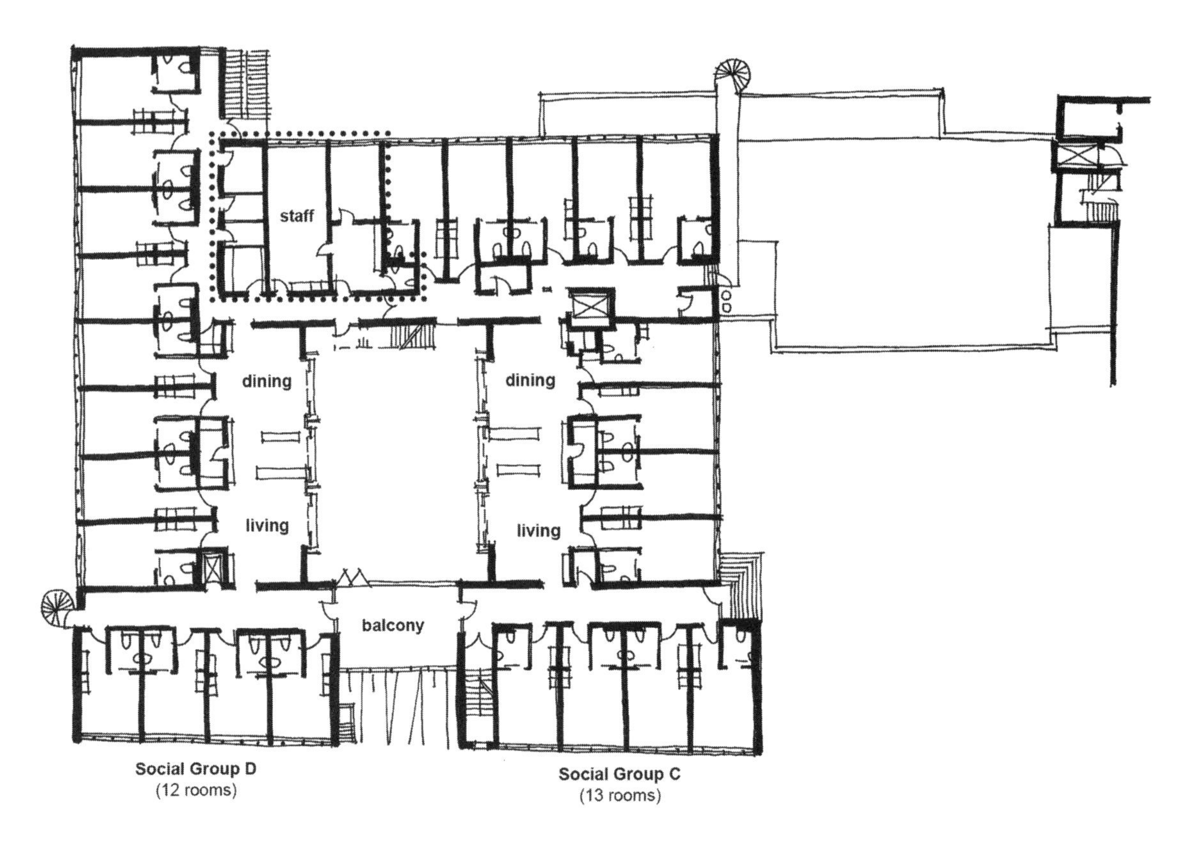

FIGURE 12-3 Upper floor plan. *Courtesy of Pozzoni LLP*

Description of the Type of Community, Including Number of Residents

Salem AELdreboliger is a nursing home located in Gentofte, an affluent suburb of Copenhagen, 10 kilometers north of the City Center.

The original care home was built in 1963 but had become outdated, thereby challenging its ability to appropriately support older people with increased dependency levels. Therefore, the building was effectively demolished, and the present Salem Nursing Home became operational in 2005.

The new building is positioned within a mixed residential and commercial area, surrounded on three sides by apartment buildings, supported housing units, private dwellings, and small businesses. A local school and variety of shops are in close proximity, thus providing a sensitive and integrated community presence.

The rear elevation faces outward onto the expansive Gentofte Municipal Park and Lake, providing an exceptional view and combined sense of openness and green space.

The nursing home supports 45 older people with predominantly high dependency support needs who live within four separate but linked households of between 8 and 13 people. The client profile includes a majority of people with dementia support needs.

Residents are required to rent their apartment and provide their own furniture, clothing, and so forth, with rental levels based on individual income and savings levels. In addition, residents fund their medical, food, laundry, and associated housekeeping costs, while all care and support costs are provided free by the state.

Most residents are from the local area, but older people from outside Gentofte who relocate to be near family support can also access the nursing home, following assessments and decisions by the Local Council.

Each household is essentially self-contained, deliberately domestic in scale with its own identity, culture, and purpose. All households, however, have strong visual links to one another and to the central common areas. This includes a large glazed atrium that replaced the original central courtyard, thus providing a combination of physical privacy, wider stimulus, and controlled independence to residents and the opportunity for sensitive observation and support by staff.

The name "Salem" in Denmark has come to mean creating a life full of joy, togetherness, and well-being for residents and such aspirations were applied to the design principles within this nursing home rebuild.

Geographics

Vernacular Design

How does the scheme/environment respond to the locality?

Extensive consultation occurred with the local community and their input on specific requirements was integrated into the final design, making the scheme well received by the community and local environment.

There was a strong locality desire for the new nursing home to present a modern version of the original building in terms of scale and materials. The community wanted a complex with the same architecture, so the building remained a two-story design (with a basement), which used the same light-color bricks, roof tiles, and materials to connect with the neighboring buildings.

The extensive use of glazed window areas, the atrium, and the building's positive relationship with its external space has enabled a traditional cubic design to have its own identity within the locality. Such final treatment has softened a somewhat utilitarian appearance, which benefits from its seamless physical integration within its immediate surroundings.

The atrium and related patio and garden areas deliver a sympathetic but powerful contribution to the adjacent Gentofte Park and Lake. Such detail as the matching and positioning of the large metal atrium support pillars with an established dramatic external tree avenue that stretches down to the lake from the nursing home, provides a seamless vista.

Care

Philosophy of Care

What is the operators' philosophy, and how does the building match this philosophy?

The philosophy of care at Salem is built around a desire to provide realistic independence and choice to older people with very dependent physical and mental support needs, the majority of whom require support with daily living tasks such as eating, dressing, and toileting.

Community representatives, staff, management, and service users participated in a 12-month consultation and design brief program prior to the new build, considering all living and working requirements, from practical washing arrangements to end-of-life care. The balance between the layers of available privacy and community involvement/stimulus was viewed as important and central to both care philosophy and building design. To provide such support it was essential the building design delivered a domestic and homey scale and environment, which helped residents to feel safe, orientated, and at home as quickly as was practicable.

The redevelopment of the building was challenged by the requirement to use the existing former nursing home footprint, which restricted any physical extension, and plans for the opening out of the basement level to the local park were viewed as too expensive. Further investigation determined the original building could not accommodate modern resident track lifts and associated technology, therefore, it was effectively demolished and only the basement and central kitchen areas were retained. Such restrictions resulted in a building that is relatively small by many modern operator standards, but provides a warm home environment and practical operational functionality.

The basement level houses all utility, staff support, training, and some administrative functions, and the ground floor front elevation is the location for reception, offices, and central kitchen, alongside a large high-profile café with views across the park.

The polarization of these utility and administrative functions enables the four households to provide a domestic environment devoid of the usual institutional presence and processes. This helps staff to focus on the individual care and support responsibilities within a house and family context rather than a larger and traditional nursing home environment.

Privacy, personal space, and socialization opportunities are deliberately structured around three integrated physical levels, or "layers," that is, the residents' own apartments, the individual households, and the wider nursing home community, which includes the café, atrium, hairdresser salon, gymnasium, and supported recreational and social activity areas.

Each resident apartment is large enough to facilitate the flexible positioning of movable furniture based on personal choice and support requirements. Large en-suite bathrooms are equipped with adjustable sinks, showers, cupboards, and grab rails to provide adaptable support to changing dependency needs. A small compact kitchenette facility is provided to allow those able to make simple snacks and drinks to do so which promotes continued independence. Every apartment has a large external window plus individual balcony with garden, lake, or open views. Front doors are recessed to provide a level of defensible and personal space, and memory cabinets and large photographs/name plates situated by resident apartment doors are used as visual prompts to aid orientation.

In each household a number of the apartments open directly into the open-plan integrated kitchen and living area and the remaining apartments open onto a short corridor. In the larger household the original footprint has necessitated the use of two short apartment corridors, which could present orientation issues in respect to dead ends and potential confusion. All corridors are wide enough to accommodate occasional furniture and end with a large glazed window wall which delivers positive light levels. The apartments are only located on the external side of the corridors, which removes any opposite facing doors, thus avoiding greater confusion and compromising privacy levels.

The household area provides the main focus for social interaction and activity, which is a central element of the operator's philosophy. A combination of fixed and movable kitchen units and worktops enables the open-plan kitchen, dining, and living space to be flexibly adapted in support of various activities and resident support requirements.

The open-plan common areas, furnished in typical Danish simple wooden furniture and neutral colors,

FIGURE 12-4 Kitchen area of social group D.
Photograph by David Hughes

provide excellent space for residents with mobility issues and strong physical visual prompts in respect to the various areas and functions, such as kitchen, dining, and living areas. They also support orientation for those residents with dementia. The use of lighting to "guide," and open shelving and cupboards to deliver links between the physical area and purpose, are successfully used within the model.

Clinical and operational practical tasks, such as individual laundry rooms with laundry chutes, are undertaken within discreet separate staff areas off the household space. This negates the need for disruptive housekeeping and institutional activity.

The independent but close proximity of the two households per floor supports the efficient deployment of staff resources, especially at night, when the staff team support is delivered on a floor basis. Staff also share an administrative base per floor, situated outside the actual household area to reduce the associated institutional and medical appearance and function.

The third level of building and community provides the general and common areas, which can be physically accessed by more able residents and visually accessed by the more dependent occupants. The operator uses an electronic tag system to discreetly monitor residents with dementia, enabling them to access the wider building safely.

The operator's philosophy in terms of activity, inclusivity, and choice relate to these building levels. For example, residents can chose to eat in their own apartments, the households, or the café, which is accessed by older people from the neighboring supported housing complex, thus providing a variety of social contact and privacy. At all three levels, the natural light has been deliberately maximized through the use of large window and glazed areas, wide verandas, and patio doors and the integration of the central full-building-height glass atrium, which provides an internal "outside" space all year round.

Such positive light levels are a direct design response to the Danish seasons with long winter periods of minimal natural light and the acknowledged impact of reduced light levels upon older people. Those with dementia, such as raised anxiety and depression, are especially affected. Light is also directed downward through the building via roof skylights and discreet glass floor panels in the first floor corridor and household areas. This is carefully monitored in respect to lessen potential anxiety for residents with dementia support needs. In contrast, lower ceiling heights and reduced light levels are applied in specific areas to deliver a deliberate calm and relaxing environment and context, which supports further visual and sensory prompts for residents.

FIGURE 12-5 The winter garden with the internal metal trellis columns reflecting the avenue of poplar trees in the garden beyond. *Photograph by David Hughes*

Community and Belonging

How do the scheme design and operation support this ideal?

As presented, the scheme design supports a strong sense of belonging and "layers" of community that reflect wider society (i.e., the ability to have choice with regard to social interaction and involvement).

The design inclusion of the central glass atrium makes a major impact on the development of a tangible sense of community and belonging. Although simple in concept, it distinguishes Salem Nursing Home from many other homes, given its relatively traditional design footprint. The design was influenced and inspired by some of the larger shopping arcades in London, which had high glass domes or ceilings with internal open balconies.

The atrium and the deliberately wide, internal visual design effectively provide a year-round visual physical and psychological link between the relationship of the four households within the scheme, which face each

FIGURE 12-6 Somewhat obscured by the trellis work, the doors and balconies from social groups A and C into the winter garden. *Photograph by David Hughes*

other across the central glass atrium, at both a floor and whole-building level. It enables residents to observe activity and interest outside their own households. This has proved to be a positive influence in increasing residents' levels of general well-being by stimulating them to have purposeful places to go and join in social events, groupings, and activities.

In addition, this internal open facility also provides subtle changes in the climate levels within the building, which appears to be positive in combating the very sedentary atmosphere that is apparent in many traditional European nursing and care homes. Even during the winter months, a sense of external "fresh air" is available. For those residents who are unable to access the outside on a regular basis, a visible and physical change in the environment, atmosphere, and physical senses can be achieved. For those residents who choose not to, or who are less able to join in at the wider nursing home level, these design and positive visual orientation prompts enable them to develop and engender a stronger sense of belonging than schemes where the households or units are physically isolated.

The design balances the operational thinking that supporting older people is better undertaken within smaller group, family, or unit type models, with concerns regarding potential lack of social interaction and stimulus. Thus, the challenge to provide older people who may have dementia with a purposeful and realistic concept of community has been successfully surmounted. Supported by a vibrant and structured activity program, involving residents coming together on a household, floor, and whole-home basis, the central operator philosophy of promoting a healthy social life is delivered by operational strategy and supported by the built environment.

Innovation

If the operator pursues a policy of innovation and pursuit of excellence, how is it demonstrated?

The principle innovation is demonstrated by the ability of very dependent older people to live as independently as the built and care environment enables, and to support individuals regardless of their increased

FIGURE 12-7 The dining area for social group B. *Photograph by David Hughes*

dependencies with meaningful choice, accessible social interaction, and visual stimulus.

The building and related care philosophy deliver a safe community, with reduced physical risk and promote the support of very dependent older people within an environment that is domestic in scale and predominantly free of any medical context. Detailed individual assessments and ongoing care plans, supportive technology, and a well-supported staff team complement the physical home.

In relation to such design innovation and its relationship to the balance between operational efficiency and the development of a real home environment, the architects, Thora Arkiteckter, recognize that Salem is a positive step in the right direction. However, further work is required within Denmark and the wider international context to balance the recent movement to design care buildings around staff and support functionality and its related economic and operational benefit, rather than the people who are to live within them.

Within the pursuit of excellence, Thora Arkiteckter are also challenging the concept that by involving older people more in the design phase the outcome will, by default, be a more homey environment. While domestic-scale care is positive, there is also evidence that older people want physical and sensory stimulus from new impressions and experiences within their lives. The building allows this to happen with a variety of spaces opening up the potential for more intergenerational and mixed-use activities to provide these extra stimuli.

Attention to detail and its impact on the resident are also delivering innovative thoughts and design solutions, as demonstrated by the introduction of two levels of lighting within resident bathrooms. On the practical and operational level, good lighting is required to support older people in basic tasks and activities, but the availability of softer and more "personal" lighting has the potential for older people to feel better about themselves, their physical appearance, and overall well-being.

Greater attention to materials and their visual impact, rather than just their functionality, is another area that is being subject to further evaluation and innovation.

FIGURE 12-8 An illustration of the adaptable fixtures in the en-suite bathroom. *Photograph by David Hughes*

Neighborhood Integration

Community Involvement

Is the scheme and service designed to integrate successfully with the local community?

The nursing home is linked to the neighboring Klockershave social enterprise–supported housing scheme. This larger community has 53 apartments and, in line with the local community requirements, the two care schemes share some common facilities such as a hairdressing salon and café/restaurant, which is used by the Klockershave Apartment tenants for lunch and evening meals. These facilities were part of an integrated local plan, but until 2011 the café was not providing support to any local older people or the wider community. Work is underway to encourage greater involvement so that the human integration matches the positive physical and building community integration.

Staff and Volunteers

Human Resources

Are policies and designs in place to attract good staff and volunteers?

Salem promotes a culture of staffing involvement, which is underpinned by Danish employment culture and regulation, as demonstrated by tangible staff contribution to the building design process.

There is a high level of longstanding staff, which promotes a low turnover rate and positive consistency for residents. Recruitment has become easier within the recent employment and economic climate, and Salem is well placed due to positive pay rates and contractual conditions. The high staff to resident ratio of one staff to four residents, provides positive care levels and higher job satisfaction. Overall there is a large staff of approximately 120, which translates to 65 full-time positions providing three direct care hours per day per client. Full induction and training programs that promote continual learning are used to support and deliver changing practice.

Environmental Sustainability

Fundamentally, this building complies with the Danish requirements for insulation and energy use. Its greatest advantage is the scale and use of its winter garden. This relatively large facility enables easier regulation of temperature in the open-plan lounges and dining areas of each of the four social groups. In either hot or cold weather, the temperature in the building does not have to be regulated with additional heating or cooling as it would if this internal courtyard did not exist.

ALTERNATIVE ENERGY SOURCES

None

WATER CONSERVATION

None

ENERGY CONSERVATION

None

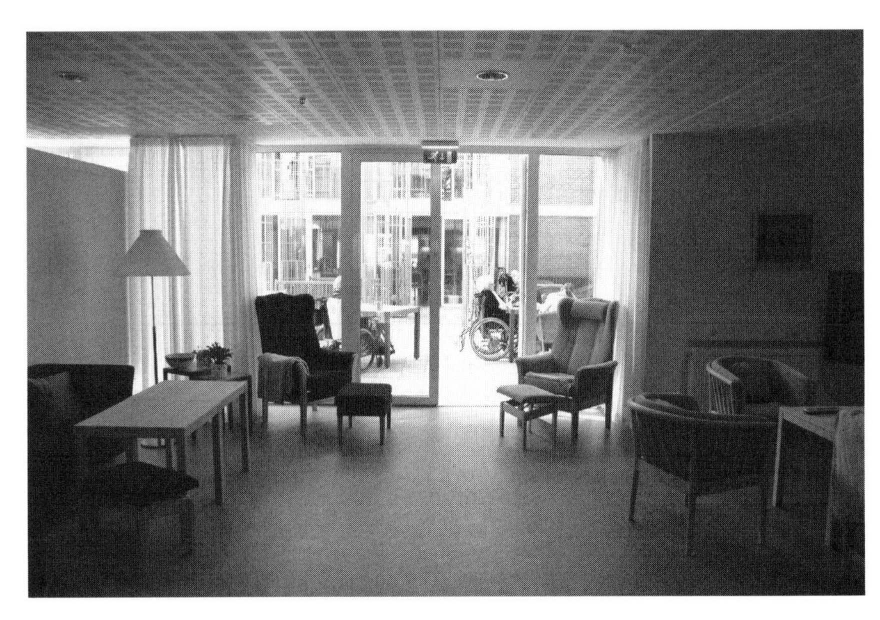

FIGURE 12-9 The lounge of social group B clearly illustrating the residents' preferred sitting area on a sunny day—out in the winter garden. *Photograph by David Hughes*

Outdoor Living

Garden

Does the garden support principles of care?

The external gardens, atrium area, large household terraces and patios, plus residents' individual verandas combine to provide a flexible variety of outside areas for occupants that offer different levels of garden privacy and stimulation.

Despite the climate, outdoor living and activity play an important part of Danish life and society. Accordingly, the garden areas support the overall principles of care and provide every opportunity for the residents to maintain independent but safe access to outside areas. These principles are important to both emotional and physical well-being.

The glass atrium that covers the original courtyard provides a safe, year-round external space for residents, hosting a range of events, activities, and simple relaxation. The use of patio heaters within the atrium and the large terraces that are shared between two households extend their practical and seasonal use, providing facilities for individual exercise, socialization, and supervised activities. The continued access and use of this area provides a positive familiarity and safeness for residents, which can be hard to establish when outside areas are often accessed and used on an occasional basis. This has proved particularly important at Salem when supporting those residents with dementia.

During warmer months the atrium can be fully opened via large-scale sliding glass doors to provide a seamless and integrated internal/external relationship, which encourages a safe "outside" area that can be effectively and subtly supervised.

The effective integration of the building to its external environment and the application of the specific extensive vistas available provide residents with safe accessible "gardens" while sharing the spectacular views beyond.

Project Data

DESIGN FIRM

Rune Ulrick Madsen
Arkitekt MAA, Direktør
THORA Arkitekter A/S
Denmark
www.thora.dk

AREAS/SIZES

Because the scheme is a partial rebuild, the care home is not distinct from the older buildings it is attached to, and the buildings share some common areas. Therefore, it is almost impossible to accurately calculate the areas/sizes.

PARKING

On the property are approximately 25 parking spaces, but parking is calculated integrally with the surrounding neighborhood.

COSTS

Danish public housing has to be constructed at a cost less than KR 23,000 per square meter, including all attributable costs, such as land acquisition and taxes. This would have been a reference point on this contract, but the complex nature of demolition, refurbishment, and new construction on this project makes costs irrelevant and confusing.

RESIDENT AGE

Average age: 89.2 years

RESIDENT PAYER MIX

Denmark is a heavily taxed society providing high levels of subsidy to those in need of health or social care. For instance, those on full pension are only expected to pay up to 15 percent of that pension on the accommodation costs of a care home. Beyond that, means testing takes place to assess the level of subsidy required from the resident.

Part V

The Netherlands Schemes

Chapter 13

A Study of Wiekslag Boerenstreek

REASONS FOR INCLUSION OF THIS SCHEME

- This scheme provides an environment that enables elderly residents with physical disabilities to live life as independently as possible when care is needed.
- This scheme highlights the importance of location of services in order to achieve the objective of community participation and encouraging resident and neighborhood interaction.

Building Description

Name of Scheme: Wiekslag Boerenstreek, a satellite nursing home of Daelhoven

Owner: Zorgpalet Baarn-Soest, a not-for-profit care organization

Address:

Wiekslag Boerenstreek
Oude Grachtje 70
3763 WK Soest
The Netherlands

Occupied since: 2006

FIGURE 13-1 Wiekslag Boerenstreek seen from the roundabout.
Courtesy of Jeanine de Zwarte

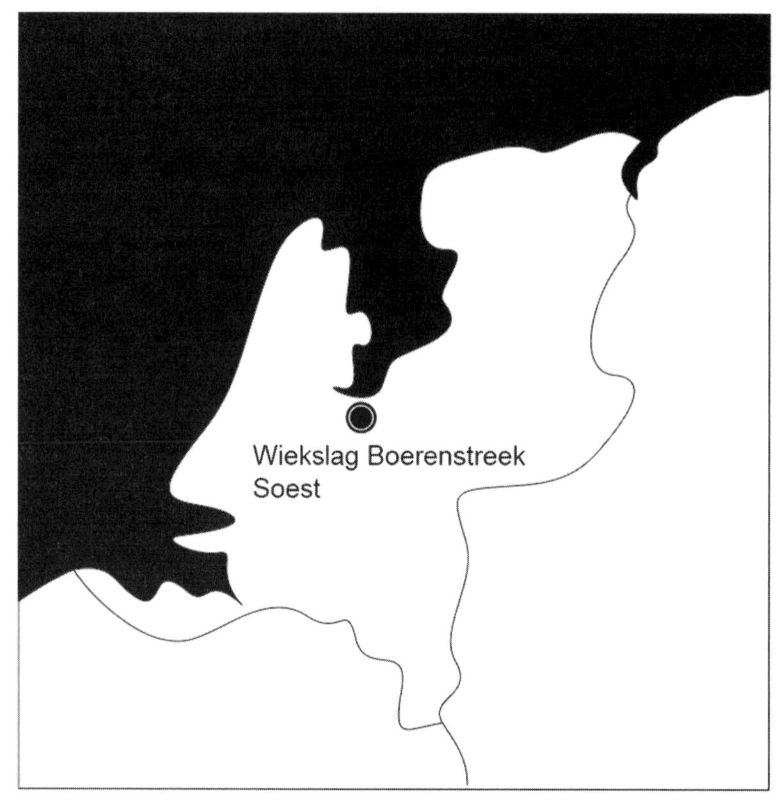

FIGURE 13-2 Scheme location. *Courtesy of Pozzoni LLP*

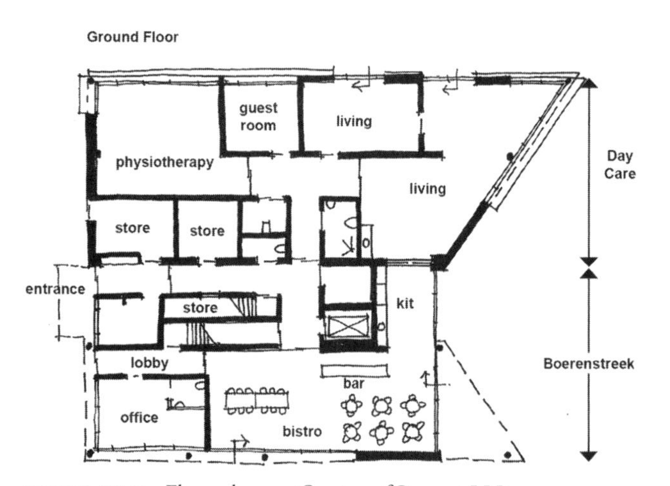

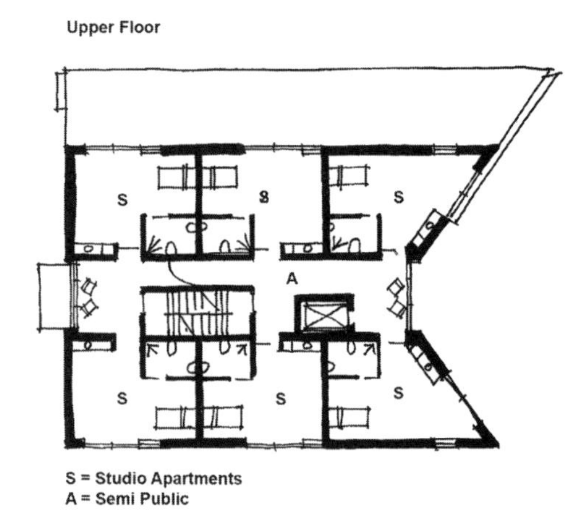

FIGURE 13-3 Floor plans. *Courtesy of Pozzoni LLP*

Description of the Type of Community, Including Number of Residents

The care association, Zorgpalet Baarn-Soest, originated in 1997 to provide nursing home care within family-sized households of six residents. Its first development was Daelhoven with 15 households for a total of 90 residents with dementia, physical disabilities, and those requiring rehabilitation treatment. In 1999 Zorgpalet Baarn-Soest opened its first satellite nursing home—Wiekslag Smitsveen—with two households for six people with dementia.

In 2006 Zorgpalet Baarn-Soest, the care organization, expanded with Wiekslag Boerenstreek, a satellite nursing home 2.5 kilometers, or about 2 miles, from Daelhoven. Wiekslag Boerenstreek provides residency for 18 residents who have physical disabilities. Unlike Daelhoven or Baarn-Soest, Wiekslag Boerenstreek provides a more independent living environment with studio apartments instead of family-like households. The residents have access to what the Dutch call a "grand café" on the ground floor. The grand café has a lounge and a dining area with a large kitchen that can be used by both staff and residents. The kitchen has wheelchair accessibility so residents can use it independently without the help of staff. Laundry, therapy gym, and staff rooms are also situated on the ground floor.

The studio apartments with en-suite bathrooms and small open kitchens are situated on the three upper floors. Each floor has six apartments and two semi-public areas where a bench or armchairs provide an alternative sitting space to one's own private room or the more public grand café.

A daycare for individuals with physical disabilities, operated by Zorgpalet Baarn-Soest, is also situated on the ground floor of the same building. Both the residents and the clients of the day care share the ground-floor gym.

Geographics

Vernacular Design

How does the scheme environment respond to the locality?

Wiekslag Boerenstreek is situated in a family neighborhood surrounded by free-standing and townhouse dwellings. It is close to shops. It responds to a busy road junction and roundabout by positioning windows to overlook this activity. Architecturally, it is a product of the internal requirements of natural light and ventilation, rather than any external stylistic influence. However, it is not located too close to the surrounding residential housing and is a prominent and striking structure facing the dominant roundabout.

Care

Philosophy of Care

What is the operators' philosophy and how does the building match this philosophy?

Zorgpalet Baarn-Soest endeavors to provide a home-like and recognizable daily life to their residents. The provision of care and the building should, therefore, be domestic, recognizable, secure, and enabling both privacy and socialization as well as enabling integration into the community.

Compared to the group homes of the care organization that are located elsewhere in Soest, Wiekslag Boerenstreek provides larger, more private studio apartments with an en-suite bathroom for people with physical disabilities, but usually with full cognition. There is no living room on each floor for the six residents residing on that floor but, rather, one hotel-like grand café for all 18 residents on the ground floor. Residents can choose to eat in the grand café or in their studio apartments. Most residents have dinner in their own apartment, either cooking their own meal or ordering a "home delivered" meal, which is provided by Zorgpalet coming from a central kitchen outside of Wiekslag Boerenstreek.

Community and Belonging

How does the scheme design and operation support this ideal?

LOCATION:

The physical location and the number of residents at each site are key expressions of the underlying philosophy to encourage the residents and the neighborhood to interact.

FIGURE 13-4 Wiekslag Boerenstreek has a lot of natural light with its floor-to-ceiling windows.
Courtesy of Jeanine de Zwarte

The choice of the location is critical to the care organization: preferably it must be close to shops, at the center of activities in the neighborhood, and with good views of those daily activities. Zorgpalet Baarn-Soest believes that a good, central location within a neighborhood enables the key objective of integration with the community and facilitates a recognizable environment. For the residents of Boerenstreek, the possibility of observing the activity of the neighborhood is one way they feel part of their community. But, more importantly, these residents of Boerenstreek with only physical disabilities are readily able to go out for shopping, either on their own, with a family member or friend, or with a staff member. At the time of this

FIGURE 13-5 Residents are welcome to meet others in the lounge area in the grand café.
Courtesy of Jeanine de Zwarte

writing, two of the residents visit a day activity center twice a week for adults with physical disabilities.

DESIGN:

Wiekslag Boerenstreek sits quite proudly on a prominent, open plot adjacent on one side to a busy road roundabout and on the other to low-rise, detached residential properties. The building has the look and feel of a modern apartment building, rather than a residential aged-care facility.

Both the grand café on the ground floor and the studios of Wiekslag Boerenstreek have large floor-to-ceiling windows. Indeed, the large amount of natural light is a feature of the building that a postoccupancy evaluation has found is highly appreciated by residents and staff alike.

The Zorgpalet Baarn-Soest experience has led to a well-equipped and highly functional design. For example, the bathrooms are designed for people with disabilities and enable residents to use them independently or with staff assistance. The kitchen in the grand café is adapted so that it readily caters to residents in wheelchairs.

One significant deficit in Wiekslag Boerenstreek is that the single elevator is small. The elevator cannot fit a bed, which means that residents who are bedridden cannot go to the grand café. The choice for an elevator of this size was made based on the experience in Daelhoven. Moreover, only one wheelchair can fit in the elevator at any one time, and the elevator is even small for some of the larger wheelchairs. While the building layout doesn't easily permit the addition of another elevator, this deficit may limit the effectiveness of the building into the future and limit who can live there.

Innovation

If the operator pursues a policy of innovation and pursuit of excellence, how is this demonstrated?

Zorgpalet Baarn-Soest is convinced small satellite nursing homes in lively locations in an average neighborhood add quality to the lives of the residents. In the residential care for people with physical disabilities, it chose to build a small satellite with the possibility to live life as independently as possible, but with the security and comfort of a small group of coresidents and the support of a care organization. The building is of high quality: the private rooms, the grand café, and the garden are all well designed. Residents are encouraged to regularly go out for activities and are welcome in the grand café for a coffee, to meet other residents, or talk to a staff member. It is the combination of all these elements in aging services that is innovative. Often, older people with physical problems can live as independently as in Boerenstreek with security and comfort, but usually this is only when their care needs are not as great. At Boerenstreek, the physical care needs of the residents are high but they are still able to make independent choices in their daily lives.

Neighborhood Integration

Community Involvement

Is the scheme and service designed to integrate successfully with the local community?

Residents of Wiekslag Boerenstreek live as independently as possible. They go out during the week for all kinds of social activities and go on their own with their scooters to the shopping mall.

Staff and Volunteers

Human Resources

Are policies and designs in place to attract good staff and volunteers?

Although for many care staff it is attractive to work in Wiekslag Boerenstreek, it can be hard to find staff to work during busy hours at the end of the afternoon and during summer holidays. The care organization offers schoolchildren in the age range of 15 to 19 small jobs in the households to work together with the care staff during the hours from 4:30 until 7 PM, depending on their age. In The Netherlands, children at the age of 15 are allowed to work for two hours a day. The older school-children can work a little longer. They help the individual residents with all kinds of activities like going into town or to the swimming pool, or with activities at home.

- Number of direct care staff: 15.84 FTE (1 FTE = 36 hours)
- Direct care hours per day per client: 4.51 hours per day per client

Environmental Sustainability

ALTERNATIVE ENERGY SOURCES

None

WATER CONSERVATION

None

ENERGY CONSERVATION

At the time the design for Wiekslag Boerenstreek started, environmental sustainability was not a major issue in The Netherlands. The Dutch Building Decree has set out technical requirements for existing and new construction including requirements on energy performance since 1995. Wiekslag Boerenstreek meets these requirements with insulation of walls, roof, and floors and double-glazing, which at the same time provides sound insulation. Wiekslag Boerenstreek does not incorporate alternative energy sources or alternative water conservation.

Outdoor Living

Garden

Does the garden support principles of care?

At Wiekslag Boerenstreek, the grand café is situated on the ground floor and has two big terraces as part of a garden with a pond. Because of the V-shape of the building, these are sheltered terraces; one terrace is accessed from the grand café and one from the day-care center. The terrace, which is accessed from the café, is very popular with residents, who are often seen outside on the terrace in their wheelchairs for a coffee and a talk or just observing both the traffic on the roundabout and on the cycle way.

FIGURE 13-6 Boerenstreek is situated in a regular neighborhood and looks like a regular apartment building. *Courtesy of Jeanine de Zwarte*

Project Data

DESIGN FIRM

Oomen Architecten
Ulvenhoutselaan 79
4803 EX Breda
The Netherlands
www.oomenarchitecten.nl

AREAS/SIZES

- Site area: 1,700 square meters; 0.42 acres (18,299 square feet)
- Total building area: 1,536 square meters (16,533 square feet)
- Typical studio apartment floor area: 44 square meters (474 square feet)
- Total area per resident: 85 square meters (919 square feet)

PARKING

One surface car park provides 14 spaces

COSTS (JANUARY 2004):

- Total building cost: €2,791,626 ($3,963,335.69 USD)
- Cost per square meter: €1,817 ($2,655 USD)
- Cost per square foot: €169 ($240 USD)
- Investment per resident: €133,181 ($189,121 USD)

RESIDENT AGE

In December 2006, the first resident, aged 56, moved in. The average age of residents in 2007 was 61 years and in 2010 it was 69 years. The residents' age varies from 46 to 84 years, with most residents in between 55 and 65 years. The average age of nursing home residents in the Netherlands is much higher. The average age of nursing home residents with physical disabilities was 81 years in 2004.[1]

RESIDENT PAYER MIX

All care is provided through the Exceptional Medical Expenses Act (EMEA or AWBZ), a Dutch national insurance scheme for long-term care. This scheme is intended to provide the insured with chronic and continuous care that involves considerable financial consequences, such as care in nursing homes, long-term nursing care at home, and care for mentally handicapped and chronic psychiatric patients. It provides a complete package that includes care, housing, food, and other housekeeping services. Residents are required to make personal contributions toward the costs. The size of this contribution depends partly on the client's age, taxable income, and domestic circumstances.

[1] M. de Klerk, "Ouderen in instellingen," The Netherlands Institute for Social Research; The Hague, 2005.

Chapter 14
A Study of Wiekslag Krabbelaan

REASONS FOR INCLUSION OF THIS SCHEME

- Wiekslag Krabbelaan provides an environment for dementia care that is familiar, enabling, and "home-like" and is as much about what goes on outside of the home as how the home itself is designed.
- It is about building a recognizable environment inside with a connection to the neighborhood outside.
- The scheme highlights the importance of locating the services in order to achieve the objective of having ongoing and actual participation in the community.
- The physical location and the number of residents at the site are key expressions of the underlying philosophy to encourage the residents and the neighborhood to interact.

Building Description

Name of Scheme: Wiekslag Krabbelaan, a satellite nursing home of Daelhoven

Owner: Zorgpalet Baarn-Soest, a not-for-profit care organization

Address:

Wiekslag Krabbelaan
Prof. Krabbelaan 50–52
3741 EN Baarn
The Netherlands

Occupied since: 2010

FIGURE 14-1 Krabbelaan seen from the public garden, with a children's playground opposite the street. *Courtesy of Jeanine de Zwarte*

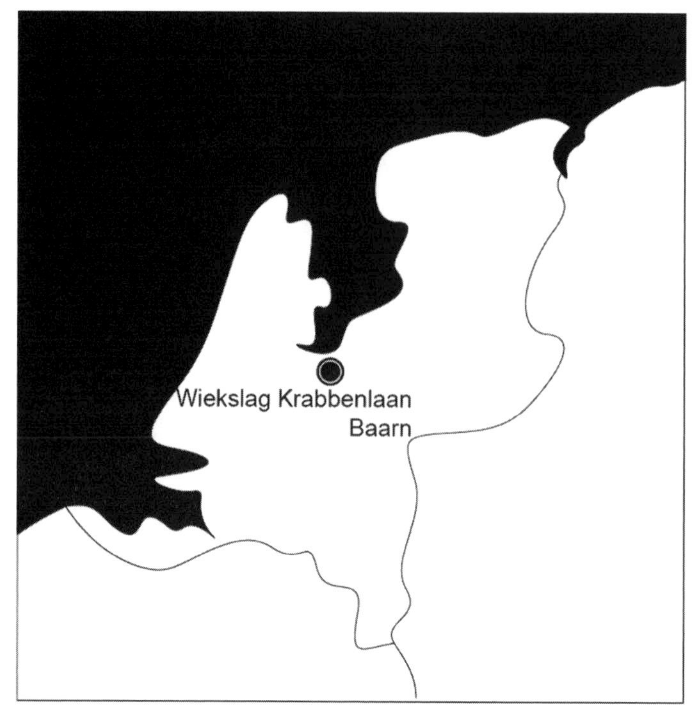

FIGURE 14-2 Scheme location. *Courtesy of Pozzoni LLP*

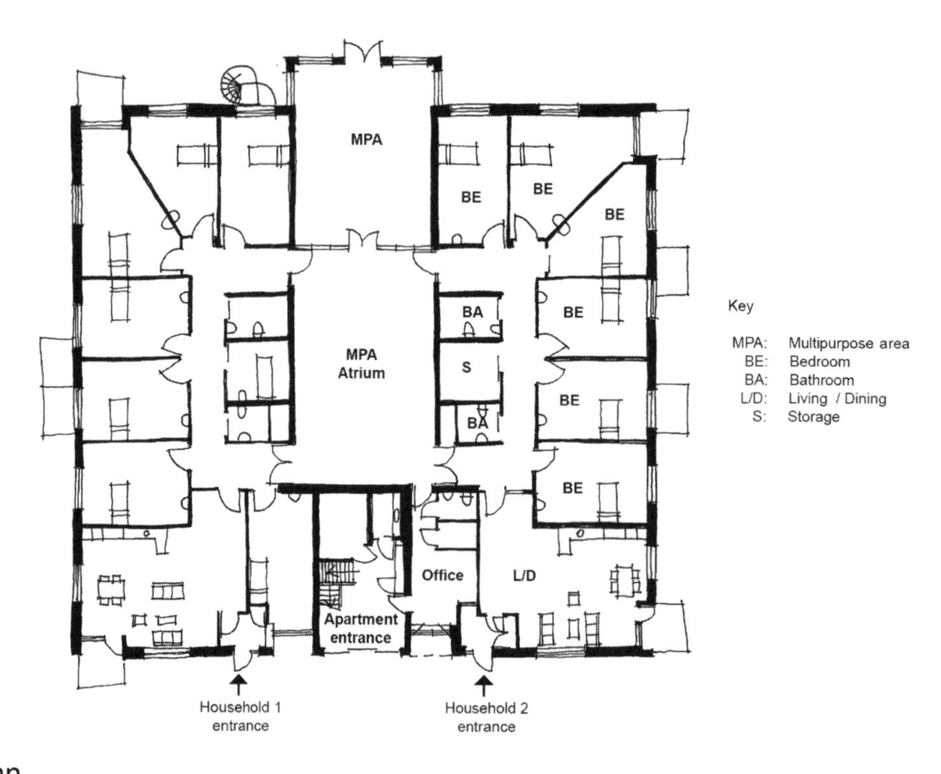

FIGURE 14-3 Floor plan. *Courtesy of Pozzoni LLP*

Description of the Type of Community, Including Number of Residents

Zorgpalet Baarn-Soest, a care association, was started in 1997 to provide nursing home care in family-sized households of six residents. Its first development was a nursing home, Daelhoven, with 15 home-like households for a total of 90 residents for people with dementia or physical disabilities, and for those requiring rehabilitation treatment.

In 1999, Zorgpalet Baarn-Soest opened Wiekslag Smitsveen, a satellite nursing home with two households for six people with dementia. Wiekslag Smitsveen is in the center of a housing estate; with the objective of emphasizing still further the concepts of providing a home-like and recognizable way of living. From 2006 to 2010, Zorgpalet Baarn-Soest expanded with two more satellite nursing homes: The first was for people with physical disabilities, Wiekslag Boerenstreek (2006), and the second was Wiekslag Krabbelaan (2010).

Wiekslag Krabbelaan is a satellite nursing home 7 kilometers (4 miles) from Daelhoven. The two households for a total of 13 persons with dementia are situated on the ground floor of a three-story apartment building. Each household has its own front door. The living areas have an open kitchen format with dining and seating areas. Each resident has a private room that is 25 square meters (270 square feet). There is one bathroom for each household but residents have a sink in the privacy of their own room. One of the bathrooms is equipped for "snoezelen," or controlled multisensory stimulation. The two households share two large multipurpose areas that are used for a variety of activities including creative and cultural activities either with staff members or with family.

The apartments on the upper three floors are all owned by the housing association Stichting Woningcorporaties Het Gooi en Omstreken. The care organization, Zorgpalet Baarn-Soest, rents one of these apartments as an office for their at-home care services. From this base, they arrange welfare and support for the residents of the apartments on the upper floors of Wiekslag Krabbelaan as well as for others in the neighborhood. The other 16 apartments, which range in size from 65 to 75 square meters (700 to 800 square feet), are rented to people who need some care but are still able to live independently. The housing association has asked Zorgpalet Baarn-Soest, as a care provider, to be responsible for assigning these apartments, preferably to people with some need for care.

Geographics

Vernacular Design

How does the scheme/environment respond to the locality?

All the schemes of this care association highlight the importance of location: Locating the services is vitally important in order to achieve the objective of having ongoing and actual participation in the community and doing the things one would normally do.

Wiekslag Krabbelaan is situated in a neighborhood where there are many families living in both standalone houses and apartment buildings. It is located opposite a public garden with a children's playground. One of the households also looks out on a public football field. Shops are within walking distance.

FIGURE 14-4 The design of Wiekslag Krabbelaan encourages the residents to participate in activities in the courtyard. *Courtesy of Jeanine de Zwarte*

Care

Philosophy of Care

What is the operators' philosophy and how does the building match this philosophy?

Zorgpalet Baarn-Soest wants to provide a home-like and recognizable daily life to their residents. The provision of care and the building should, therefore, be domestic, recognizable, secure, and enabling both privacy and socialization, as well as enabling integration into the community. Organizing daily activities in a way the residents would have performed them prior to their need for care is the key in this concept.

The size of the household is important to provide both a domestic feeling and a feeling of belonging, therefore, each household consists of six or seven members, which is considered to be the size of a large domestic family in The Netherlands. Dinner is prepared within the household with groceries bought in the nearby shop. It is possible to cook for this group on a typical residential stove and have dinner at a single dining table. Laundry and cleaning are undertaken within each household with the possibility of residents helping the staff. Multitasking staff take care of everything that has to be done: helping residents to wash and get dressed, shopping for groceries, preparing meals, and cleaning up.

The households in Wiekslag Krabbelaan for people with dementia have six or seven residents each. The household contains everything a normal home would have: a front door (accessible from the street), a living area with a kitchen, a dining table and a lounge area, private bedrooms, and shared bathrooms.

Wiekslag Krabbelaan is distinctive to the original nursing home, Daelhoven, because it only has two households containing 13 residents in this location. It is also different from most other schemes for dementia care in The Netherlands, which typically have a number of households combined for financial reasons. The choice for a satellite nursing home of this size is quite deliberate. If there are only two households with a total of 13 residents embedded in the community, it almost *forces* the services to interact with the surrounding neighborhood with shopping and socialization.

Community and Belonging

How do the scheme design and operation support this ideal?

LOCATION:

For Wiekslag Krabbelaan the physical location and the number of residents at each site are key expressions of the underlying philosophy to encourage the residents and the neighborhood to interact.

The choice of the location for a nursing home is critical to Zorgpalet Baarn-Soest: preferably it must be close to shops, at the center of activities in the neighborhood, and with good views of those daily activities. Zorgpalet Baarn-Soest believes that a good, central location within a neighborhood enables their key objective of integration with the community and facilitates a recognizable (home-like) environment. It means that it is easy for residents to go out for shopping, either with a staff member or with family, and because the activity of the neighborhood can be observed, it also provides the feeling of being part of the neighborhood.

DESIGN:

Wiekslag Krabbelaan has the look and feel of a modern apartment building, rather than residential aged care facilities. The building fits in comfortably with the surrounding buildings.

Wiekslag Krabbelaan is designed to allow natural light to help illuminate the building. Both living rooms have large windows on two sides while one of the multipurpose areas is in a courtyard in the center of the building which has a glass-roofed atrium which also introduces natural daylight.

The design of Wiekslag Krabbelaan has been specifically tailored to the needs of dementia care in households. However, if in the future the building needs to

FIGURE 14-5 Private bedroom with residents' own furniture. *Courtesy of Jeanine de Zwarte*

FIGURE 14-6 One of the two lounge areas in the living room. *Courtesy of Jeanine de Zwarte*

be adapted for other uses, this can readily be achieved. The apartments for independent living on the upper three stories lend themselves readily to a variety of residential accommodation while the ground floor can be remodeled into two or more additional apartments or for other uses.

The building has been specifically built with a frame structure and non-load-bearing internal walls to offer ultimate flexibility and sustainability in the future.

Innovation

If the operator pursues a policy of innovation and pursuit of excellence, how is this demonstrated?

Zorgpalet Baarn-Soest is an experienced care organization in residential care households and uses this experience to keep improving the care provided and the quality of life of their residents. They not only have a focus on "adding days to the life of the residents" but more importantly on "adding life to the days of their residents."

With the positive experience in their first satellite nursing home called Wiekslag Smitsveen they continue to develop satellites for 13 to 20 residents, unlike other Dutch care organizations who do not choose to develop such small, independent services for financial reasons. Zorgpalet Baarn-Soest is convinced the small satellites in lively locations in an average neighborhood add quality to the lives of the residents. The buildings are of high quality. The private rooms, living rooms, and the spaces for common use like the atrium and the other multipurpose areas are all well designed.

Neighborhood Integration

Community Involvement

Is the scheme and service designed to integrate successfully with the local community?

The residents of Wiekslag Krabbelaan that require care for dementia, do need staff, volunteers, or family members to go out for shopping. Their neighborhood integration is limited because of their disabilities. All activities are organized within the building.

Because of the location and the small size of Wiekslag Krabbelaan, the residents are attached to the neighborhood simply by watching what is going on outside their homes and by going to the local shops. Family members are invited to come in and be part of and take part in daily life in the group home. For instance, family members might join their relatives and the other residents in the household for a coffee or lunch.

FIGURE 14-7 Living room with lounge area and kitchen. *Courtesy of Jeanine de Zwarte*

Staff and Volunteers

Human Resources

Are policies and designs in place to attract good staff and volunteers?

Although for a lot of care staff it is attractive to work in the Wiekslag Krabbelaan, it can be hard to find staff to work during busy hours at the end of the afternoon and during summer holidays. Zorgpalet Baarn-Soest offers schoolchildren in the age range of 15 to 19 small jobs in the households to work together with the care staff during the hours from 4:30 until 7 PM, depending on their age. Children at the age of 15 are allowed to work for two hours a day. The elder school children can work a little longer. They work in the household helping prepare dinner, having dinner together with the residents, and helping them get ready for the evening.

Apart from the family members who take part in the daily life in the household, at the time of this writing Wiekslag Krabbelaan does not have many volunteers. The Care organization has found that it takes a while before a nursing home has gained a group of volunteers. Often volunteers are family members from former residents, and the neighborhood needs time to become acquainted with the nursing home. Since Wiekslag Krabbelaan has only been open since 2010, more volunteers are expected in the future. Wiekslag Krabbelaan is inviting people to come in and find out more about the possibilities of becoming a volunteer in several ways—for instance, through the local door-to-door newspaper.

- Number of direct care staff: 11.35 FTE (1 FTE = 36 hours)
- Direct care hours per day per client: 4.48 hours per day per client

Environmental Sustainability

ALTERNATIVE ENERGY SOURCES

None

WATER CONSERVATION

None

ENERGY CONSERVATION

The Dutch Building Decree has set out technical requirements for existing and new construction, including requirements on energy performance since 1995. Wiekslag Krabbelaan meets these requirements with insulation of walls, roof, and floors and double glazing, which at the same time provides sound insulation. Wiekslag Krabbelaan also has a ground source heat pump to provide the ground-floor households with central heating during the winter and a cooling system in summer.

Outdoor Living

Garden

Does the garden support principles of care?

Both households at Wiekslag Krabbelaan have a garden that can be entered from the living areas. From the gardens, residents have a better look at the activities in their neighborhood.

Importantly, these features emphasize a key aspect of some of the Dutch schemes in this book: Building an environment that is familiar and enabling and "home-like" is as much about what goes on outside of the home as how the home itself is designed. It is about building a recognizable environment outside as much as inside.[1]

[1] For further detail on Daelhoven, see Damian Utton, *Design for Dementia*, London, 2005.

Project Data

DESIGN FIRM

Jorissen Simonetti Architecten
Planetenbaan 16
3606 AK Maarssen
The Netherlands
http://www.jorissensimonettiarchitecten.nl/

AREAS/SIZES

- Site area: 2,700 square meters (29,063 square feet)
- Building footprint: 900 square meters (9,688 square feet)
- Total building area (Wiekslag + apartments): 2,578 square meters (27,749 square feet)
- Total Wiekslag building area not including apartments: 871 square meters (9,375 square feet)
- Typical bedroom floor areas (non-en-suite): 25 square meters (269 square feet)
- Floor area of each household: 331 square meters (3,563 square feet)
- Total area per resident: 67 square meters (721 square feet)

PARKING

One car park (above ground) provides 11 spaces

COSTS (2010)

- Total building cost Wiekslag: €790,222 ($2,523,063 USD)
- Cost per square meter: €2,005 ($2,826 USD)
- Cost per square foot: €91 ($269 USD)
- Investment per resident: €137,709 ($201,189 USD)

RESIDENT AGE

Average age of residents: 87 years

RESIDENT PAYER MIX

All care is provided through the Exceptional Medical Expenses Act (EMEA or AWBZ), a Dutch national insurance scheme for long-term care. This scheme is intended to provide the insured with chronic and continuous care that involves considerable financial consequences, such as care in nursing homes, long-term nursing home care, and care for mentally handicapped and chronic psychiatric patients. The scheme provides a complete package, including nursing care, housing, food, and house-cleaning services. Residents are required to make personal contributions toward the costs. The size of this contribution depends partly on the client's age, taxable income, and domestic circumstances.

Chapter 15

A Study of De Hogeweyk

REASONS FOR INCLUSION OF THIS SCHEME

- The scheme challenges thoughts about issues of creating and building community.
- The intersection of care and housing are hallmarks of the design.
- The issues of security and independence are creatively addressed.
- Engaging with the environment and being protected from it are key elements of the scheme.

Building Description

Name of Scheme: De Hogeweyk
Owner: Vivium Hogewey, a Dutch not-for-profit care organization
Address:
De Hogeweyk
Heemraadweg 1
1382 GV Weesp
The Netherlands
Occupied since: 2009

De Hogeweyk was built in two phases. The first phase, including 15 households, part of the offices and the theater, was occupied beginning in April 2008. The second phase, including eight households and the boulevard and passageway, was occupied beginning in December 2009. Since January 2010, De Hogeweyk has been fully occupied.

FIGURE 15-1 De Hogeweyk has attractive gardens, streets, and squares to enable the residents to daily experience the outdoors. *Photographer Madeleine Sars*

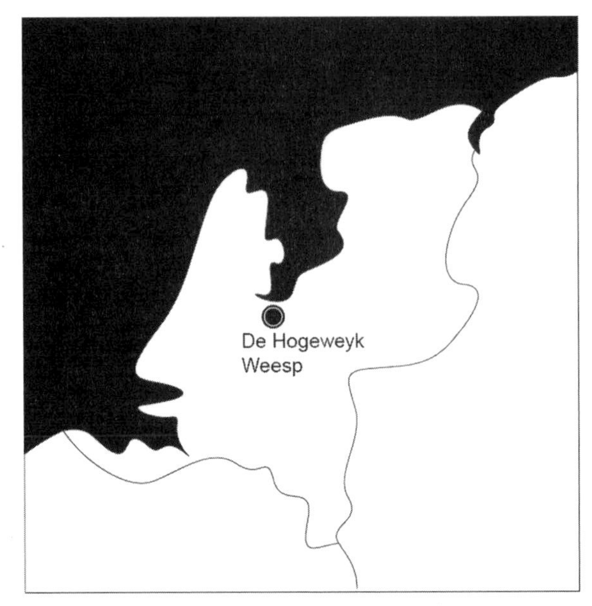

FIGURE 15-2 Scheme location. *Courtesy of Pozzoni LLP*

De Hogeweyk: The Netherlands

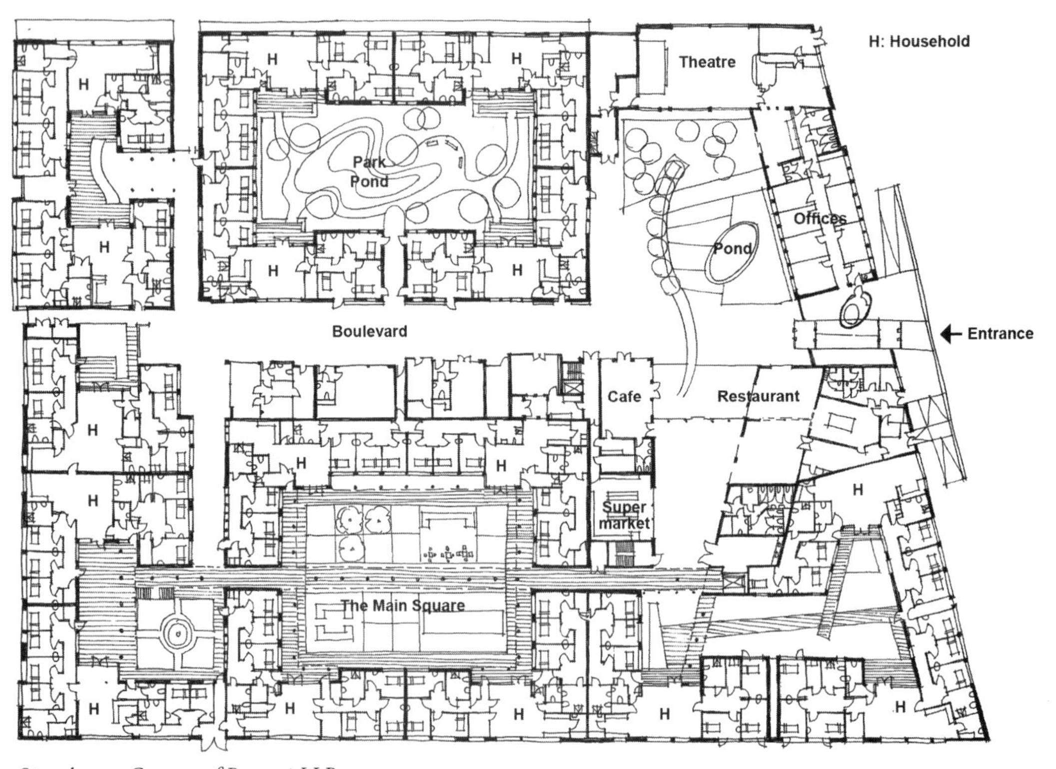

FIGURE 15-3 Site plan. *Courtesy of Pozzoni LLP*

Description of the Type of Community, Including Number of Residents

De Hogeweyk provides nursing home care to 152 people with dementia. However, De Hogeweyk has little in common with a traditional nursing home. Rather, it is designed as a small, self-contained village with 23 individual homes. Except for one household with seven bedrooms, all households have six bedrooms.

Each of the 23 homes is a self-contained household, and the village has its own amenities all contained within the village, including a theater, a supermarket, a hair and beauty salon, a café/bistro, and a restaurant. Moreover, De Hogeweyk has challenged the "one size fits all" care and design approach to aged-care settings. It has attempted to provide the residents with the ability to live the lifestyle they enjoyed prior to their need for care. Therefore, the households are designed according to seven quite different, well-articulated lifestyles. For example, if a resident had been a laborer with a traditional profession, he or she can live with other laborers; if a resident used to follow and be interested in the arts, he or she can live with others interested in the arts. The facilities of De Hogeweyk are open to all 17,000 inhabitants of Weesp, the surrounding community, as well as others.

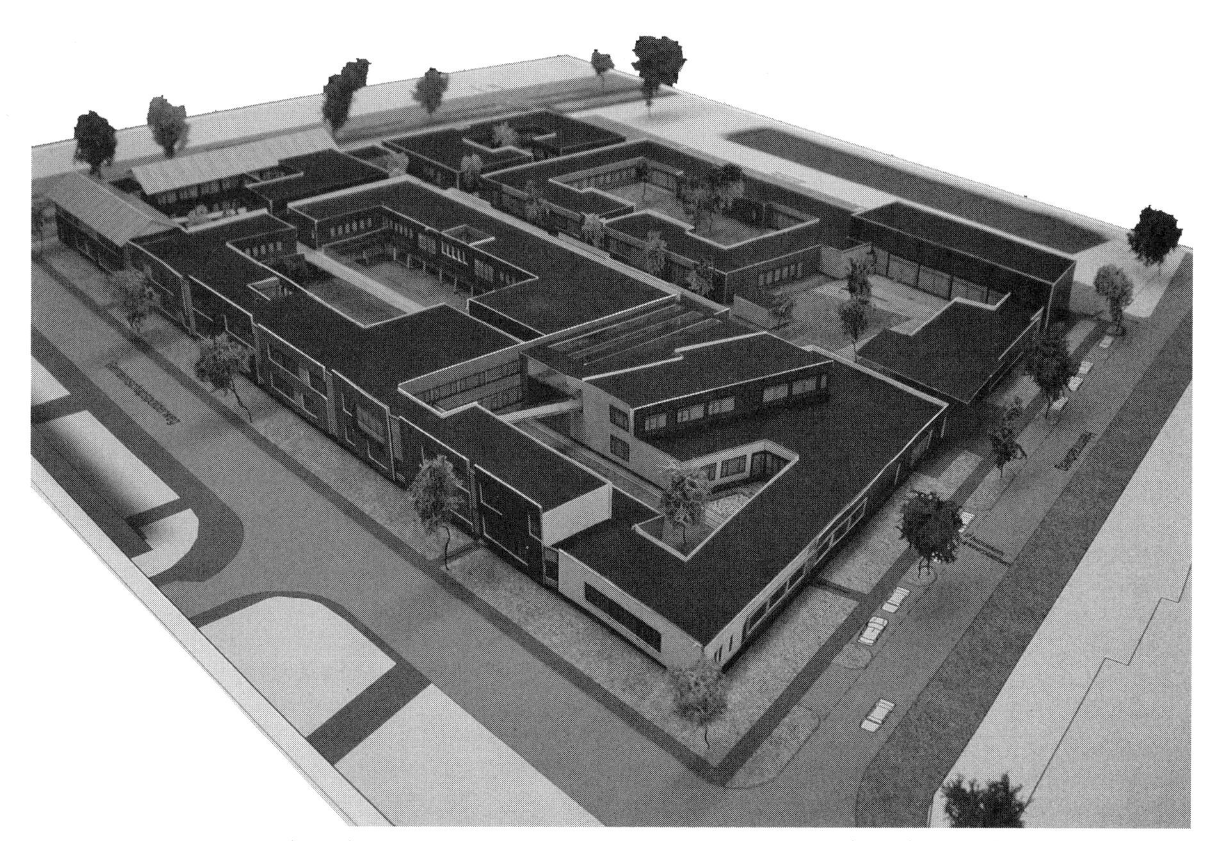

FIGURE 15-4 De Hogeweyk is a dementia-caring neighborhood. *Courtesy of Molenaar & Bol & VanDillen Architects*

Geographics

Vernacular Design

How does the scheme/environment respond to the locality?

Upon approach, De Hogeweyk looks quite severe and appears to be a large square building with an undefined use or function. This is the result of the architectural decision to design the site using the opposite design of an average city block with the households built to the perimeter and the square, gardens, and streets on the inside. Although the main entrance to De Hogeweyk is easily recognizable once in the village of Weesp, due to the site design, it is not visible as one enters Weesp by car. Upon entering De Hogeweyk and passing the reception desk, it may be surprising to see the often vibrant Theater Square and all the resident amenities, such as the restaurant with terrace.

Care

Philosophy of Care

What is the operators' philosophy, and how does the building match this philosophy?

Vivium Hogewey, the organization that developed and owns De Hogeweyk, embraces the philosophy that people with dementia should be able to live their lives the way they had been used to living, even though they may no longer be capable of full independence. The implications of this philosophy have guided De Hogeweyk to what it has become: a safe environment for people with dementia to live the way they were used to prior to their need for care. Regardless of the fact that De Hogeweyk's residents need nursing home care, because they can no longer live completely independently in the community, they still have the opportunity to be engaged, safely, in all aspects of a normal life.

This approach has not been an easy transition at De Hogeweyk. In 1993, the Vivium Hogewey organization started exploring the lifestyles of its residents prior to their need for care and arranging households around seven different lifestyles identified among its residents. In De Hogeweyk, residents can continue their lifestyle with like-minded people in a group size that is familiar to how they had been living. Households with approximately six to eight residents are today a widely accepted phenomenon in the care for people with dementia in the Netherlands. But in 1993, this was not the case and was an approach that was just gaining acceptance. The differentiator for De Hogeweyk was the combining of

FIGURE 15-5 From the outside, De Hogeweyk does not show its function or the vibrant neighborhood it is. *Photographer Madeleine Sars*

FIGURE 15-6 The main entrance is a corridor to a safe environment for people with dementia. *Photographer Madeleine Sars*

this new development of small households with defined and varied lifestyles within the homes. In the 1990s, De Hogeweyk put this change into practice within the limitations and confines of the old building located on the site of the current village. This older building was designed as a traditional four-story concrete nursing home building with surrounding gardens. After the transformation to care focused on lifestyles, each floor of the old nursing home replicated a street with three living rooms, each with its own defined lifestyle. The gardens surrounding the nursing home provided a pleasant view for the residents and perhaps even more pleasant for those passing by the nursing home looking into the gardens. But the old building still had many restrictions. For example, it was not safe for residents to go into the gardens without supervision. Also, although De Hogeweyk was able to arrange households within the old building, the nursing home did not have the look or feel of a typical, domestic, living environment.

As a result, Vivium Hogewey decided to demolish the old building and build a new Hogewey with all the elements of a neighborhood providing a natural environment for each of the seven different lifestyles. Twenty-three households were needed to house a total of 152 residents, which is the resident population needed to support all the amenities that the organization wished to include, such as the theater, bar, supermarket, and restaurant. The new building contained everything needed to replicate a neighborhood. And so the organization changed the name of the nursing home from De Hogewey to De Hogeweyk because "weyk" sounds like the Dutch word for neighborhood.

FIGURE 15-7 At De Hogeweyk, the buildings embrace the streets and gardens. *Photographer Madeleine Sars*

THE SEVEN LIFESTYLES INTO WHICH DE HOGEWEYK'S HOUSEHOLDS ARE DIVIDED ARE:

1. **Traditional:** for residents whose pride and identity came from carrying out a traditional profession or managing a small business
2. **City:** for "urbanized" residents whose life had been spent in the center of the city
3. **"Het Gooi":** for residents who attach importance to correct manners, etiquette, and proper external appearance (named after an area close to Weesp)
4. **Cultural:** for residents who appreciate art and fine culture
5. **Christian:** for residents for whom practicing their Christian religion is an important part of daily life
6. **Indonesian:** with Indonesia being a former colony of the Netherlands, De Hogeweyk has a lifestyle for residents with an Indonesian background, which determines their daily routines to a large extent
7. **Homey:** for residents who believe that caring for the family and household is important, and for whom domestic rhythms are as important as for those who have a traditional lifestyle

Each household has either six or seven bedrooms, two bathrooms, and a living room with kitchen providing a home for residents living together as a group. Every household in De Hogeweyk has one shared-occupancy bedroom. Thirteen of those shared bedrooms are shared by two residents. Which rooms are used by two residents depends on the preferences of the residents' lifestyle. This works very well for many residents because, to some, it is more familiar to have another person around, thus contributing to a less stressful situation. Because this is often unknown to relatives, new residents are initially offered a bed in a two-person bedroom becoming the seventh person in that household. When there is a vacancy in the household, the residents in the double room are offered a single-occupancy room. De Hogeweyk has found that a considerable number of the families prefer their family member to stay in the shared-occupancy room because of the benefit of having a companion.

De Hogeweyk: The Netherlands

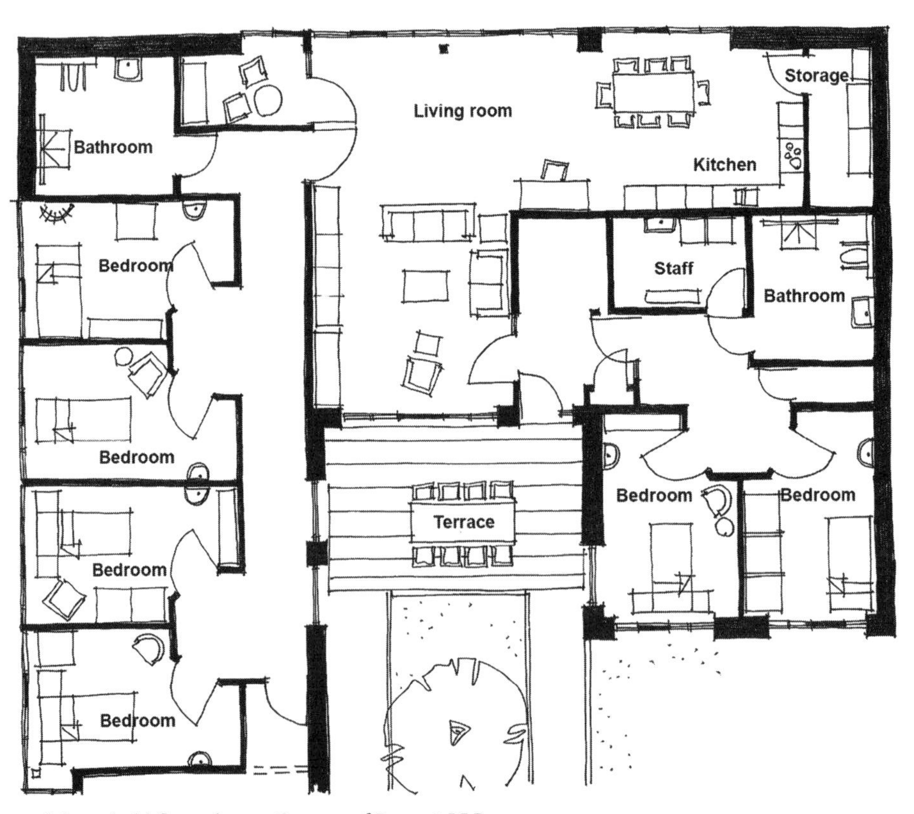

FIGURE 15-8 De Hogeweyk household floor plan. *Courtesy of Pozzoni LLP*

Community and Belonging

How does the scheme design and operation support this ideal?

The difference between the old scheme and the new De Hogeweyk is quite distinct. The old nursing home was placed in the center of the site and was surrounded by gardens. The new De Hogeweyk is completely different, with the village built to the very edge of the site's perimeter and the scheme being inwardly focused. The gardens, squares, and streets of the new De Hogeweyk are surrounded by the households and the associated facilities.

In October 2002, the design architect proposed the new De Hogeweyk as "a little village of memories." He started with the opposite design of a normal city grid. By using this tactic, the houses surround the streets, gardens, and squares rather than the other way around. This also had the effect that the living environment—that is, the village—became a safe place for residents with dementia. They could leave their homes and go into the garden and streets quite safely. De Hogeweyk's design architect also created houses with different internal layouts and exteriors. This served to be a cueing device as much as an aesthetic device, assisting the residents who had dementia in their wayfinding.

This differentiation between households also suited the organization's philosophy to provide different lifestyles in each household. Together, Vivium Hogewey and the architect translated into the building's design the dual objectives of having seven distinct lifestyles as well as the desire to provide the residents a normalized life. The result was that the specifically designed households for resident lifestyle were situated in different parts of De Hogeweyk. For example, those houses intended for a lively urban lifestyle have a similar neighborhood to that of homes in an urban setting, which is quite different than the neighborhood of those living in a traditional household. The lifestyle even determines the point and way of entry of a resident to the household. In some, it would only be proper if a visitor came in through the front door. But in others, the approach is less formal and visitors can come in directly after knocking on the door, or during the summer, enter through the garden doors. The lifestyle and home choice of the resident also determine whether they eat in a more formal dining area or in an open kitchen.

De Hogeweyk has a determined focus on meaningful activities outside the household. The reality of an individual's life is that not every aspect of life takes place inside the home. Normalization, in its richest form, means allowing the resident to go out for grocery shopping, go out to have lunch, or go out to the theater. It also means leaving the home to see the doctor. And, yet, so many older people in aged-care settings do not experience these normal activities because they are in a nursing home, which precludes such excursions for a variety of reasons. De Hogeweyk has, in perhaps a controversial and challenging way, chosen to arrange all aspects of residents' daily life as it would be outside a nursing home in their own community, but within the confines of the village so that it can remain safe and secure for people with

FIGURE 15-9 Interior of household with city lifestyle. *Courtesy of Vivium De Hogeweyk*

FIGURE 15-10 People in De Hogeweyk live their life as they were used to, including going to the supermarket. *Courtesy of Vivium De Hogeweyk*

dementia. It is a challenging task but one in which De Hogeweyk has succeeded. This does not mean that residents don't at times wander. But that manifestation of dementia is allowed to occur safely.

The organization believes that it is very important to enable the residents to experience the outdoors as they had done prior to moving into De Hogeweyk, and there are three key elements of outdoor life in the scheme: attractive gardens, streets, and squares. The streets and gardens of De Hogeweyk were designed with a variation of associations with normal life such as street signs, streetlights, ponds, and benches as well as squares in which people can congregate. It would be easy for this to become artificial but their familiarity and "normality," as well as the fact that they are outside, prevent this from occurring.

Innovation

If the operator pursues a policy of innovation and excellence, how is this demonstrated?

In the Netherlands in 2005, at least 10 percent of the residents in nursing homes for dementia care lived in households. This was expected to rise to 25 percent in 2010.[1] Ideally, life in these households is as normal as possible. For this reason, households are situated in regular neighborhoods. De Hogeweyk has chosen to realize this goal in a very different way. Rather than having a small number of group homes in a typical village or suburban neighborhood, it has chosen to build a complete village of households in such a way that residents can live as independently as possible. De Hogeweyk's staff converts the philosophy of the design and care program into the daily life of the residents. Before designing the new building, they considered every aspect of daily life, asking themselves two primary questions: "What had the residents been doing at home?" and "What will we have to create in order to match this?" For instance, while living at home, one may go to the supermarket. At most, nursing homes residents don't go out for daily grocery shopping. At De Hogeweyk, residents go out to the supermarket to collect all ingredients for their home-cooked meals. Of course, some household members go to the supermarket more often than others, and sometimes, they go out for dinner. One might ask if residents go out in winter when the streets are covered with snow. Usually not, but then someone else will bring groceries to the resident instead. Therefore, De Hogeweyk has its own supermarket where staff can only buy groceries when accompanied by a resident.

In the same way, consideration was given to other aspects of daily life, from going to see the doctor to going out for dinner or to the theater, and a whole range of other activities. The result is that De Hogeweyk is unique in terms of how residents can maintain the lifestyle they had previously enjoyed.

The initial plans for De Hogeweyk involved a flexible building system that could, in the future, be converted

[1] *De Toekomst Van Kleinschalig Wonen Voor Mensen Met Dementie*; Utrecht, October 2007; Aedes-Actiz Kenniscentrum Wonen-Zorg, Hugo van Waarde, Monique Wijnties.

FIGURE 15-11 De Hogeweyk is a neighborhood on its own. *Photographer Madeleine Sars*

into different care schemes or, indeed, into residential housing. However, the cost of this initial proposal was too high. Nevertheless, the modified scheme ultimately selected still allows the transformation of any of the households into two or three apartments.

One of the key innovative elements of the design is the fact that the physical therapist, the doctor, and the maintenance service are highly visible on the main street. So many aged-care schemes put these, for understandable reasons, at the back of house. However, in De Hogeweyk, they are part of the streetscape, with shop-front visibility, so that people can see where the maintenance men are and what they are doing.

De Hogeweyk is a village for residents with dementia that challenges the design to accommodate the residents' memory loss. The households are very small and intimate, but the village itself is quite large, accommodating numerous residents. The households are very domestic and residential in scale. The design is familiar to the residents and the passion of the residents for a particular lifestyle means that the familiarity will be enhanced. The collaboration of the design and care program promotes self-esteem, autonomy, and independence. And there is security for the residents within their own households and in the larger village.

Neighborhood Integration

Community Involvement

Is the scheme and service designed to integrate successfully with the local community?

De Hogeweyk is a secure "community" occurring within a "memory village" simply by the fact that normal life is integrated into the design and operation of De Hogeweyk. However, the outside walls of the village and the entrance to the village itself are somewhat less than inviting to outside community members.

De Hogeweyk is open to anyone, not just residents and their families. Anyone can come in and have dinner in the restaurant or go to a concert in the theater. Additionally, there is evidence that outside community members participate in these activities because of the numerous amenities available at De Hogeweyk, and many consider it a treat to visit relatives at De Hogeweyk and accompany them to the pub, the restaurant, or the theater. Nevertheless, Vivium Hogewey's desire is to increase participation, and the organization continues its efforts to attract people from the outside community to volunteer as well as use the available amenities.

De Hogeweyk has been designed with its entrance from the central street situated so that it would connect with the central street of an anticipated plan for a piece of land opposite of De Hogeweyk. Unfortunately, this plan has been delayed, with the result that De Hogeweyk's entrance is situated opposite a large, vacant lot of undeveloped land and is thus less attractive.

Next to the car park on the northern side of De Hogeweyk there is an apartment block with eight stories above ground. The owners of these apartments have been very pleased with the development of De Hogeweyk and feel a connection with the building and its residents. During the building process, De Hogeweyk stayed in touch with the surrounding community of owners to inform them of the building activity and to find a way to make it less disturbing for the neighbors. When the building was finished, the neighbors of the adjacent apartment blocks donated a little statue to express their connection to De Hogeweyk.

Staff and Volunteers

Human Resources

Are policies and designs in place to attract good staff and volunteers?

De Hogeweyk has 120 volunteers, not including family members. Family members primarily come in to visit their relatives and might help in the caregiving process. For instance, in the Indonesian households family members sometimes help with preparing the Indonesian meals.

De Hogeweyk's philosophy of care is attractive to staff and volunteers. It provides staff members the opportunity to work in a household with a lifestyle and atmosphere one relates to. Vivium Hogewey is well known for its philosophy, and this alone attracts enough staff and volunteers even though other organizations do have problems attracting staff and volunteers.

- Direct care hours per day per client: 4.89

FIGURE 15-12 The gardens have different designs according to the lifestyles of De Hogeweyk. *Courtesy of Vivium De Hogewek*

Environmental Sustainability

In 2002, at the time the design for De Hogeweyk started, environmental sustainability was not a major issue in the Netherlands. The Dutch Building Decree has set out technical requirements for existing and new construction including requirements on energy performance since 1995. De Hogeweyk meets these requirements with insulation of walls, roof, and floors and double-window glazing, which at the same time, provides sound insulation. De Hogeweyk does not incorporate alternative energy sources or alternative water conversation.

Outdoor Living

Garden

Does the garden support principles of care?

The residents' ability to go outside on their own is an important part of the care philosophy. Therefore, De Hogeweyk had a focus on designing not just households but a neighborhood with an outdoor space that is both interesting and safe to residents. When making plans for the new building, the organization tried to find a larger site, preferably more centrally located in the village of Weesp, to be able to offer all residents a room in a household on the ground floor and to encourage the inhabitants of Weesp to use the amenities at De Hogeweyk. Since a suitable larger, more centrally located site was not found, the organization decided to rebuild De Hogeweyk on the same site as the old nursing home, even though this would require households to be located on the ground and second floors.

De Hogeweyk has several gardens and public squares within the premises. Each garden and site design is unique and correlates to the custom interior designs representing the lifestyles supported in the households, being mindful of their individualized care and their location within the neighborhood. Households are located in an area of the plan that might replicate the particular lifestyle of the home. For example, households with a city lifestyle are close to a big square, while households with a traditional lifestyle are situated on a more private part of the plan. Gardens and squares attached to the households are designed in a style according to the lifestyle of the household, therefore, some are more urban while others are more traditional.

Project Data

Design Team

DESIGN ARCHITECT

Molenaar & Bol & VanDillen Architecten
Taalstraat 112
5261 BH Vught
The Netherlands
www.mbvda.nl

LANDSCAPE DESIGN ARCHITECT

Niek Roozen
Ossenmarkt 36
1381 LX Weesp
The Netherlands
www.niekroozen.com

INTERIOR DESIGN

Vivium Hogewey's approach to the interior design was unique. Much of the interior design was done by De Hogeweyk's staff. Throughout the process, staff members described the ambience they were looking for and made the final choice in furniture, upholstery, and finish. In the first phase, staffers worked together with Kembo's design bureau (www.kembo.com). In the second phase, De Hogeweyk did not contract with any interior designer. For the restaurant, De Hogeweyk worked together with Klaasen Interior (www.klaasenhekker.nl).

AREAS/SIZES

- Site area: 15,310 square meters (164,735 square feet, 3.78 acres)
- Building footprint: 7,607 square meters (81,851 square feet)
- Total building area: 10,772 square meters (115,907 square feet)
- Total area per resident: 70.87 square meters (762.55 square feet)

PARKING

Surface parking provides 56 spaces: 46 on the site and 10 in cooperation with the municipality on public space in front of the building.

COSTS (JUNE 2005)

- Building cost: €19,268,808 including taxes ($27,836,906 USD)
- Cost per square meters: €1,789 ($2,584 USD)
- Cost per square feet: €166 ($240 USD)
- Investment per resident: €126,768 ($183,110 USD)

RESIDENT AGE

Average age of residents: men 79.5 years and women 83.7 years

RESIDENT PAYER MIX

All care is provided through the Exceptional Medical Expenses Act (EMEA or AWBZ), a Dutch national insurance scheme for long-term care. This scheme is intended to provide the insured with chronic and continuous care that involves considerable financial consequences, such as care in nursing homes, long-term nursing care at home, care for mentally handicapped and chronic psychiatric patients. It provides care, housing, food, and housekeeping services. Residents are required to make personal contributions toward the costs. The size of this contribution depends partly on the client's age, taxable income, and domestic circumstances.

Most of De Hogeweyk's realization costs, €17,800,000 ($25,707,331 USD), were supplied through regular budget funds. However, De Hogeweyk spent more on housing than the budget allowed to be able to translate its philosophy into the required environment. An extra €1.5 million ($2,166,348 USD) was received from other funds, sponsors, and donors.

Chapter 16
A Study of Weidevogelhof

REASONS FOR INCLUSION OF THIS SCHEME

- This scheme is a neighborhood development in which collaborative housing associations and care organizations work together.
- Differing types of welfare and care housing are scattered throughout the neighborhood in different parts of the development.
- This scheme's philosophy is strongly translated into the built environment of mostly affordable housing, attractive not only to elderly but others who might need shelter or care.
- Facilities for the entire suburb Pijnacker-South are situated within Weidevogelhof, which assists in making Weidevogelhof an integrated part of the suburb.

Building Description

Name of Scheme: Weidevogelhof

Owners: The local housing association Rondom Wonen developed the whole of Weidevogelhof (meaning "Meadow Bird Court"). In order to finance Weidevogelhof, Rondom Wonen collaborated with other housing associations. The original intention was that Rondom Wonen would buy the property from its financing partners after a period of 10 years. However, during development, this part of the plan was modified so that ownership would remain with the housing associations financing the project. Mooiland will be the owner of the buildings realized in phase one, Habion of the buildings in phase two, and Rondom Wonen in phase three. Rondom Wonen will be responsible for the administration and management of all property.

In the Netherlands, a care organization has the possibility either to develop and own property or to work together with a housing association. In the development of Weidevogelhof, the housing association is responsible for the built environment, tenants rent the apartments, and

FIGURE 16-1 Weidevogelhof and the family homes opposite the Floralaan. *Courtesy of Jeanine de Zwarte*

the care associations are responsible for delivery of care. As a result, at Pijnacker, there are several care organizations, each with its own specific expertise and services, involved in the program. Phase one of Weidevogelhof was developed in cooperation with Pieter van Foreest (elderly care). Parts of phase two were developed in cooperation with Fokus Wonen (providing Fokus Housing for people with physical disabilities). Phase three was partly developed with *IPSE* (care for people with intellectual disabilities). All housing associations and care organizations involved in this development are not-for-profit organizations.

Address:
Weidevogelhof
Floralaan (area in between Floralaan and railway)
Pijnacker-Nootdorp
The Netherlands

Occupied since: The first buildings were completed in September 2010. Phase one and phase two were finished at the end of 2010. Phase three was scheduled to be ready at the end of 2011. The first tenants moved in during October 2010. It is expected that the last tenants will move in during early to mid-2012.

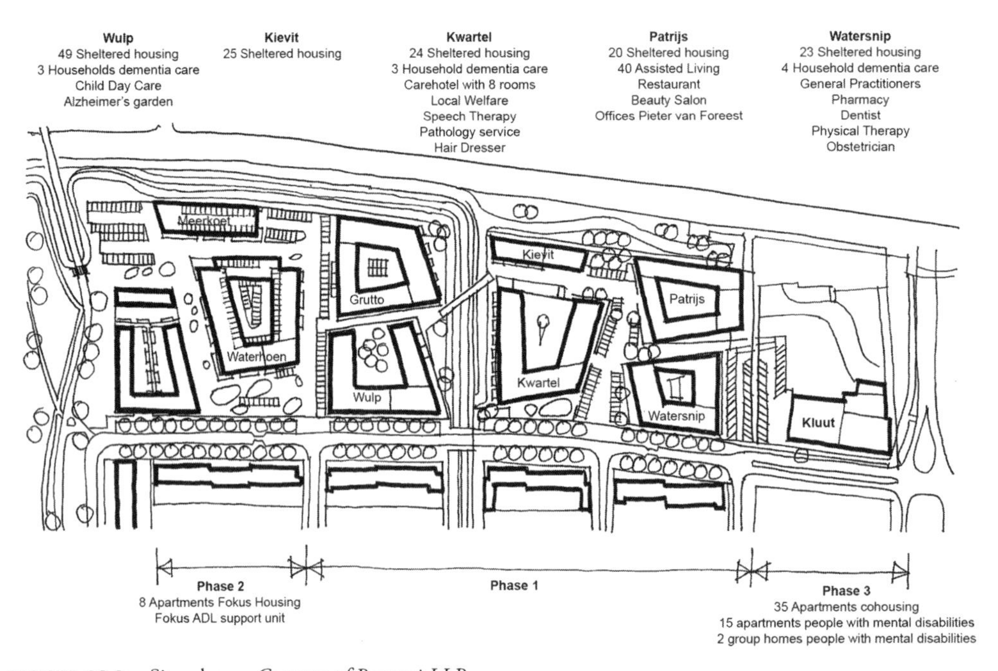

FIGURE 16-2 Site plan. *Courtesy of Pozzoni LLP*

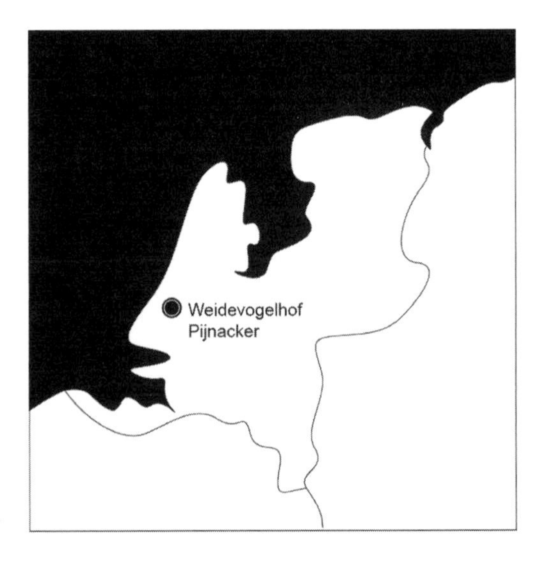

FIGURE 16-3 Scheme location. *Courtesy of Pozzoni LLP*

Description of the Type of Community, Including Number of Residents

Weidevogelhof is a development of nine buildings with a total of 354 apartments, some of which are affordable. The development is a part of the 2,300 houses in Keijzershof in Pijnacker-South, a newly built suburb of Pijnacker-Nootdorp. The other part of Pijnacker-South is Tolhek, with 1,700 houses situated on the opposite side of a railway line. Facilities for the entire new suburb Pijnacker-South are integrated in Weidevogelhof.

Almost a quarter of the inhabitants of Pijnacker live in affordable housing. It is likely that the demand for affordable housing will grow given the demographic and socioeconomic profile of Pijnacker. Fueling this demand for affordable housing, house owners who are older increasingly want to sell their homes and rent in order to free themselves from the demands associated with homeownership, such as maintenance. Still others want to downsize and leave their large family home for the comfort of an apartment without stairs, which will serve their needs as they age. With this in mind, it is not surprising that the local housing association, Rondom Wonen, took the opportunity to develop Weidevogelhof.

What Rondom Wonen has done in Weidevogelhof is build a complete housing development in which several care associations provide a comprehensive range of services. Weidevogelhof is a "lifetime" neighborhood with sheltered housing, assisted living, primary care, welfare and other services, as well as at-home nursing care, a care hotel, and dementia care. The distinctiveness of this development is that the developers have not aggregated specific services; rather, they have scattered them across the site in an attempt to develop true integration of community.

Weidevogelhof: The Netherlands

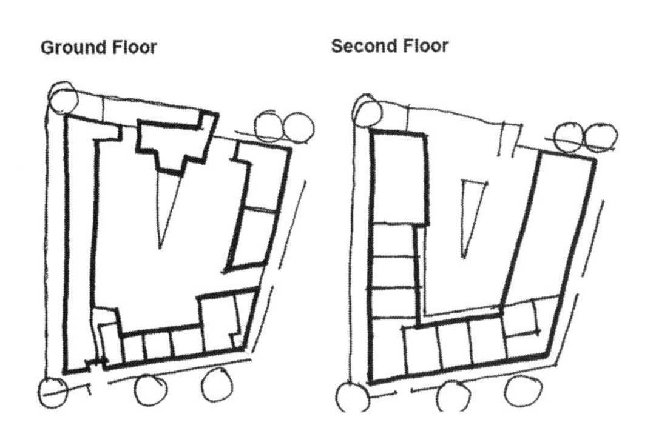

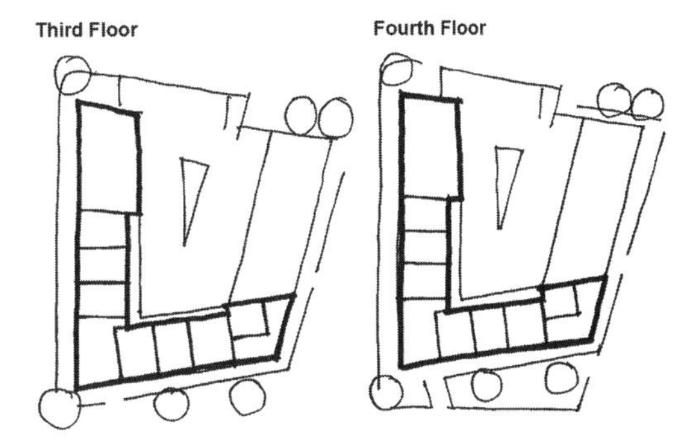

Ground Floor
Left: Care Hotel
Bottom: Speech therapy, pathology service, hair dresser
Right: Pieter van Foreest

Second Floor
Top Left: Household for dementia care
Bottom left & bottom: Apartments
Right: Local welfare

Third Floor & Fourth Floor:
Top Left: Household for dementia care
Bottom left & bottom: Apartments

Kwartel

FIGURE 16-4 Weidevogelhof, with the buildings in phase one in the middle, phase two on the right, and phase three on the left. *Courtesy of Pozzoni LLP*

PHASE ONE

Sheltered Housing Apartments

Keijzershof phase one includes 201 sheltered housing rental apartments varied from one- to four-bedrooms, of which 176 are affordable housing. Twenty-five larger apartments, up to 150 square meters (1,615 square feet), were developed for market rental rather than as affordable-housing rental units.

To create a community with a mix of people regardless of their need for care, a maximum of 82 of these 201 apartments are reserved for people who need nursing home care. Pieter van Foreest can deliver this nursing care in any of the 201 apartments because all apartments meet the requirements of care and assistance. Weidevogelhof provides individuals with the opportunity to rent an apartment from the housing association even if no care is required. These rentals are made with the knowledge that care is on hand if needed in the future, thus allowing them to stay in their own apartment and in a familiar environment as they age. Two of the six buildings within phase one are solely dedicated to sheltered housing apartments. The remaining four buildings comprise a mix of apartments and other facilities.

Assisted Living Apartments

Forty one-bedroom assisted-living apartments have been acquired for clients of Pieter van Foreest. While this form of housing with care is now part of Dutch legislation, it is anticipated that in the future these apartments will not be needed because the demand will be for larger apartments. As a result, these sheltered apartments are all concentrated on two floors in one building with a flexible layout so that, if they are not required in the future, two apartments can be transformed into one large apartment or several apartments can be put together to form a household for dementia care.

FIGURE 16-5 Weidevogelhof is developed with the prevailing view that it is crucial to provide good housing as a basis for integrating welfare and care. *Courtesy of Jeanine de Zwarte*

FIGURE 16-6 Waiting room for primary-care health services. *Courtesy of Jeanine de Zwarte*

Households with Dementia Care

On behalf of Pieter van Foreest, 10 households, each for six people with dementia, were added and distributed over three of the six buildings in order to provide the maximum reminiscence of being "at home" and living in a normal neighborhood. In each building, three or four group homes are situated above one another from the second floor and above.

Also Pieter van Foreest provides services at a day care center in Pijnacker-South to independently living people suffering from dementia and their caregivers.

Care Hotel

The Pieter van Foreest care hotel has six rooms with en-suite bathrooms and the supporting facilities for rehabilitation and hospice care. Rehabilitation and hospice care are separate, and each has its own entrance at both ends of a straight hallway. The care hotel uses four rooms for rehabilitation and two for hospice care. These functions are interchangeable, providing a flexibility that is achieved by having two sliding doors to divide the spaces according to demand.

Facilities for All 4,000 Houses of Pijnacker-South

All facilities a neighborhood the size of Pijnacker-South needs are realized within Weidevogelhof, including a restaurant, hairdresser, and a beauty salon. Also within Weidevogelhof is a wide range of primary-care health services, including a group practice of general practitioners, pharmacy, dentist, and specialist physicians for the whole of the Pijnacker-South community, as well as physical therapy, pathology services, and speech therapy. Only the supermarket and other shops were planned elsewhere in Keijzershof.

Special Facilities for the Elderly

In addition to the facilities for the entire suburb of Pijnacker-South, Weidevogelhof offers a community center attached to the 40 assisted-living apartments as well as facilities for the local welfare for elderly Stichting Welzijn Ouderen Pijnacker. Next to the local welfare facilities, a home care office provides a central information point for future clients. Pieter van Foreest houses its specialist nursing home physicians and physical and occupational therapists specialized in elderly care in a central location next to the home care office.

PHASE TWO

The number of apartments in phase one that will, in the future, be rented to people without a need for care was determined to be too low for an optimum mixture of housing and care, an essential part of the philosophy at Weidevogelhof. This was also determined not to provide enough affordable housing compared to the amount of elderly people looking for such within Pijnacker. Therefore, Rondom Wonen decided to build a second phase of 100 affordable apartments for people over 55 years of age, divided over two buildings just north of phase one.

Also situated in phase two is a cluster in which care association Fokus Wonen provides independent living with Activities in Daily Life (ADL) support for people with severe physical disabilities.

With this type of support, the people living in Fokus Housing are able to live a "normal" life. Eight two- and three-bedroom apartments and the ADL support units are situated in Weidevogelhof. Another eight two-bedroom apartments are situated outside Weidevogelhof elsewhere in Keijzershof no more than 300 meters (984 feet) from the ADL support unit. These eight apartments were developed together with a private housing developer. They are situated on the ground floor on the corners of two blocks of family housing, and each has its own garden.

PHASE THREE

Phase three consists of one building, which will look as if it has two sections and was to be completed around the end of 2011. The lower section with housing for people with intellectual disabilities has five apartments for independent living, 10 apartments for assisted living, and two households totaling nine residents. The higher, more tower-like, section is developed as cohousing with 35 two- and three-bedroom apartments.

Geographics

Vernacular Design

How does the scheme/environment respond to the locality?

The Pijnacker-Nootdorp municipality of 37 square kilometers (14 square miles) and 48,000 inhabitants is situated in the western part of the Netherlands halfway between the two cities of The Hague and Rotterdam. Though Pijnacker desires the retention of the look and feel of a small village, the location of Weidevogelhof also has urban elements. Pijnacker, at the south, is more or less connected to Rotterdam by a concentration of recently built neighborhoods, a part of which are Tolhek and Keijzershof. Keijzershof is adjacent to the older part of Pijnacker, to grassland with ditches, but also to the railway that divides Pijnacker-South into a western part, Keijzershof, and an eastern part, Tolhek. Weidevogelhof is situated in the Keijzershof section on a strip of land of 7.7 acres (31,160 square meters, 335,403 square feet) along the railway and next to the station of Pijnacker-South.

The architect's design brief for Weidevogelhof was challenging. To create the required number of apartments on a relatively small area, the design had to be dense. The ambition of the municipality of Pijnacker-Nootdorp was to retain the ambience of a village and that this dense design should not lead to an anonymous or too urban environment. And with the future inhabitants and the care functions in mind, the design had to be useful. To solve this, the architect did not choose a historic or organic design, but a contemporary design with a strong recognizable character that is not interchangeable with other neighborhoods in the Netherlands.

To further address these issues, the architect chose to divide the area into smaller neighborhoods. He then

FIGURE 16-7 View from the top floor of building Wulp (B) over Weidevogelhof toward Tolhek. *Courtesy of Jeanine de Zwarte*

dedicated two of these areas to open space, one of which was for a station square. In an attempt to create even more interest, additional openness and a softness within this high-density solution, the design consists of varying neighborhood solutions, including "C"-shaped buildings, square buildings, and three buildings that are linear. Subtle twists, angles, towers, and extensions of building mass for each structure on the site increase the sense of anticipation for pedestrians as they wander around the development. Finally, public green spaces were added, and zones for pedestrians, cyclists, and car parking were defined. By combining all of these approaches into the design, the architect created an open, inviting, and at the same time, warm and safe area on a human scale.

Care

Philosophy of Care

What is the operators' philosophy, and how does the development match this philosophy?

Providing housing for people is the housing association Rondom Wonen's core business regardless of whether people are in need of care and support, at home or in a homelike environment. The majority of people in need of care are elderly, but persons with disabilities can also rely on Rondom Wonen. Irrespective of age or disabilities, living an independent life and living in your own home is the common goal and is the basis for government policy in the Netherlands today.

In order to achieve this objective, the three elements of housing, at-home care and welfare services all have to be developed simultaneously and in one process. Living in close proximity to a care provider and especially living in an area with available welfare services is necessary to live, not just independently, but more importantly, to stay in control of one's own life if one becomes more dependent with age.

In Weidevogelhof, housing with care is a mix of independent and care-supported living. Such a mix of housing, care, and services has to be developed by housing associations and care organizations cooperating while each focuses on its own core business and expertise.

By providing the range of housing, welfare, and care, individuals can stay home as long as possible or, when needed, move into a care environment and stay within the same neighborhood. Couples can stay close to one another when one is in need of care even if this is specialized dementia care. With the 10 households within the scheme providing dementia care to 60 people, dementia care is easily accessible. In this situation, not only can the partner easily visit the household, but the person suffering from dementia can also easily go back home for a short period of time, go out with relatives for a walk, or have coffee in a familiar environment.

The foundation for this philosophy is provided by modern, fully equipped apartments of 70 to 140 square meters (750 to 1,500 square feet) some with more than

FIGURE 16-8 View from the terrace attached to the local welfare service. *Courtesy of Jeanine de Zwarte*

one bedroom and with suitable outside space in the form of either a balcony or garden. For privacy reasons, a second separate toilet is provided in the scheme.

The apartments and the apartment buildings are designed as lifetime housing. The apartments enable the tenants to live independently even when mobility and transportation aids are used and simultaneously enable the care organization to provide care. In the central entrance, hallways and elevators are easy to access by people using walkers, wheelchairs, or motorized scooters. Central scooter parking on the ground floor is provided in several of the buildings.

Community and Belonging

How does the scheme design and operation support this ideal?

With the philosophical objective to provide a normal environment, all the apartments and facilities are not brought together in one huge building but are designed as a neighborhood called Weidevogelhof. In addition, because Keijzershof is a completely new suburb, the design of Weidevogelhof had to be strong enough not only to provide housing as well as care and welfare but also to create a sense of belonging. In short, Weidevogelhof had to be recognizable and have its own character within the wider neighborhood of Keijzershof. The presence and location of all facilities support the individual sense of belonging. The restaurant is close to the station square, and welfare and health services are situated on the ground and second floor of the buildings next to the restaurant and close to the station square.

Innovation

If the operator pursues a policy of innovation and pursuit of excellence, how is this demonstrated?

Weidevogelhof is not a building, nor is it even a series of buildings. It is an entire neighborhood with all facilities one could wish for at any age cloaked in a strong design in a high-quality and mostly affordable-housing environment. The place in which it is situated is desirable with a promising future because it provides a heart for the new suburb Keijzershof, something many new suburbs lack.

Neighborhood Integration

Community Involvement

Is the scheme and service designed to integrate successfully with the local community?

Rondom Wonen realizes the importance of creating a safe neighborhood with readily available services and activities and has achieved this goal in Weidevogelhof. If people want to live independently as long as possible, they must stay in control of their own life. Three issues can undermine this: physical or cognitive deterioration, insecurity, and loneliness.

The fear of deterioration can lead to insecurity. With the complete range of services and care, from at-home care to dementia care and a care hotel, provided at Weidevogelhof, as well as a modern technical alarm system, residents can feel secure and can be sure of support and care when needed.

Loneliness can be a major threat to the quality of life and often occurs among elderly people, even when they are living together as a couple. Meeting other people and being able to participate in activities is important for almost everyone to experience a good quality of life. Therefore, the presence of local welfare services for all Pijnacker-South—with a center for meeting and activities as well as a public restaurant and services like transportation, meals on wheels, and so forth—is essential. With the restaurant and all of the health services, the neighborhood of Weidevogelhof attracts other people to the community, especially people living in the larger suburb of Pijnacker-South. This way meeting others happens naturally, but is also formally and specifically organized as well. With the various facilities offered, Weidevogelhof has a long-term goal to be "the place to be" for the elderly of Pijnacker and especially for the people living in Keijzershof.

Staff and Volunteers

Human Resources

Are policies and designs in place to attract good staff and volunteers?

This is the second facility in Pijnacker for local welfare provider Stichting Welzijn Ouderen Pijnacker. This welfare organization already has several hundred volunteers in its facility in the center of Pijnacker. The organization expects to find enough volunteers for its new facility in Weidevogelhof.

Weidevogelhof, with its modern approach to care and design, is an attractive environment in which to work especially for the people living in Pijnacker-South in one of the 4,000 family houses. Even child care is available in Weidevogelhof. For people from outside Keijzershof, Weidevogelhof can be reached easily by car or public transport, and it is just 10 to

15 minutes by bicycle from almost any location in Pijnacker.

Environmental Sustainability

ALTERNATIVE ENERGY SOURCES

The Dutch Building Decree has set out technical requirements for existing and new construction including requirements on energy performance since 1995. Weidevogelhof meets these requirements with insulation of walls, roof, and floors and double glazing which at the same time provides sound insulation. Weidevogelhof also has a ground source heat pump with Aquifer Thermal Energy Storage (ATES) to provide central heating during the winter and a cooling system in summer.

WATER CONSERVATION

None

ENERGY CONSERVATION

Some of the lower roofs are covered with plantings of sedum. These absorb rainwater and provide insulation as well as providing an attractive external aesthetic.

Outdoor Living

Garden

Does the garden support principles of care?

A primary focus of Weidevogelhof's philosophy is on housing in an environment with a feeling of belonging. The private gardens and public green spaces providing access to the outdoors support this philosophy. Each apartment has its own garden or balcony, and all the households for dementia care, which are never situated on the ground floor, have their own balcony.

To enhance the sense of community and belonging, a public meeting point is being developed and sponsored by the Lions Club. This meeting point is situated on a central spot next to Kwartel building. It is opposite the family homes across the Floralaan in order to encourage individuals from these homes to meet with the seniors renting the apartments of Weidevogelhof.

FIGURE 16-9 Outdoor public meeting point. *Courtesy of Dat de architectenwerkgroep tilburg*

FIGURE 16-10 Alzheimer's garden next to households for dementia care and child day care. *Courtesy of Jeanine de Zwarte*

Another public green area in the neighborhood is the garden of the C-shaped Wulp building with a private childcare garden next to the Alzheimer's garden. Though separated by a low fence, interaction between the children and people in the Alzheimer's garden is possible. The Alzheimer's garden is subsidized by a local organization advocating care and cure in Pijnacker. It is secure and has the only gate that one will find in Weidevogelhof.

Project Data

Design Team

ARCHITECT

DAT De Architectenwerkgroep Tilburg
Theo van Es
Walter van der Hamsvoord, project architect
Prof. Cobbenhagenlaan 47; 5037 DB Tilburg
The Netherlands
www.datarchitecten.nl

LANDSCAPE ARCHITECT

Karres en Brands Landscape Architects
Oude Amersfoortseweg 123
1212 AA Hilversum

The Netherlands
www.karresenbrands.nl

AREAS/SIZES

- Total site area: 31,160 square meters (335,403 square feet; 7.7 acres)
  - Phase one: 21,451 square meters (230,897 square feet; 5.3 acres)
  - Phase two: 7,791 square meters (83,862 square feet; 1.93 acres)
  - Phase three: 0.47 acres, 1,918 square meters (20,645 square feet; 0.47 acres)
- Building Footprint
  - Building A: 2,460 square meters (26,479 square feet)
  - Building B: 2,595 square meters (27,932 square feet)
  - Building C: 614 square meters (6,609 square feet)
  - Building D: 2,981 square meters (32,087 square feet)
  - Building E: 2,115 square meters (22,766 square feet)
  - Building F: 1,714 square meters (18,449 square feet)
  - Total building footprint phase one: 12,479 square meters (134,322 square feet)
  - Total footprint phase two: unknown
  - Total footprint phase three: 1,792 square meters (19,289 square feet)
- Total Building area:
  - Building A: 7,086 square meters (76,276 square feet)
  - Building B: 6,835 square meters (73,570 square feet)
  - Building C: 3,151 square meters (33,912 square feet)
  - Building D: 5,376 square meters (57,867 square feet)
  - Building E: 7,796 square meters (83,913 square feet)
  - Building F: 5,606 square meters (60,341 square feet)
  - Total building area phase one: 35,850 square meters (385,879 square feet)
- Total building area for phase two and three are unknown.
- Apartments: 70 to 150 square meters (753 to 1,615 square feet)

PARKING

Weidevogelhof provides 188 spaces inside buildings (on ground floor) and 61 places outside. Phase one provides 114 spaces inside and 42 spaces outside. Phase two has 39 inside and 19 outside parking spaces, and phase three has 35 inside but no outside parking spaces.

Also, all buildings provide central bicycle parking inside, and two buildings with apartments for independent living also provide central scooter parking within the building.

COSTS (2010)

- Total building cost
  - Building cost phase one: €71,895,000 ($102,896,467.13 USD)
  - Building cost phase two: €26,900,000 ($38,500,870.26 USD)
  - Building cost phase three: €10,775,000 ($15,421,221.27 USD)
- Cost per square meter
  - Phase one: €2,005 per square meter ($2,869.10 USD; or $266.65 USD per square foot).
  - Costs for phase two and phase three are unavailable.

RESIDENT AGE

At the time of this writing, two-thirds of the development was complete. The tenants of the rental homes for independent living as well as the residents of the care schemes were moving in. It is, therefore, not possible to confirm the average resident age at scheme opening.

RESIDENT PAYER MIX

The care hotel, the households for dementia care, and the houses for individuals with intellectual disabilities are being paid out of the Exceptional Medical Expenses Act (EMEA or AWBZ), a Dutch national insurance scheme for long-term care.

All other apartments were built according to the regulations for developing houses and partially affordable housing. Tenants pay rent and tenants in affordable housing can be supported by individual housing benefit.

If care is needed in these rented apartments, it is partially paid out of the AWBZ and partially out of the Social Support Act for domestic care and welfare, such as social activities and meeting opportunities. The intention of this Act is to enable everybody, old and young, disabled and able-bodied, with and without problems, to participate in society. The Ministry of Health, Welfare and Sport defines the framework in which each municipality can make its own policy, based on the composition and demands of its inhabitants.

Part VI

United Kingdom Schemes

GIVE
WAY

Chapter 17

A Study of Belong Atherton

REASONS FOR INCLUSION OF THIS SCHEME

- This scheme is located in an urban neighborhood, town center.
- This scheme integrates the concept of long-term care and independent living in close proximity in the same development.
- This scheme responds to the frailties of older people with various levels of care needs, including dementia, through the building design.

Building Description

Name of Scheme: Belong Atherton
Owner: Belong
Address:
Mealhouse Lane
Atherton
Wigan
Lancashire
M46 0DR
United Kingdom
Occupied since: April 2011

FIGURE 17-1 Belong Atherton entrance and café at the ground-floor corner and community room on the second floor above ground. *Photo courtesy of Damian Utton*

FIGURE 17-2 Scheme location. *Courtesy of Pozzoni LLP*

FIGURE 17-3 Site plan. *Courtesy of Pozzoni LLP*

Description of the Type of Community, Including the Number of Residents

The owner of Belong Atherton has created a number of schemes for older persons in the United Kingdom and with this past experience has developed a lifestyle concept for older people that is intended to prevent isolation and to protect, promote, and maintain a person's autonomy and independence. The design and operation of the several Belong villages creates and balances noninstitutional spaces in which people feel at home in their own personal and private space, while simultaneously being in close proximity to a range of support, facilities, and activities. Belong Atherton is a three-story, predominantly brick-built scheme and is the fourth project to be built and opened by Belong since it embarked on its mission in the new millennium to enhance residential, dementia, and nursing care services across the northwest of England.

The Belong company was born out of CLS and Borough Care Services, two not-for-profit care organizations that, until the early 1990s, had originally been the Local Authority providers of the County of Cheshire and the Borough of Wigan, respectively. Between them, these two organizations owned a total of 54 homes, mostly dating from the 1960s and 1970s and built to the model of that time with small bedrooms and shared toilet and washing facilities. The size of these homes varied, but generally had a total of 40 residents in common. Although most of these homes were refurbished during the 1990s with many rooms being provided with en-suite facilities, a few homes were deemed surplus for a variety of reasons, and there are fewer than 30 still operating. The locations of four of these original homes were selected for their size and redevelopment opportunity. This fourth scheme, Belong Atherton, was considered particularly interesting because of its location in the center of the Victorian mill town of Atherton within the busy Borough of Wigan.

Belong specifically required a building that would house six self-contained households of 12 residents each under one roof. Within wider financial constraints, it attempted to keep households of a size that enables the lifestyle of an "extended family" to be realized. Each household is designed in a domestic contemporary style. Of the six households, the scheme manages three distinct layouts. Each revolves around a large open-plan communal center that contains living, dining, and kitchen areas.

Private bedrooms that include en-suite bathrooms open onto the central open-plan communal area or onto short lengths of corridor. This ensures that residents can find their way around the household easily and that staff members can easily and discreetly monitor the entire household. Some residents report feeling safer in this household design than in their previous care home because they can see staff around all the time. These residents indicated that they previously felt as if they had been left alone if they could not see staff.

In addition to providing a homey and noninstitutional environment, Belong requested, in its design brief, building flexibility for both current and future use. Its long, exhausting experience of trying to sensibly upgrade cheap, tired, inflexible structures from the 1960s was ingrained in Belong's recent memory. Affordable and flexible use of space became a driving mantra of the organization. Bedroom floor areas and communal space areas comfortably exceed national minimum standards for the United Kingdom. These larger floor areas, particularly in the bedrooms, allow space for residents' personal possessions to be brought in if they wish and for additional equipment to be used if a resident's needs change.

Belong continues to respond to both theoretical and practical precedent. One such example is a Joseph Rowntree Foundation report titled "My Home not the Home" of 2001.[1] Within that publication, residents encourage providers to consider variation in shapeand size of their bedroom. Although obviously compromised by other practical factors, such as economic considerations, the principle is considered in all Belong developments. At Belong Atherton, it manifests itself in several different shapes and sizes of bedrooms. For example, there are large window bays that help to delineate sitting areas within each resident's private room.

All individual bedrooms have en-suite barrier-free shower rooms with toilets visible from bed-heads when the doors remain open. Bedrooms and shower rooms are deliberately paired up to allow easy conversion in the future into small apartments should demographics and

[1] *My Home not the Home*; published by Joseph Rowntree Foundation, 2001. Edited by Tim Dwelly; Research by Eleanor McKee and Caroline Oakes.

demand change. Two en-suite bedrooms can easily convert in the future to a one-bedroom apartment with a separate kitchen, bedroom, and living space. Outside each bedroom is a small recess with a lowered ceiling and down-light, creating the impression of a "front porch." This helps to define the transition from the semi-private domain of the household communal space to the private domain of the bedroom.

The kitchen is open and accessible and forms a lively hub around which all activity revolves. Dining, craft, and living areas are clearly separate, and along with other smaller alcoves and sitting spaces, provide several possibilities for the resident to choose their preferred activity at any time of the day, whether it is views of the activity on the street or the quiet garden or balcony.

The team of designers, with the client, has become familiar with the principles of good design for people with dementia as discussed in the publication, "Design for Dementia" by Judd, Marshall, and Phippen.[2] That is, good design for individuals with dementia should compensate for impairments, maximize independence, and enhance self-esteem and confidence. It should also demonstrate care for staff, be orientating and understandable, reinforce personal identity, welcome relatives and the local community, and allow the control of stimuli. Certainly the layout and interior décor of the households and individual bedrooms strive to meet these principles. Now commonly seen solutions such as glass-fronted kitchen cupboards, hidden service doors, memory boxes, and familiar fixtures and fittings are used extensively. Less common is the overwhelming feeling of being comfortably at ease in someone's private home. No access is possible to any of the Belong Atherton households without ringing a doorbell, a procedure that is strictly followed by even the most senior of company staff. No household is a thoroughfare but is the residents' home, and everyone else needs permission to enter.

Much thought has also gone into the need for clear color and shade contrast where necessary to accommodate the eyesight problems associated with dementia, and guidelines published by the Royal National Institute for the Blind (RNIB) have been adopted. In time, it is anticipated that all six households could be occupied predominantly by people suffering from some level of dementia. The design has taken this possibility into consideration by providing large balconies on the upper-floor households, which enable easy access to the outside without compromising safety, in addition to providing a well-appointed garden at grade level.

Belong Atherton is registered with the United Kingdom Care Quality Commission to provide 72 "care homes with nursing and dementia care" beds. While there are not currently 72 residents with nursing and care needs, the design layout and details, along with the operational and management policies, allow for "future-proofing" should the needs of current and future residents change. Belong is a home for life; the building and staff change to suit the residents' needs.

FIGURE 17-4 Café/bistro open to the surrounding community. *Photo courtesy of Damian Utton*

---

[2] S. Judd, M. Marshall, and P. Phippen, "Design for Dementia," *Journal of Dementia Care,* London, England, 1998.

Beyond the six households, the central core of the village on the ground floor consists of a bistro served by a central, fully equipped catering kitchen. This kitchen can provide meals to the households by way of a temperature-controlled cart and a separate service elevator. However, most meals are cooked in the households by the staff and residents, as a family. The bistro is accessed directly from the main street entrance to the scheme. A curved, staffed reception desk swings gracefully around from the reception area into the bistro service line where a range of meals and snacks are available throughout the day. A hair salon sits close by, and another set of automatic doors leads clearly out to a rear parking area.

On the upper floor, there are other common facilities such as community rooms, an Internet café, and a small shop. Ideally, Belong admits, these rooms would generally be more successful if they were at the ground-floor level, but space prohibited that option, and the compromised location was selected and is well managed.

The hub facilities are open to the general public and, as with the other completed Belong villages, this is successful in providing the opportunities for interaction between residents and the community. As a result, residents do not feel isolated and still feel they are part of the community and the wider neighborhood. A spinoff benefit is in showcasing the home to future residents and staff and generating an additional income stream.

With all Belong schemes, the emphasis is on the pedestrian. The main entrance is never accessed through a sea of cars, but either through gardens or directly off the street, which emphasizes the importance of the non-driving resident, and not the car. Vehicular access is kept discreet but readily accessible.

The last ingredient of a Belong village development is the assisted-living apartments. At Belong Atherton, there are 27 one- and two-bedroom apartments that are provided over three stories and are almost indistinguishable externally from the three-story care facility. They are, however, accessed externally with their own controlled door to common carpeted corridors and stairwells. A separate elevator is provided adjacent to the entrance. The independence of these residents is emphasized but with an easy access to the community facilities of the hub.

Residents of these apartments are provided with a range of purchase or rental options, depending on their needs. These apartments are particularly popular, probably because of the town center location of the development. Residents can also avail themselves of the care and support services available if they need to, but are in no way required to do so. Although this is a newer scheme, elsewhere Belong has witnessed an increasing need for the spouse to have a neighboring apartment if his or her partner needs to live in a care household.

FIGURE 17-5 Façade on Mealhouse Lane with the bedrooms behind the bay windows and lounge areas behind the balconies. *Photo courtesy of Damian Utton*

Geographics

Vernacular Design

How does the scheme/environment respond to the locality?

From the outset, Belong was particularly excited about the opportunities presented by this location. The site was occupied by one of its older residential care homes managed by its sister company Borough Care Services. This existing development faced inward and, architecturally, refused to recognize its neighbors in any way whatsoever. Cold, unattractive, gray bricks give the building an almost prison-like feel. Located centrally on a busy crossroads in a small, but vibrant, town center, the possibility of integration with the town and community on an architectural and social scale was immediately obvious.

It was decided that the building should strongly present itself to the street. The bistro would sit prominently on the corner of the crossroads and beckon the public in. Common areas would have views onto the vibrancy and activity of the town wherever possible. At higher levels, balconies would be located to overlook the town.

The scheme succeeds in recreating the Victorian street pattern of the neighborhood by closely following the sidewalk. The architects and developer wanted to build much closer to this sidewalk, but the local planning authority insisted on a buffer zone of several meters. This zone consists of soft landscaping to the residential blocks and hard surfacing to the more public areas of the central "village" communal areas of the bistro and hair and beauty salon.

Facing materials were chosen to complement the predominant vernacular of brick with slate roofs. A mixture of brick and contrasting colored stucco is softened in parts with cedar cladding to give the whole a more defined and varied feel. The building is large relative to the adjacent smaller domestic and local retail units, and it was deemed important to break up the scale with projecting bays and balconies. Stone window surrounds are a modern interpretation of the solid stone lintels and sills of the Victorian, workmanlike neighbors. The roof is clad in economic gray concrete tiles, which sit well with the Welsh gray slates elsewhere.

Care

Philosophy of Care

What is the operators' philosophy, and how does the building match this philosophy?

BELONG HAS FOUR OVERRIDING PRINCIPLES WHEN APPROACHING A NEW PROJECT:

- The home should accommodate current demands and design in the flexibility for change in the future as attitudes and expectations change.
- The design should give residents the choice and the independence to make their own decisions.
- The built environment should facilitate and enhance the delivery of care.
- The entire team should always remember that the design and layout of the care home is just one aspect of a total person-centered care approach.

It is this last principle that totally underpins the holistic care philosophy of Belong. It can be clearly witnessed in the households that the staff are committed to preventing social isolation and promoting people's control and independence. To assist this, the design is not only based on the latest research and thinking in respect to the support of the elderly, but it specifically conforms to RNIB and disabled-access guidelines.

Interestingly, the staff members in each household, often at a ratio of one staff to four residents, are multitasked. They live as part of the household, carrying out all the specific tasks necessary to meet the overall philosophy of Belong. They will assist with care needs but also cook, clean, and provide activity stimulus with their wider "family." Where possible, the resident will join in with these tasks, with assistance as needed.

This can be a burden on these members of staff and, thus, a wider support network is available. For instance, although the staff on the household will make beds and carry out some basic cleaning on a day-to-day basis, the

FIGURE 17-6 Open-plan household lounge and dining area with access to garden beyond the domestic-style kitchen. *Photo courtesy of Damian Utton*

whole household is thoroughly cleaned by professional cleaners once a week. Again, although the main course of the main daily meal might be cooked in the household, the dessert course would be delivered from the central kitchen to lighten the load on staff. This assistance, along with laundry assistance, helps to share workload but maintains a thoroughly domestic feel. This philosophy, along with the open-plan design, appears to allow the resident to feel at ease, and there is a massive reduction in individuals' anxiety levels to the point where aimless wandering, for instance, has been almost eliminated.

This familiar, safe, and comfortable home life is pursued as well in the assisted-living apartments. If the resident engages with the care provision, then he or she will find therapeutic activity is valued. Pets, for instance, are encouraged throughout the building. Time and again, one is struck by the fact that people actually do all seem to "belong" to the "village."

FIGURE 17-7 Community room with chairs set out for a presentation. The licensed bar is in the background. *Photo courtesy of Damian Utton*

Community and Belonging

How does the scheme design and operation support this ideal?

The entire concept of the building revolves around community and belonging. The households themselves are designed with their large open-plan floors and bedrooms accessed directly off this space. Privacy is available in one's own room, but interaction is easily available at the resident's choice. Some residents say that they like the opportunity of listening to the activity of the living or kitchen area when they choose to do this from the privacy of their own room, particularly if they are bedridden for a period of time.

The wider village is also the wider community, and it is clear that it is used in that way. Residents on their own or with family or caregivers clearly quite often visit the range of facilities offered by the village.

Innovation

If the operator pursues a policy of innovation and pursuit of excellence, how is this demonstrated?

An important aspect of the Belong concept that sets the design apart is the fire engineering strategy, which integrates the open-plan design on multilevel floors with a fire-suppression system and the operational management plan. The fire-engineered solution is a combination of a water-mist system and fire compartmentalization layout with a thorough and robust fire evacuation and management procedure, with both aspects being integral to the success of the other. Careful and full consultation with the local fire officer has enabled a layout that previously had only been seen in single-story dwellings with multiple fire-escape options.

In the United Kingdom, fire officers are more familiar with separate rooms, fire doors and a particularly institutional approach to fire safety. In this instance, a series of detailed reviews with all parties established potential fire and smoke risks, which could then be addressed in the strategy. One good outcome of this is the minimal use of heavy overhead fire closers, which would previously have been used on all bedroom doors and prevented them from staying open. They would also have been more difficult to open and close for frail residents. The end result is a more domestic feel.

The fire strategy is clearly one innovation. Another has to be the intense effort witnessed in making Belong a thriving part of the community and dismantling any negative perceptions of care homes and the contribution that older people have to offer within society. The public access to the hub facilities goes a long way toward achieving this.

Neighborhood Integration

Community Involvement

Is the scheme and service designed to integrate successfully with the local community?

The central "hub" provides a bistro, hair and beauty salon, community room, shop, and Internet café. These are designed and fitted out as if they were independent

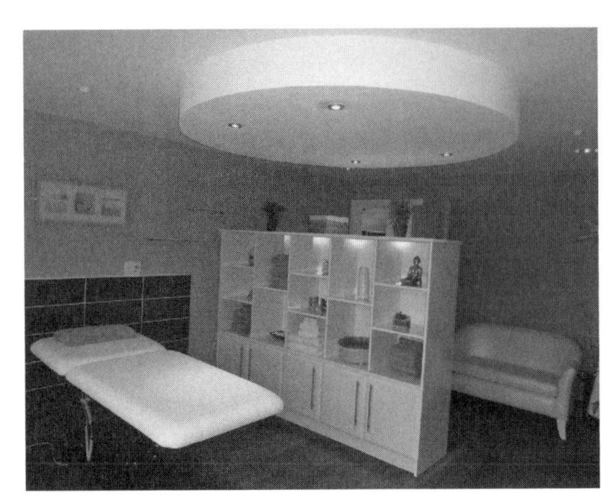

FIGURE 17-8 The "well-being suite" fitted out to create a spa-like ambience. *Photo courtesy of Damian Utton*

businesses and are clearly expected to act as such. The bistro is positioned on a prominent corner of the plot to attract passing pedestrians. It is designed deliberately to be part of the wider community and is clearly seen by Belong as the strongest ammunition in the armory of community attractions.

Elsewhere on other Belong villages, the Bistro attracts people into the village from outside, but in this instance, it is overwhelmingly successful because of its location in a town center. It is clear that the welcome given by the architecture, interior design, and staff helps to encourage use by all generations, breaking down the perception of elderly institutions. The hair salon is a similarly popular attraction, again open to the wider community.

Although still working through its relative newness, it is anticipated that the community rooms will be used by a variety of local groups. In other Belong villages, a good deal of effort has gone into attracting cinema clubs, exercise groups, and even the occasional use by Brownie Scouts.

The "well-being suite" provided at Belong Atherton also has possibilities for use by local, independent, alternative practitioners, for such things as aromatherapy or reflexology, who could hire the room out to service their own clients as well as a service for residents and staff, furthering community integration.

Staff and Volunteers

Human Resources

Are policies and designs in place to attract good staff and volunteers?

With ever-increasing difficulties of attracting the right type of committed person to work within an elderly people's home, Belong has attempted to consider this within the design. The policy of multitasking, which goes beyond that of a standard caregiver, arguably requires a buy-in from the prospective employee. Not all the staff from the previous Borough Care Service home on the site were employed for this new concept. The clean, contemporary, but homey design is clearly an attraction to staff as well as residents. The open nature of the layout allows easy monitoring and therefore does appear to encourage the staff to spend quality time with the residents.

Each household team is tasked with self-managing themselves, to think creatively and to have fun. This manifests itself in different activities, meals and, it could be said, the overall atmosphere in each household. In much the same way as domestic houses can feel quite different once entered, these households clearly have their own personalities and are certainly not institutional in any way. Cost of building and operation was never far off the agenda during the design of the building. For that reason, the households operate as pairs on each floor at night to assist staffing costs.

Traditional staff rooms are completely absent. The team at Belong have learned from their earlier schemes that staff want to stay in their respective households, living the family life with the residents. Obviously, there are quiet rooms or even the bistro, for staff if they so wish, but gone are the stark locker rooms of the old, institutional models.

The village is also fitted with a sophisticated nurse-call system that covers all bedrooms and communal areas. Each bedroom, for instance, has a specialist dementia installation that provides:

- Automatic light guidance for the en-suite bathroom and bed
- 16 behavior profiles
- Fall notification
- Bed exit and en-suite bathroom activity sensors
- A server that records all nurse-call activity

Each room has a call unit that uses speech, call lead and pull cords dependent on individual requirements. All calls go to a wireless phone carried by staff members, which is cascade programmed such that when a call is not answered within a time period, the call is repeated to a higher level of staffing.

FIGURE 17-9 The separate entrance for the apartments; residents must cross the courtyard to access the communal facilities. *Photo courtesy of Damian Utton*

Environmental Sustainability

ALTERNATIVE ENERGY SOURCES
None

WATER CONSERVATION
None

ENERGY CONSERVATION
The building structure has load-bearing masonry walls with concrete floors for thermal mass. A dynamic thermal model was produced, allowing for an in-depth energy appraisal of the building design.

Glazing is installed, which minimizes solar gain and heat loss. At the same time, the design exceeds all minimum daylighting requirements. The large areas of glazing allow natural light to flood into the building, helping to minimize the need for artificial lighting, but also helping with the real issues of depression and eyesight problems that are particular problems for older people.

High levels of thermal insulation, low-energy light fittings, and individual room heating controls are intended to reduce the demand for energy.

Future maintenance is minimized with the choice of external materials such as PVC-clad windows, factory-treated cedar, and through-colored stucco. Local tradespeople were also sought out by the building contractor to reduce transport to and from the construction site. Building materials were obtained from sustainable sources.

Outdoor Living

Garden

Does the garden support principles of care?

Belong relies heavily on its knowledge of dementia to influence the design of the outdoor spaces. Households have access to either private, secure, sensory gardens, if they are situated at ground level, or to balconies on upper floors. The attractive balconies are planned to be

FIGURE 17-10 The balcony accessed from the household lounge area is large enough for several people to sit comfortably.
Photo courtesy of Damian Utton

large enough to seat most, if not all, of the residents of each household. This would depend on the number of wheelchairs required, but appears possible, particularly on the larger balconies at the rear of the scheme. Those balconies looking onto Mealhouse Lane, the main thoroughfare, have the advantage of being south-facing and having an active aspect onto this street, which has much activity. As with the other Belong villages, the gardens and balconies become outdoor rooms, and each household brings its own identity. Growing tomatoes, potted flowers, or bird feeders and baths are examples of the use of external spaces for purposeful activity.

Project Data

DESIGN FIRM

Pozzoni LLP
Woodville House
2 Woodville Road
Altrincham
Cheshire
WA14 2FH
United Kingdom
www.pozzoni.co.uk

AREAS/SIZES

- Site area: 6,400 square meters (68,889.03 square feet; 1.58 acres)
- Building footprint: 2,280 square meters (24,541.72 square feet)
- Total building area: 5,830 square meters (62,753.60 square feet)
- Total area per resident: 59.48 square meters (640.24 square feet)

PARKING

Spaces for 31 automobiles including 5 disabled access spaces on surface lots

COSTS (APRIL 2011)

- Total building cost: £6,670,896 ($10,810,116.57 USD)
- Cost per square meter: £114 ($185 USD)
- Cost per square foot: £106 ($172 USD)
- Investment per resident: £92,651.33 ($150,141 USD)

RESIDENT AGE

Average age of residents: 80 years

RESIDENT PAYER MIX

The social services agencies in the United Kingdom provide funding for care of the residents.

Chapter 18

A Study of Heald Farm Court

REASONS FOR INCLUSION OF THIS SCHEME

- Heald Farm Court has a well-designed external architecture; the contemporary style sits well in its surroundings.
- It is a large development that is reduced in scale with several buildings.
- The scheme is an example of partnership between several organizations.

Building Description

Name of Scheme: Heald Farm Court

Owner: Methodist Homes for the Aging Care Group (MHA) manages Heald Farm Court on behalf of Helena Partnerships (a Registered Social Landlord) who owns the building

Address:
Sturgess Street
Newton-le-Willows
Merseyside
WA12 9HP
United Kingdom

Occupied since: October 2009

FIGURE 18-1 Detail of Sturgess Street frontage with gable-fronted apartments with copper cladding and balconies. *Courtesy of Damian Utton*

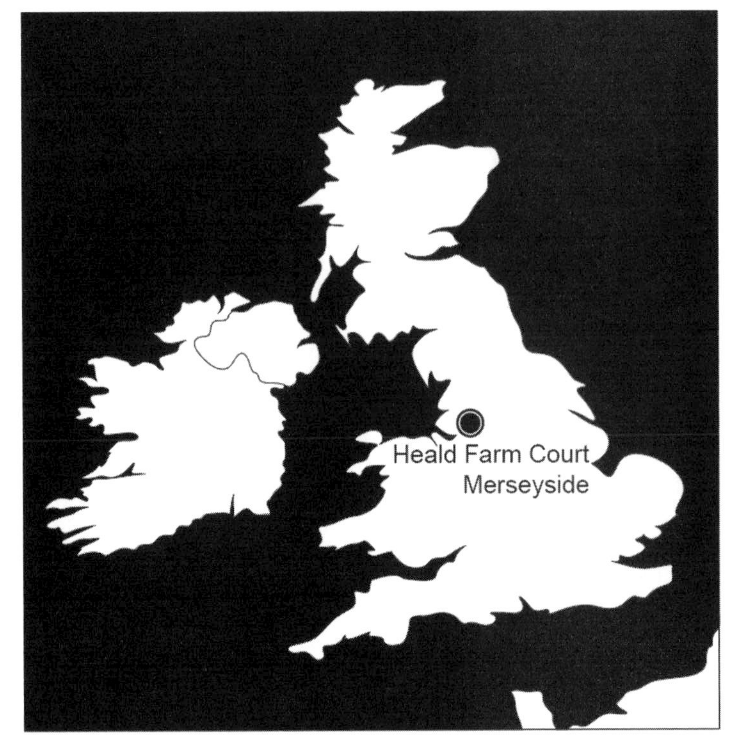

FIGURE 18-2 Scheme location. *Courtesy of Pozzoni LLP*

Heald Farm Court: United Kingdom

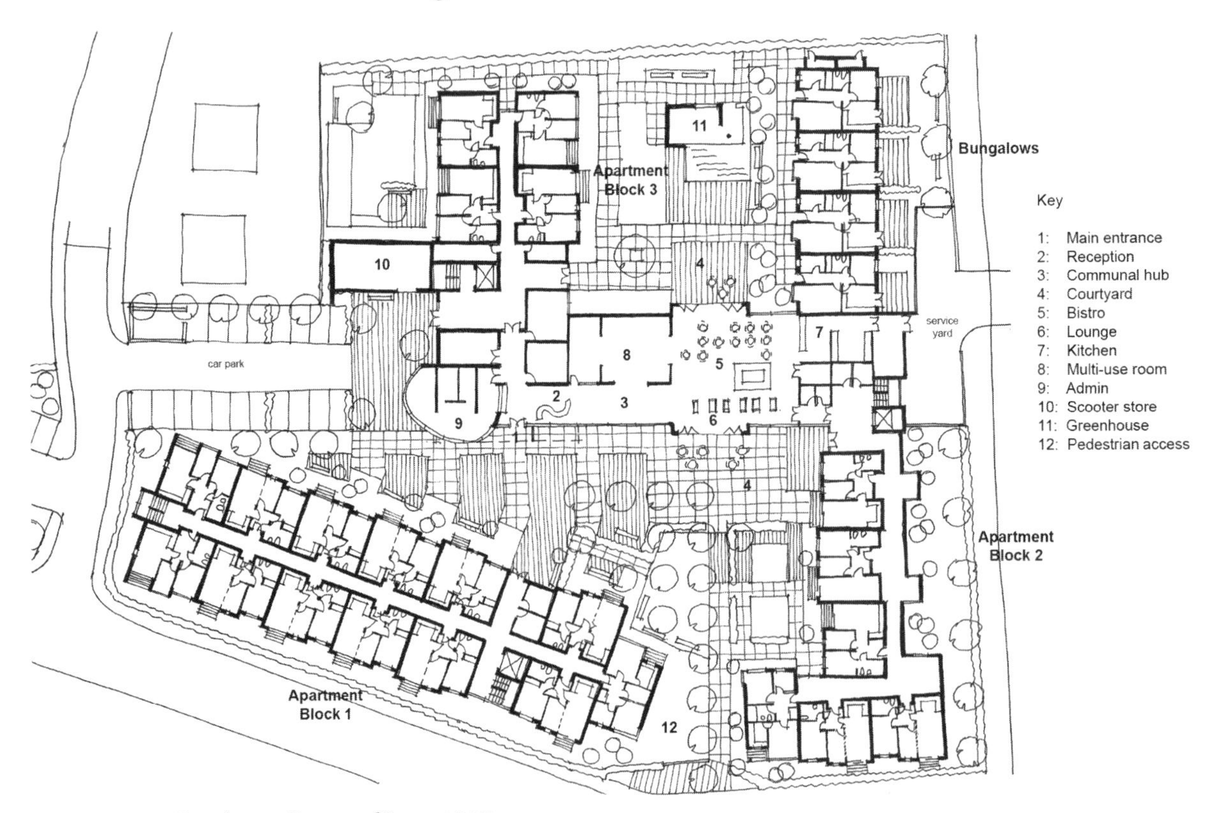

FIGURE 18-3 Site plan. *Courtesy of Pozzoni LLP*

Description of the Type of Community, Including Number of Residents

Heald Farm Court is an attractive development of 86 extra care apartments and three bungalows in the town of Newton-le-Willows in northwest England, located midway between Manchester and Liverpool. The region grew prosperous with the Industrial Revolution and the main employer in the region was the railway carriage manufacturing works. The town declined as manufacturing moved away from the area and the railway works closed in 1953. The main employer today is a food manufacturer and numerous smaller businesses.

The previous use of the site was a local authority care home dating from the 1960s. The local authority, St Helens Council, owned the land and gifted it to Helena Partnerships to redevelop the site for extra care housing. The design was developed with Helena Partnerships, MHA Care Group and DK-Architects and was partially funded by a Department of Health grant, which was secured by St Helens Council.

The development contains three separate buildings, which are two and three stories high, grouped around the central communal facilities and two courtyard spaces. Externally, the buildings are constructed of dark-red brickwork and copper cladding with gray roofing slates. Granite paving leads to courtyard areas with hardwood seating benches, and mature trees have been planted.

Heald Farm Court is impressive at first contact. It is clear that a great deal of attention has been paid to the design and to the use of expensive materials. Some might be attracted to Heald Court when entering the central courtyard and being surrounded by the three different buildings; others might feel it is too monumental and prefer a more human scale. Whatever one's preference, there is no doubt this is a development that demands consideration.

Heald Farm Court has apartments for rent, shared ownership, and purchase. The two-bedroom apartments and bungalows are all wheelchair accessible and suitable for individuals and couples alike. Of the 86 apartments, all have two bedrooms and there are 10 different apartment types with a variety of designs—some with balconies, terraces, or gardens.

The apartments are designed with open-plan living and kitchen areas to create the feeling of space and ease of access between these two areas, as well as allowing additional daylight into the kitchen area. All the apartments have been fitted with built-in kitchen units with integrated hob (warming tray), oven, and extractor fans. Heating of the apartments is with low surface

FIGURE 18-4 Main entrance under canopy with apartments over. Canopy also links to street frontage apartments to the left. Car park is in the distance. *Courtesy of Damian Utton*

FIGURE 18-5 Communal café/lounge with rooflight and views and access to courtyards via glazed doors. *Courtesy of Damian Utton*

FIGURE 18-6 Walnut veneer internal wall cladding shown here to the café. Multiuse room is behind the closed sliding doors. *Courtesy of Damian Utton*

temperature radiators, not the more commonly used under-floor heating.

The en-suite baths are the wet-room style and can be accessed from either the hallway or the master bedroom. This means that if a resident calls for help on the call system, there will always be access to the room, even if someone had collapsed against one of the doors.

Staff are available 24 hours every day and are able to use their electronic key fobs to access all private residential areas. There is door entry video phone for visitors, and security cameras throughout the village contribute to the safe and secure environment for residents.

Pets are not allowed, which is unusual—many extra care schemes allow pets at the manager's discretion.

The communal and leisure facilities form the heart of the development and include a café, lounge, health and well-being center, and landscaped gardens, encouraging interest and socialization. There is also a sensory garden, multi-activity room, hair salon, prayer room, launderette, gymnasium, greenhouse, and a guest suite.

The communal facilities serve as a village hub for another 166 properties in the surrounding area, including new bungalows developed simultaneously on a site some distance away from Heald Farm Court.

Geographics

Vernacular Design

How does the scheme/environment respond to the locality?

Heald Farm Court was the winner in the "Housing our Aging Population" category for the U.K. Housing Design Awards 2010.

The first impression of the courtyard areas and the architecture lining the courtyard is of a university courtyard. Many of the apartments are presented as terraces of gable-fronted villas. The external finishes are dark-red brickwork and bronzed copper cladding with dark powder–coated windows and generous balconies in a smartly detailed and well-proportioned arrangement.

However, one has to question the architectural language of a university campus as appropriate for a domestic setting for older people. While the overall scheme is popular for a variety of reasons, the courtyards are spacious but lack an intimacy that is often found in other developments for older people.

The use of copper cladding is unusual and helps to give the development a striking feature. The dark tone complements the brickwork well. However, much copper cladding has been used and possibly overused which can detract from the impact. The roof to the scooter store is copper clad. While this roof is visible from a stairwell and several apartments, the cost of this

FIGURE 18-7 Front courtyard: Communal facilities are in the copper clad structure with apartments behind the brickwork walls. Main entrance is to the left under the canopy. *Courtesy of Damian Utton*

expensive material should also be questioned in terms of value. Would the money have been better spent on features that residents can use and touch on a daily basis?

THE LAYOUT WORKS FOR THREE DIFFERENT USER GROUPS:

- Visitors who must feel welcome
- The more independent residents who want to feel they are in a domestic environment
- Residents with higher dependency needs who need to feel secure

The design accomplishes these objectives by dividing apartments into three blocks around the central hub of communal facilities. The residents who are most independent live in the street frontage block along Sturgess Street and can access the hub under a covered walkway. Residents with higher dependency needs are able to access the services without going outside, with short and direct access routes.

Internally, the communal corridors and stairs are very generously proportioned, and a luxury feel has been created with the use of high-quality materials such as internal walnut and oak veneers and handrails, along with a number of warm wall colors and contemporary furniture and fittings, but the height at which the handrails have been fixed does seem high.

However, while the corridors may be wide enough for two scooters to pass each other, the proportion of the corridors means that they can feel "empty." And yet, while the communal and circulation spaces are generously proportioned, the apartment floor areas are relatively standard housing association floor areas. Similarly, the internal finishes in the apartments are also relatively standard for housing associations. One has to question if the space would have been better utilized in the apartments and if the cost for the luxury corridor and stair finishes would have been better spent on a higher specification of kitchen and bathroom finishes in the apartments.

FIGURE 18-8 Wide corridor and stair landing to upper floor in apartment area. *Courtesy of Damian Utton*

Many apartments have very generous-sized balconies, and these are well used. The balustrading detail is of a timber handrail supported by a thick sheet of glass. While this allows uninterrupted views out, vertigo is a common issue with many older people. There may also be costly ongoing issues with keeping this exposed double-fronted glass clean.

Care

Philosophy of Care

What is the operators' philosophy, and how does the building match this philosophy?

Heald Farm Court is an example of two organizations—Helena Partnerships and Methodist Homes—working together, with one organization focused on the housing and the other on care delivery. Helena Partnerships' philosophy is about enjoying life to the fullest with comfort, security, and independence with the ability to live free from worry. As a registered social landlord, Helena Partnerships provides affordable homes, neighborhoods, and communities that people want to live in. Their aim is to be an innovative and well-respected housing company working with their tenants, employees, and partners creating thriving neighborhoods with modern homes and services.

Methodist Homes for the Aging's philosophy, which also underpins the design and operation of Heald Farm Court, is to improve the quality of life for older people. MHA places an emphasis on the spiritual well-being of older people, which is an important and integral part of their service. The personal beliefs of each individual, and the choices of older people to participate, or not, in activities and events within the home or scheme are always respected. At Heald Farm Court, this philosophy of care translates to:

- Improving the lives of the residents who live there, based on the principles of love, compassion, and respect
- High-quality, person-centered care
- An emphasis on nurturing a person's spiritual as well as physical well-being
- A respect for individuality, personal choice, dignity, and potential

FIGURE 18-9 Communal lounge area in use. *Courtesy of Damian Utton*

Community and Belonging

How does the scheme operation support this ideal?

There are 89 apartments at Heald Farm Court, of which two are reserved transitional flats for people requiring accommodation between a high-dependency needs unit and those returning home. These transitional units can also be booked by people who are "trying before they buy" and may subsequently move back to the village of Newton-le-Willows. Forty-six apartments are contracted by St Helens social services, who refer residents directly to the scheme.

Having the communal facilities located in the central block makes them equidistant for everyone to reach. The properties facing Sturgess Street are in a standalone block, and residents must walk under a covered walkway across the front courtyard to reach the hub. For more able-bodied people this works well. The other two blocks are accessed via internal corridors and are more suitable for less able-bodied residents.

The hub itself is of a large assembly space that acts as the restaurant and lounge areas. Windows and doors give access to both courtyards and allow for cross ventilation. Large doors allow the adjoining multipurpose space to open up into the restaurant, or to be closed off. The other communal facilities are located in the same block as separate rooms.

Innovation

If the operator pursues a policy of innovation and pursuit of excellence, how is this demonstrated?

The partnership between Helena Partnerships and MHA Care Group is in itself an innovative example of working together with shared goals, each organization bringing to the table their own expertise and working together to drive the design and operation of Heald Farm Court.

Staff are in daily contact with residents to ensure their well-being. Social activities and events are also organized. The specialist team enables residents to continue to live independently in their own home and maintain a good quality of life. Additional support is also available with personal care, medication, meal preparation, cleaning, and laundry.

A care team is available onsite 24 hours every day, providing flexible support tailored to individual needs and in case of an emergency.

Neighborhood Integration

Community Involvement

Is the scheme and service designed to integrate successfully with the local community?

Heald Farm Court is set in an urban context of a "working-class/blue-collar" residential area. Such a development has to integrate with the local community on several levels.

All of the extra care apartments are designated for "affordable housing," which means that the rent is fixed at a lower than market level and residents must satisfy certain criteria in terms of assets and savings to live at Heald Farm Court. The social services department of St Helens Council has reserved 46 apartments for their own referrals. As most of the residents will have lived in the surrounding neighborhood most of their lives, and most will have family who also live nearby, providing this "affordable" housing for local people assists ongoing social integration. Social integration is also assisted by the employment of many staff who live in the immediate local area.

Heald Farm Court is situated in the suburb of Earlestown, Newton-le-Willows. The town center is just a five-minute walk away, offering a wide range of shops, banks, pubs, cafeterias, and a twice-weekly open air market. There is also a community church, medical practice, and pharmacy nearby. The nearby towns of St Helens and Warrington are easily accessible via frequent bus services (there is a bus stop next to the development). These town centers offer an even greater choice of amenities including cinemas, restaurants, and shopping facilities.

The local urban context of Heald Farm Court is one that has traditionally been characterized by two-story terraced houses, which were mostly built in the late-nineteenth century to house workers in the nearby factories. This style of housing still dominates the east side of the site. On the opposite side of Sturgess Street are 65 single-story sheltered housing bungalows and open parkland. To the north is a relatively new development of two-story semi-detached houses. To the west is the access road to the new housing, open space, and a housing estate.

People from the wider community are encouraged to participate in activities offered at Heald Farm, with the aim that the development will become a community facility. For example, the bistro-style restaurant found onsite is available to the residents of the local community as well. Although the facilities are aimed at older people, no one interested in joining in is turned away and MHA reports that the hub has become the area's liveliest center.

On the opposite side of Sturgess Street there are 65 sheltered housing bungalows. Heald Farm Court staff provides the support services to the bungalows and all who reside at the bungalows are encouraged to use the facilities at Heald Farm Court.

Regular contact is maintained with the local primary schools and there are currently discussions underway with school teachers with a view to developing joint educational programs and activities.

The architectural appearance uses the local red brick and the Sturgess Street frontage is in the style of gable-fronted three-story villas. As Heald Farm is much larger than surrounding houses, its appearance to the street does reduce the scale of what could be perceived as a very long and uniform apartment block. The three bungalows, accessed from the rear courtyard, have apartments to the upper floor (accessed from the hub), so they look like two-story houses.

There are two routes for the visitor into the hub: pedestrian and vehicular, which converge at the concierge desk at the entrance to the central hub. Visitors have access to all the communal facilities without crossing into private residential areas.

FIGURE 18-10 Multiuse room. *Courtesy of Damian Utton*

Staff and Volunteers

Human Resources

Are policies and designs in place to attract good staff and volunteers?

MHA Care Group offers staff and volunteers a counseling service, discounts at supermarkets and other leading retail suppliers, and the option to join a pension plan. A competitive salary and a flexible working policy are also offered, plus MHA Care Group is considered to be an employer of choice.

Employee retention is critical to the long-term health and success of the site. Investment in training is also key to staff retention and MHA Care Group invests in the development of their employees. By investing in the professional development of employees, quality care and support of the residents is improved.

Ensuring that employees are regularly recognized and rewarded for the contribution they make to the service, MHA Care Group recognizes that staff loyalty, happiness, and satisfaction can be achieved.

One-to-one reviews with staff are completed regularly as is an annual appraisal. Exit interviews with departing employees are also undertaken, which provides valuable information for continuous improvement.

- Direct care hours per day per client: 0.6 to .08 or more hours per day. It should be noted that there are relatively low levels of care required for residents at Heald Farm Court.

Environment Sustainability

"Sustainability" refers to the overall viability of a project as well as the environmental impact. The regeneration of the site is in itself a major sustainable feature. Building on "brownfield" sites has far less environmental impact than building on undeveloped "greenfield" sites.

By creating affordable and attractive housing for older people, the family home that residents may have been living in is released back to the open market. This family home is often a house (rather than an apartment), which now becomes available for a new family, Thus, the wider housing market generally is kept flowing with supply and demand and is, therefore, sustainable.

The United Kingdom government is aiming for all new residential developments to be zero-carbon by 2016, and the building regulations are becoming more stringent, particularly with regard to energy efficiency. Renewable energy is also becoming a requirement.

ALTERNATIVE ENERGY SOURCES

Hot water is provided by a solar panel thermal system.

WATER CONSERVATION

None

ENERGY CONSERVATION

The scheme is both heated and cooled with ground source heat pumps feeding off 10 deep bore holes. Heat recovery units fitted to the ventilation system increase energy efficiency. Thermostatic controlled showers and water taps also contribute toward energy efficiency, and resident safety. There is also a sedum roof, aiding thermal insulation and providing a small amount of biodiversity.

Corridor lighting is operated by passive infra-red detectors, switching the lights on only when someone is in the corridor, saving energy. However, the perception of the corridor in the distance can be dark and gloomy until one walks along it and the lights come on.

Large windows to the apartments maximize daylight, reducing the need for electric lighting during the day.

The external envelopes of all buildings have been designed to comply and in some instances exceed current building regulations. Double glazing to windows, high levels of insulation to walls, floors, and roofs all contribute to the energy efficiency.

FIGURE 18-11 Ground-floor units have their own front door accessed from the courtyard. First-floor apartments are accessed through an internal corridor, but the overall appearance is of a two-story house. *Courtesy of Damian Utton*

Outdoor Living

Garden

Does the garden support principles of care?

Between the hub and accommodation blocks are landscaped spaces, which are fully enclosed for protection to the back of the site but are more open on the street side so visitors can also enjoy them, although widely overlooked creating a natural surveillance.

The front courtyard is quite formal in appearance and is accessible by the general public. The pathway is finished in granite paving with quadrangles of planting and perimeter planting creating a defensible space to the ground-floor apartments. There is also bench seating and bollard-style lighting.

The rear courtyard is accessible only via the communal or apartment areas and is thus only accessible to the residents or guests. While the layout is still quite formal, there are grassy areas plus raised planting beds and a greenhouse for residents to engage in gardening activities. There is also bench seating, a pergola area, and planting to the perimeter in the front courtyard.

Project Data

DESIGN FIRM

DK-Architects, Liverpool
26 Old Haymarket
Liverpool
Merseyside L 1 6ER
United Kingdom
www.dk-architects.com

AREAS/SIZES

- Site area: 10,000 square meters (107,639 square feet)
- Total building area: 9,762 square meters (10,077 square feet)
- There are 10 different variations of two-bedroom apartments: 61 square meters (656 square feet)– through 75 square meters (807 square feet)
- Total of communal facilities: 850 square meters (9,150 square feet)

PARKING

Forty-four car parking spaces including four disabled parking spaces. There is also an enclosed "garage" for parking and recharging mobility scooters. A bus stop is also outside on Sturgess Street for staff and visitors arriving by public transport.

COSTS (2009)

- Total building cost: £12,500,000 ($20,242,193 USD)
- Cost per square meter: £1,068 ($1,729 USD)
- Cost per square foot: £1,280 ($2,009 USD)
- Investment per resident: Unable to determine as each apartment houses a different number of residents

RESIDENT AGE

Residents range in age from 55 to 94 years old

RESIDENT PAYER MIX

Forty-six apartments are for rent, 40 are for shared ownership and/or outright purchase. Rent is subsidized in that the rent is lower than current market rent levels but there are eligibility criteria to ensure that only those on lower incomes are entitled to live here.

Chapter 19

A Study of Sandford Station

FIGURE 19-1 Exterior of Sherwood House with covered veranda and bowls/croquet lawn. *www.zedphoto.com*

REASONS FOR INCLUSION OF THIS SCHEME

- Sandford Station is a redeveloped brownfields site in a rural setting.
- It is a successful creation of a village within a village, addressing a wide range of clinical and accommodation needs.
- Sanford Station employs an Australian design and model of dementia care, which has been successfully implemented in the United Kingdom through this scheme.

Building Description

Name of Scheme: Sandford Station
Owner: St. Monica Trust
Address:
Station Road
Sandford
North Somerset
BS25 5RF
United Kingdom
Occupied since: Phased completion: first residents moved in October 2009, last residents moved in June 2010

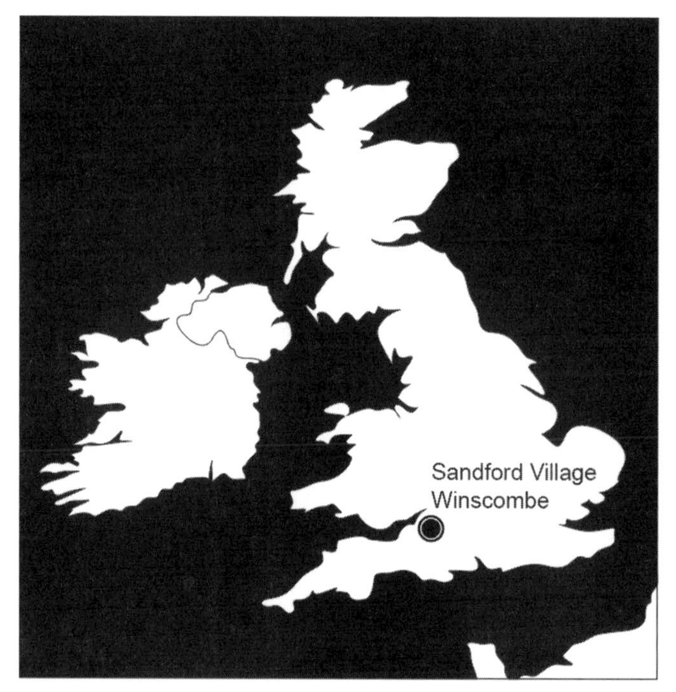

FIGURE 19-2 Scheme location. *Courtesy of Pozzoni LLP*

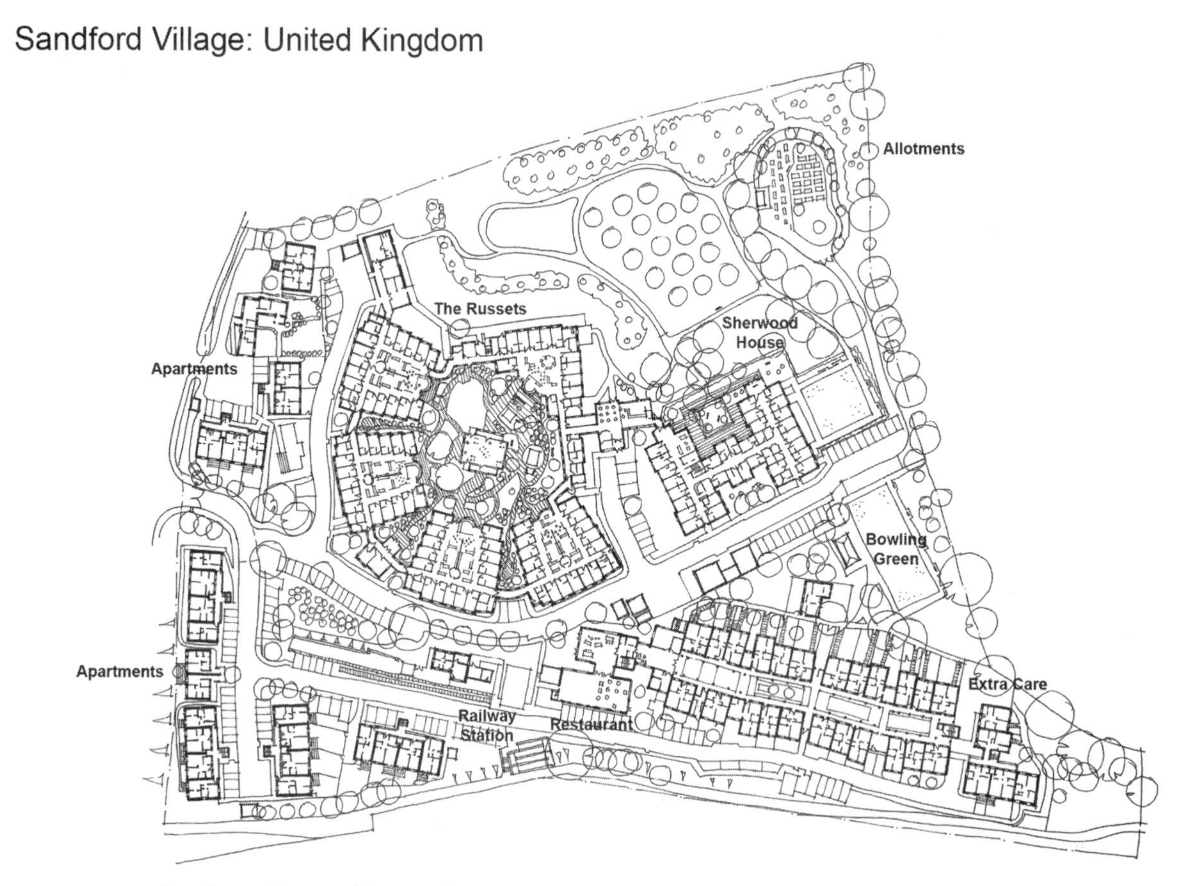

FIGURE 19-3 Site plan. *Courtesy of Pozzoni LLP*

Description of the Type of Community, Including Number of Residents

The Sandford Station development can be described as a village within a village. Sandford itself is a historic village in the Somerset region of the United Kingdom, the site of an ancient crossing point across the rolling Mendip Hills and located within the Mendip Hills Area of Outstanding Natural Beauty. It is part of the Parish of Winscombe and Sandford, with all the elements that enhance rural community village life and that has a population of about 4,500 people.

Sandford Station is the fourth retirement development from the St Monica Trust, a registered charity and provider of high-quality care, support, and accommodation for older people. The Trust is committed to creating an environment of enrichment and independence, and this development aims to deliver a range of high-quality properties, extensive amenities, and the peace of mind that comes from dedicated, onsite support and care.

Sandford Station is a continuing care retirement community with different types of accommodation and levels of care. To live at Sandford Station the only stipulation is to be over 60 years of age. Apart from this, everyone is welcome.

SANDFORD STATION PROVIDES THE FOLLOWING RESIDENTIAL MIX:

- 108 independent living and extra care apartments
- Sherwood House: 30-resident nursing with care home
- The Russets: 73-resident nursing with dementia care home
- Communal facilities
- Refurbished railway station museum

The independent living and extra care apartments are self-contained apartments, each with their own front door and one, two, or three bedrooms. The independent living apartments are located in several two-story buildings with the front door accessed by way of a secure covered deck. The extra care apartments are located on either side of a central two-story covered street where also is located some of the communal facilities and activities spaces. In both instances the appearance is of traditional looking railway workers cottages.

The concept of independent living and extra care are to promote independence for older people. In the United Kingdom, "independent living" is also sometimes known as retirement housing or sheltered housing and is typically for people who are still physically and mentally active but wish to live in a sheltered environment with others of a similar age and outlook. "Extra care" is also known as assisted living or "home-for-life." This type of housing is essentially self-contained apartments for people who still wish to maintain their independence but do have some care requirements. Care is brought to residents as and when needed and if an individual's care needs change, then the building is adaptable accordingly. A resident does not have to relocate because their needs change.

Sherwood House is a 30-resident nursing with care home and was completed in June 2010. This is a single-story building with a central dining area and kitchen along with smaller lounge/sitting areas dispersed throughout the building. A secure garden area and a bowling green are available for the residents of Sherwood House.

FIGURE 19-4 The Russets clubhouse within the garden courtyard. *www.zedphoto.com*

The Russets is the 73-resident nursing with dementia care home designed as five connected bungalows. Four bungalows are for 15 residents and one bungalow is designed for 13 residents. Each bungalow is self-contained with its own open-plan design which includes a living room, dining room, adjacent kitchen, and a separate front door. This allows families and staff to enter, and deliveries to be made to each bungalow without disturbing other bungalows. The overall building forms a perimeter around an enclosed garden and clubhouse, which is used for a variety of activities. The garden itself is varied in its layout and also contains an aviary.

Communal facilities include the original railway station buildings, which have been converted to a museum that is run in conjunction with the local railway heritage society, a restaurant, the main lounge, a grocers shop, a hydrotherapy pool, a gymnasium, activities rooms, and the office and administration buildings. In addition to the enclosed communal facilities, there is a large crown green lawn bowling area with an adjacent shaded pavilion and plots for residents to grow vegetables. A substantial grass-covered parkland area complete with accessible walking paths is also available for use by all residents of Sandford Station.

RESIDENTS PAY A COMMUNITY FEE IN ADDITION TO THEIR RENT WHICH COVERS THE COST OF:

- 24-hour emergency response
- 24-hour security
- Housekeeping in both the apartments and common spaces

FIGURE 19-5 One-half of a Russets household lounge. Bedroom doors open onto this space and colored panels help identify each bedroom. *Courtesy of Damian Utton*

- Use of health spa and gymnasium
- Recreational activities and entertainment
- Transportation
- Electrified wheelchair (scooters) parks and recharging facilities
- Welfare benefits advice
- Security equipment through closed-circuit television
- Communal television connections
- Building insurance
- Use of restaurant, computer suite, library
- Window cleaning, maintenance of alarm calls, fire alarms, and lifts

THERE ARE ADDITIONAL CHARGES FOR:

- Hairdressing
- Chiropody
- Personal laundry
- Domiciliary support (personal care)
- Reflexology

Residents have the choice of three different levels of tenancy: rent, lease-purchase, or shared equity. With the option of purchasing an apartment on a lease-purchase scheme, the capital payment is a one-time payment calculated at 90 percent of the market value of the apartment. When a resident moves out of the apartment, the capital payment is repaid in full to the lease-owner. The St Monica Trust resumes ownership of the property and sells it to the next lease-owner. As of November 2010, 66 of the independent living and extra care apartments have been sold this way. A small number of apartments are occupied through "shared ownership" in which a resident pays a smaller capital payment and an additional monthly rental amount for the remaining amount of the property. In addition, there are a few apartments which are available for a straight monthly rental fee.

The site for this aged care development is a former railway station in a small village south of Bristol. The local industry is cider brewing and to the south of the site is an apple orchard with a cider brewery located nearby. The railway theme is continued throughout the development with the original Great Western railway signage style and livery colors of cream and brown used throughout the design scheme. This design approach relates to the local vernacular and to the site history. Many of the residents can still remember the era of steam trains and of Sandford Station as a working place of the transportation industry.

Geographics

Vernacular Design

How does the scheme/environment respond to the locality?

Sandford Station is a rural, countryside environment on the edge of a small village and in an area designated as one of outstanding natural beauty. The town planning requirements called for the architecture to be small-scale and domestic in appearance and to use local building materials for the façades. A "traditional" architectural vocabulary has been used, rather than a "modern" style—mostly due to requirements of the town planners.

All the buildings are either single-story or two-story with open spaces between, giving the impression of a village that has naturally grown over time. The independent living and extra care apartments, when viewed from the outside, look like individual two-story cottages that are more familiar to a rural setting.

Local stone, brickwork, and synthetic stucco are used as facing materials for walls. Stepped wall planes and the incorporation of recesses and projections help to break down the larger buildings to a domestic scale. Roof tiles, not slates, are a recognized local building material. Their use with different colors and profiles set into varying heights also help to break down the overall scale and create variety.

Automobile parking is spread throughout the community, avoiding large areas of hard surfacing with the added benefit of parking being closer to the residents' own front doors. Car parking areas are delineated with brick paving, while the access roads are finished in black tarmacadam. This mix of finishes reduces the scale of a single material. Likewise, public footpaths are finished in black tarmac, but courtyards and similar areas are finished in a more natural and inviting stone paving material.

FIGURE 19-6 Exterior of the extra care apartments designed to look like railway cottages. *Courtesy of Damian Utton*

Care

Philosophy of Care

What is the operators' philosophy, and how does the building match this philosophy?

As stated in their printed material, the St Monica Trust promotes independence, dignity, and fulfillment for more than 750 residents. The work of the St Monica Trust is based on Christian principles, which include compassion, service to others, and treating individuals with dignity and respect. The services are open to all older people irrespective of their beliefs. The Trust

FIGURE 19-7 Covered "street" with the extra care apartments to each side. The street becomes a social area with activities and sitting areas. *www.zedphoto.com*

regularly sets benchmarks for the very best practice in the care and support of elderly people and continues to provide a welcome financial resource for local organizations and individuals in need.

The layout of the independent living and extra care apartments, particularly with the covered street and easy access to communal facilities, supports the St Monica Trust philosophy. Of course promoting independence, dignity, and fulfillment, and making the most of life as a resident is more than just simply bricks and mortar. This support can range from help with domestic chores to assistance with bathing or dressing. These services can be accessed by everyone, giving residents just the support they need, whenever they might need it. Residents in the independent living apartments may bring their own furniture to their apartments and may choose their room decoration. In addition, residents can bring their pets with them as they move into Sandford Station, adding to their "fulfillment" as a retiree.

Sherwood House provides high-quality nursing care and companionship for those needing this level of care. There is 24-hour general needs care in an open and airy environment. Each of the 30 en-suite apartments at Sherwood House has wonderful views of the nearby hills, giving residents maximum opportunity to enjoy their surroundings, at least visually. Bedrooms are fitted with ceiling-mounted lifts, and en-suite "wet-room" showers are also fully equipped for nursing care requirements. Each bedroom has patio doors with direct access to the outside.

The communal kitchen and dining area in Sherwood House allow all residents an opportunity to gather together. Several smaller lounge areas and alcove sitting areas provide a more intimate social scale and setting, thus giving residents several choices for social interaction.

A covered veranda gives views over the adjoining orchard and hills and is directly accessible to the lawn bowling green. Residents can sit outside on the veranda in wet weather and, while protected from rain, still enjoy the fresh air and views.

As it is in the Russets, activity and engagement at Sherwood House is supported through positive personal care and regular opportunities for purposeful participation in discussion groups, therapies, events, and entertainment. Well-being is also explored holistically, addressing physical, social, psychological, emotional, and spiritual matters and concerns of the residents.

The key driver behind the design of the Russets was to provide a successful dementia facility in the countryside, based on the models pioneered by Brightwater Care in Western Australia. The St Monica Trust recruited the first manager for the Russets to relocate from Australia to

FIGURE 19-8 Interior of a Russets household. The kitchen area in the background can be seen from both spaces.
Green Hat

assist in the development of the design and care philosophy and to then manage the completed building.

Four of the five households in the Russets is a home for 15 residents, while the fifth is home for 13 residents. Each household has its own living, dining, and kitchen areas. An innovative care service, combined with the specially created living environment, is designed to support the individual needs of people living with dementia, including those who are still quite active. Each household is named after a different type of apple: Encore, Discovery, Crispin, Bramley, and Ashmead, further reinforcing the local site context.

Residents in the Russets are free to move between the households, and different visual cues, decoration, fixtures, and fittings give each household an identity, helping residents recognize where they are and where they might be going.

The design of the Russets household is focused on making them home-like, relaxed, and to encourage independence among the residents. The five bungalows are each divided into two halves, creating smaller households of seven and eight people. Both halves share a communal kitchen, accessible for all residents to help prepare food, two dining areas, and two sitting areas,

FIGURE 19-9 The Russets household kitchen in a familiar domestic style. Glass-fronted cupboard doors allow residents to see the contents, compensating for impaired memory. *Courtesy of Damian Utton*

each with a fireplace. The open-plan kitchen area also serves as a cue to people with dementia, providing the sounds and smells of food being prepared in order to stimulate appetite. An easily accessible kitchen also promotes independence. For example, a resident can get a glass of water or a cup of tea without having to ask staff who may be busy elsewhere. This provides a sense of independence and self-worth to the residents.

Simple visual cues throughout the households are an integral part of the interior design, helping residents identify their surroundings and encouraging them to explore other places such as neighboring households, the club house, or the courtyard garden areas. These visual cues help people with impaired memory to identify their surroundings and encourage residents to explore. Colors, layout, furniture, fittings, and signage are all designed to make purpose and function clear, to aid understanding and orientation.

Within the bedrooms in the Russets, wardrobes with clear doors help residents select their choice of clothes each day. Sensors in every bedroom control the lights in the en-suite bathroom, turning on when someone leaves their bed, turning off when the bed is reoccupied. One of the households has additional equipment to support the needs of residents who are very frail or who have limited mobility.

A flexible approach to the daily resident routine encourages choice and variety so that residents have structure to their day, but can also make decisions about what to do and when to do it. Purposeful activity is encouraged by the staff, be it tidying up, helping with meal preparation, or gardening. Creating the opportunity for regular interaction and participation with staff, other residents, family members, and visitors is a significant consideration in the design of the households. Regular activities are organized that are suitable and engaging for the residents, ensuring they do not become withdrawn or isolated.

The central clubhouse at the Russets has a larger hall for group gatherings or activities, a kitchen, and a hairdressing salon. There are several social, physical, and spiritual activities that take place in this location which are also open to residents throughout Sandford Station, not just residents of the Russets.

Full-time care is focused on the needs of each individual Russets resident and is flexible, with few routines, so that residents have the freedom and choice to live their lives as independently and fully as possible, just as they might choose to do in their own homes. Friends and family can also visit whenever they choose without restrictive visiting hours. Each household has its own external front door and vestibule, further emphasizing the individual household and domestic nature of the scheme.

The net result is an environment that reassures residents, enables freedom for the resident, and provides an opportunity for residents to move about without restriction and to find fulfillment in the different environments and daily activities.

Community and Belonging

How does the scheme design and operation support this ideal?

Sandford Station is a community in itself, and the St Monica Trust aims to make all residents, staff, and the residents' families feel part of that community. The village community facilities, located in Darlisette House, of the restaurant, lounge, shop, hydrotherapy pool, gym, bowling green, croquet lawn, and gardening allotments are open and accessible to all the residents.

FIGURE 19-10 The Russets space between households is used as a library. *Courtesy of Damian Utton*

Located centrally within the village this is the "hub" of village life and the railway station in particular serves as a focal landmark. From a design perspective there are ramps for wheelchair and scooter access, floor finishes are easy for wheelchairs and scooters to negotiate, doors are wide but not too heavy to push or pull, internal spaces are light and airy without feeling empty, signage is clear and easy to read.

The village owns and operates its own minibus to take residents, with or without their families and staff, to the neighboring villages or towns for visits, shopping, or other social occasions.

The residents of Sherwood House and the Russets may not be able to access the main hub facilities because of their physical or cognitive impairments. Both Sherwood House and the Russets have their own internal and external communal spaces for social and group activities, while the design and operation also respects the residents' needs for privacy.

Residents are offered the opportunity to participate in social and recreational activities and an individual plan for each resident identifies their established skills and aspirations. This can then be used as a tool to promote individual creativity.

Activities are arranged on a daily basis within each of the five households at the Russets, with the aim of supporting individuals to maintain roles, routines, and expressing individual identity. There is also a therapeutic activity program that provides opportunities for engaging in stimulating and creative activities. These can be on either a one-to-one or a group basis.

At the Russets there is also a regular program of social events and entertainment, including singing and music, which often takes place in the clubhouse. Relatives and friends are invited and often take part.

There is also a pastoral care team at Sandford Station to look after residents' spiritual, religious, and pastoral needs and requirements. For many residents who may have been active in church or religious activities in their own local communities, this continued sense of belonging is very important.

Innovation

If the operator pursues a policy of innovation and pursuit of excellence, how is this demonstrated?

Inspired by the success of innovative dementia schemes in Australia, and in particular Brightwater Care in Western Australia, senior staff of the St Monica Trust traveled to Australia to see for themselves the design and operation and, as previously mentioned, recruited the manager from Australia to oversee and manage the Russets.

The CCRC model, while common in the United States, Australia, and New Zealand, is less common in the United Kingdom. High land values and onerous planning development policies often restrict development. In economic terms, with the independent living and extra care apartments for sale/lease purchase, this can cross-subsidize the "less profitable" areas of high-dependency care and the community hub facilities.

A land-hungry single-story development, such as Sherwood House or the Russets, as a standalone development would more than likely be uneconomical to build and operate but this cross-subsidy allows the vision of a single-story development to be realized. For these reasons most care homes in the United Kingdom are two or three stories in height to maximize land value.

As explained previously, the design of the Russets draws on and develops the best and innovative experiences of dementia care design from elsewhere.

Bringing the wider community into the village, with the historic railway station and museum, is a welcome change for the all-too-familiar concept of gated communities and of taking residents out into the community only.

Neighborhood Integration

Community Involvement

Is the scheme and service designed to integrate successfully with the local community?

Sandford Station is located in a small rural community, and such a large physical development within a rural community has to integrate with the local community on several levels.

Some of the extra care apartments are designated as "affordable housing" where the rent is fixed at a lower than market level. Specific tenants for these apartments are referred to Sandford Station by the local authority's housing and/or social services departments. United Kingdom town planning policy is for all developments over a certain size to allocate a percentage of the dwellings for affordable housing. The dwellings are scattered throughout the development and there are no differences in size or finishes to the apartments for the affordable housing and those at market rate. This mix of social classes at Sandford Station ensures a social integration.

While the appeal of Sandford Station is to people who have lived in a rural or semi-rural context, Sandford Village is also appealing for staff and is an important employer of staff in this rural location. Many of the staff working at Sandford Village live in the local villages and this also serves to help integrate the retirement village into the wider community.

The architectural appearance of the village is in the style of the local surrounding rural vernacular. External finishes, differing roof pitches, changing wall lines, window sizes and styles all are intended to reduce the scale of the development to a more human scale and one familiar to a rural village.

The railway station platform, ticket office, and waiting rooms that have been retained on campus have been refurbished and maintained by the local railway heritage preservation group as a museum. Sections of railway track, railway cars, and station paraphernalia have been restored as well as the buildings themselves. Residents of the retirement village are also involved in this ongoing project. Visitors coming to the museum have the opportunity to experience the retirement village and to meet some of the residents. Any negative preconceptions from visitors about a retirement village are quickly overcome largely in part due to the incorporation of the historic buildings as well as the overall design of the campus structures.

Staff and Volunteers

Human Resources

Are policies and designs in place to attract good staff and volunteers?

The St Monica Trust employs over 700 staff across their four villages and main headquarters. They have national recognition for excellence as an employer and for exceptional provision of training and development opportunities for all staff. In 2007 the Trust won the "Skills for Care Accolades" as best employer for more than 250 staff.

"Equality and diversity amongst our staff is a key feature of our day to day working lives." The Trust is committed to a positive attitude toward people with disabilities, employing and retaining such individuals whenever possible.

STAFF MEMBERS ARE ENCOURAGED TO REACH THEIR FULL POTENTIAL AND ARE SUPPORTED IN THIS BY SEVERAL WAYS:

1. New staff members are provided with a full and comprehensive induction to the St Monica Trust and their role within the organization.
2. Staff members receive regular supervision, support, and annual review and are encouraged to identify their own training and development needs. There are also opportunities created to participate in courses or learning on a regular basis.
3. A learning skills and development department offers a comprehensive in-house training program that includes an approved National Vocational Qualification (NVQ) assessment center.
4. Participation in the organization's decision making and communication processes is encouraged via a staff consultation group, the staff newsletter, as well as through smaller teams and other groups.

There is a Practice Development Department within the Trust, and it has developed training courses covering a range of different aspects relating to the provision of care services. These courses have been and continue to be refined over the years. All staff members undertake mandatory training to comply with the U.K. care standards requirements, and staff are also encouraged to participate in their own continuing professional development.

SOME OF THE STAFF BENEFITS AT ST MONICA TRUST INCLUDE:

- Competitive salaries and benefits
- Good leave entitlement
- Positive training and qualification opportunities
- Flexible pension scheme with employer contribution
- Free uniforms (where applicable)
- Subsidized meals

Environmental Sustainability

"Sustainability" refers to the overall viability of a project as well as the environmental impact. The regeneration of the existing railway station site is in itself a major sustainable feature as it avoids razing these buildings and carting the debris to a nearby landfill. Building on and reclaiming "brownfield" sites such as this, has a far less environmental impact than building on undeveloped "greenfield" sites.

There are several couples living at Sandford Station where one partner requires dementia or nursing care and lives in the Russets or Sherwood House but the other partner does not require such care and lives in one of the extra care or independent living apartments; allowing them to access the right support for their needs while remaining together in the same location. By doing this, the family home that the couple may have been living in is released back to the open market. This family home is often a larger property, which now becomes available for a new family; thus the wider housing market generally is kept flowing with supply and demand and is, therefore, sustainable.

FIGURE 19-11 Bowling green in use. Sherwood House and the open meadow area are in the background. *Green Hat*

The government of the United Kingdom is pushing toward requiring all new residential developments to be zero-carbon by 2016 and the building regulations are becoming more stringent, particularly with regard to energy efficiency. Renewable energy is also becoming a requirement of town planning, although there is not a nationwide U.K. policy on this.

There is a central biomass boiler plant providing combined heat and power on campus. This is fueled by woodchip pellets, obtained from sustainable sources. However, there have been ongoing maintenance issues with this equipment.

The external envelopes of all the buildings have been designed to comply with and, in some instances, exceed current building regulations. Double glazing at all windows as well as high levels of insulation in walls, floors, and roofs contribute to the energy efficiency.

The covered street that is along the extra care portion of campus is unheated but relies on passive heating and ventilation to warm and cool the space. The glazed roof allows daylight and solar gain, but a controllable ventilation opening allows excess heat to rise and escape. The dwellings that have an external wall facing onto this covered space experience less heat loss because of the reduced temperature differential between inside and outside.

Building materials have been obtained from local sources as far as possible, reducing the embodied energy in transporting materials over long distances. The open grass walking areas and allotments also sustain a biodiversity as a natural habitat for flora and fauna.

Outdoor Living

Garden

Does the garden support principles of care?

Several open, recreational spaces are provided at Sandford Station. There is a lawn bowling green, allotments for growing vegetables, and open grassland with paths for walking. The external spaces are just as important as the interior spaces for all residents and are well used by residents.

Careful landscaping and planting is used for public areas as well as the more private courtyard areas. The gardens at Sherwood House and the Russets demonstrate that great care and pride has been taken in the appearance and maintenance of the external spaces.

The main garden area of Sherwood House is accessed from several points within Sherwood House and is clearly well thought through with regard to selection of plants and flowers and their ongoing maintenance. A wooden picket fence provides an unobtrusive yet secure boundary and the view from the garden is to the grass parkland with the walking paths and to the orchard and hills beyond. Each bedroom at Sherwood House has direct access to an external patio space, and the surrounding landscaping has been carefully designed to allow views but also to create privacy and a sense of security for each private door.

At the heart of the Russets is a sensory garden with a circular walkway through seven different landscaped areas, with raised beds for resident gardening activities and also with an aviary. This garden has been created as a central courtyard with the households forming a perimeter and the clubhouse as a standalone building in the center. Residents are able to walk safely into the garden areas and to other households but they are secure and unable to directly access the wider development. Seating benches, garden sheds, a vegetable plot with a scarecrow, and covered veranda areas provide a variety of activities and choices for residents. Careful selection of plants and flowers provide variety, stimulation, and interest. In addition to the busier central courtyard area there are also more intimate garden areas between households with seating and planting, giving residents a choice of a more private external space.

Project Data

DESIGN FIRM

KWL Architects, Newport, Wales
Poplar House
Hazell Drive
Newport South Wales
United Kingdom

AREAS/SIZES

- Site area: 50,051 square meters (12.37 acres)
- Total building area: 17,760 square meters (191,160 square feet)
- 1-bedroom apartment: 49.7 square meters (536 square feet)
- 2-bedroom apartment: 56.4 to 84.5 square meters (607 to 910 square feet)
- 3-bedroom apartment: 92.6 to 122.8 square meters (997 to 1,322 square feet)

PARKING

Adequate parking for all residents is scattered throughout the development on surface lots.

COSTS

- Total building cost: £23.8 million ($38,380,804 USD)
- Cost per square meter: £1,562 ($2,520 USD)
- Cost per square foot: £122 ($201 USD)
- Investment per resident: Not available

RESIDENT AGE

Minimum age: 60 years old

RESIDENT PAYER MIX

Properties at Sandford Station are purchased on a lease arrangement; a one-off capital payment that covers the cost of ownership and is totally refundable when the resident leaves or dies. In this instance there would not be a government contribution to the capital payment, it is private pay.

THE
BROOK
FOLD

Chapter 20

A Study of the Brook Coleraine

REASONS FOR INCLUSION OF THIS SCHEME

- The Brook offers care to the most vulnerable individuals in society.
- This scheme makes care as accessible as possible, regardless of a person's age or financial status, and makes people aware of the care that is offered.
- The Brook incorporates existing bungalows used for care and knits seamlessly into an existing urban fabric.

Building Description

Name of Scheme: The Brook Coleraine
Owner: Fold Housing Association, Care Provider, and Northern Health Care Trust
Address:
Brookgreen
Brook Street
Coleraine
Co. Londonderry
BT52 1QG
Northern Ireland
United Kingdom
Occupied Since: 2005 (Phase One); 2007 (Phase Two)

FIGURE 20-1 Entrance to the Brook Coleraine. *Courtesy of Pozzoni LLP*

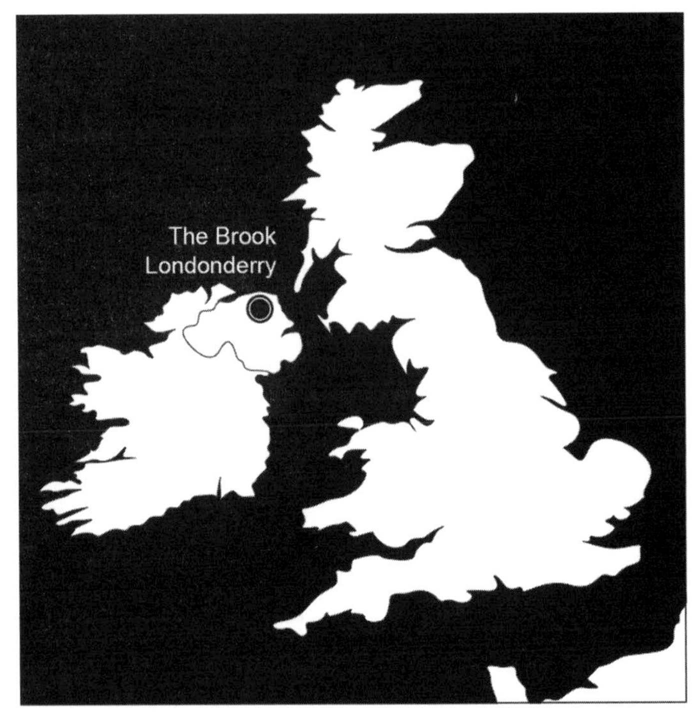

FIGURE 20-2 Scheme location. *Courtesy of Pozzoni LLP*

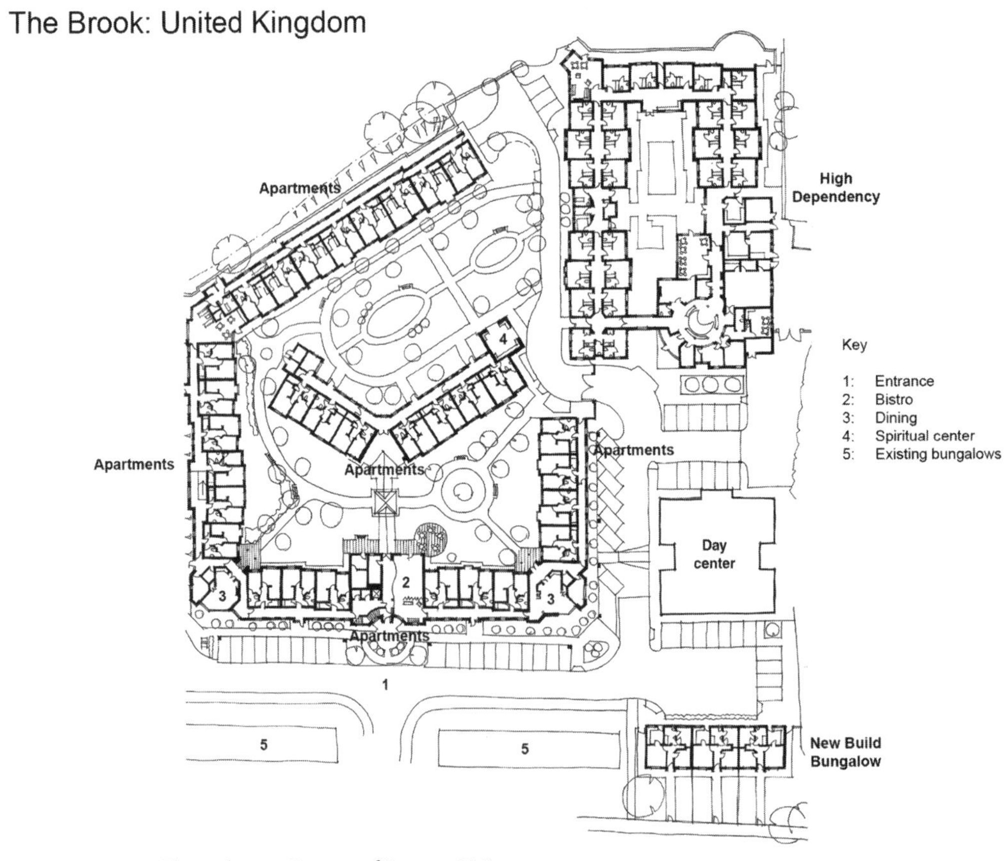

FIGURE 20-3 Floor plan. *Courtesy of Pozzoni LLP*

Description of the Type of Community, Including Number of Residents

The Brook is an innovative development of supported housing for people with dementia with no age limitation for residents. The development was made possible through the partnership between Northern Healthcare Trust, Fold Housing Association, and the Northern Ireland Housing Executive. The Brook provides specialized yet home-like living accommodation within a safe environment for 61 people. There are 25 bedrooms, each with en-suite facilities. Six of these bedrooms are reserved specifically for people requiring a high level of dependency care. The design provides for 31 one-bedroom apartments, all situated in the main building, and five two-bedroom bungalows. The bungalows are for couples, designed to suit the needs of the person with dementia and their care provider as a "live-in" provider. An adult day center accessible to the local community is also located on the site and provides respite day care for individuals with dementia.

The scheme is predominantly single story with all living accommodation at ground-floor level. The apartments and bungalows have a high-quality finish, in keeping with the aesthetic of a private accommodation. Communal facilities on the campus include a café, a beauty/barber salon, and a spiritual center, as well as accessible landscaped gardens and an internal landscaped courtyard.

While the residents of the bungalows are free to come and go in and around the surrounding community, the residents within the main building are more restricted and take more advantage of the communal facilities and activities offered directly on campus.

Payments on behalf of the residents made to the development are done so in agreement with the development partners through an allocation panel. These allocations are nondiscriminatory with regard to religion, age, culture, or ethnic background.

Geographics

Vernacular Design

How does the scheme/environment respond to the locality?

The scheme is close to Coleraine City Center but is sited within a residential area. Several existing bungalows were retained on the site from a previous development. These face onto Brook Street. Both pedestrian and vehicular access to the site emanate from Brook Street, and these are set between the bungalows. A two-story building greets the visitor, and it is here where the café and main communal facilities are sited. On either side of this main building the scheme returns to single story. Because of this design feature and because there is a drop in grade level across the site, most of the scheme is hidden from view from the street.

The scale of the building is appropriate for the area and, despite being quite an extensive structure and plan, manages to retain a domestic style and feel in its architecture. The palette of materials of stone, stucco, and brickwork has been used to great effect in order to break up what could have become a somewhat monotonous façade. The materials are indigenous to the area but have been used in a contemporary manner on the Brook.

Care

Philosophy of Care

What is the operators' philosophy, and how does the building match this philosophy?

At the heart of the philosophy of both Fold Housing Association and Northern Health Care Trust (NHT)

FIGURE 20-4 Typical façades at the apartments showing the change in materials. *Courtesy of Pozzoni LLP*

FIGURE 20-5 Typical bay detail at the apartments. *Courtesy of Pozzoni LLP*

FIGURE 20-6 Memory wall displaying artifacts belonging to residents. *Courtesy of Pozzoni LLP*

is keeping a clear focus on the needs and wishes of each of their tenants ensuring that they retain in their daily lives choice, privacy, dignity, fulfillment rights, and independence. The Brook has proved to make a significant difference in the lives of socioeconomically vulnerable residents who may have dementia. The tenants maintain a sense of individuality, choice, and control through both the service delivery and the design of the Brook. In 2001, only 45 percent of people with dementia were actually known to the NHT dementia services team. The integrated approach, integrating the care philosophy with the design of the Brook, where NHT offices are also situated, has significantly increased the number of individuals with dementia who are now known to NHT.

The delivery of care at the Brook strives to meet individual choices, including their likes and dislikes. This is achieved by the establishment of a tailored care and support plan for each resident, often involving family members, which is constantly under review through a key worker system. The scheme is an accessible model of care and support and answers community needs both through the variety of accommodations that are offered and through daytime support and respite service for care providers in the integrated day center. The design has incorporated the latest innovative assistive technology allowing tenants to live with privacy and dignity. For each tenant the Brook provides a home of their own with an emphasis placed on personalization of furniture, personal items, and décor. Residents are actively encouraged to decorate and personalize their homes. Additionally, art and craft work designed and made by the residents adorns the lounges and circulation areas. A "memory wall" situated in the entrance foyer displays memorabilia from the residents' lives and is maintained with artifacts supplied by the residents and their families, providing excellent conversation starters, a reminder of people's lives, and a destination to which residents can walk.

The variety of amenity spaces in the Brook, including the café, spiritual center, residents lounges, and resident rooms, allows residents the choice to be social or maintain their privacy, while the security of the complex allows people to walk freely from household to household and throughout the communal areas.

Community and Belonging

How does the scheme design and operation support this ideal?

FIGURE 20-7 Back-lit café scene in the communal café area. *Courtesy of Pozzoni LLP*

FIGURE 20-8 Decoration by residents in one of their private dining areas. *Courtesy of Pozzoni LLP*

The Brook has been planned with a hierarchy of spaces. Central to the plan are the most public areas, including the café, which has access to an external terrace, a communal lounge with pool table, beauty/barber salon, and a laundry. The café area is well used by residents who enjoy meeting for a chat with their friends and people coming and going to collect their morning newspaper. These areas allow all of the residents to have a meeting point either by arrangement or incidental to their simply being in the space. A secondary area is the spiritual center, which is less central to the scheme but is accessible to all residents. By its location, this spiritual center encourages residents to walk through the landscaped gardens, although a covered route is available for days of inclement weather. The spiritual center provides an area for more formal or contemplative meetings and a place for the residents to worship as a community or individually.

Smaller, more private lounges and dining areas are provided throughout the scheme, serving approximately eight residents in each location. These lounges are personalized by the residents living nearest to them and have differing activities than those in the public areas. The ability to have control over how they decorate their surroundings draws the residents together as a close-knit group.

The corridors linking the apartments have "breakout" spaces with seating areas that provide resting points and also enable the incidental meeting and opportunity for socialization of residents enabling them to strike up new friendships or engage with their neighbors.

Residents take great pride in their surroundings, particularly their own private spaces. Every resident can bring their own furniture and possessions to the Brook. This automatically provides residents with a sense of their own identity within the scheme and a strong sense of place. The variety of hierarchical spaces allows residents to form more intimate relationships with their neighbors while having the option to connect with the more extensive community when they choose.

Innovation

If the operator pursues a policy of innovation and pursuit of excellence, how is it demonstrated?

The partnership between Fold Housing Association and the Northern Health Care Trust was formed to provide an all-encompassing service for people with dementia, removing boundaries that might prevent people requiring care from obtaining it regardless of their ability to pay for the services. This is achieved by integrating their services on a single site offering a range of care, but also including on that site the NHT offices and a daycare center, making care as accessible to the local community as possible.

The most recent innovation at the Brook is the "brain bus," which is a mobile therapy unit for people with dementia bringing the latest technology to all areas of the community. Through light exercise and mental challenges to stimulate the mind and body, people are encouraged to manage their condition. Technology that is offered includes:

- Puzzles, quizzes, and games
- Music, photographs, videos from yesteryear
- Cycling, driving, and flying simulations
- Social interaction through web cams

Neighborhood Integration

Community Involvement

Is the scheme and service designed to integrate successfully with the local community?

The Brook retains links to the wider community through the services offered within the day center and through an onsite activities co-coordinator. The co-coordinator plans programs to include the tenants of the Brook in activities occurring within the local community such as tea dances. Alternatively, local schools and music groups are invited into the Brook to provide entertainment for residents. Regular meetings between staff, relatives, and an Alzheimer's outreach worker take place to offer advice and support to both residents and family members.

Staff and Volunteers

Human Resources

Are policies and designs in place to attract good staff and volunteers?

Staff vacancies are advertised in NHT-published procedures. The high retention of staff is due to the training programs that are in place and performance appraisals that occur. Staff members have their own restrooms and a sleepover facility is provided. The assistive technology that is in place in the scheme allows staff to be more flexible in their delivery of care and be alerted to situations that may require immediate action. This reduces the pressure on staff by increasing their control over situations that may arise or to anticipate situations before they do arise.

- Direct care hours per day per client: Not available

Environmental Sustainability

ALTERNATIVE ENERGY SOURCES

None

FIGURE 20-9 One of the larger daylight lanterns bringing light into internal spaces.
Courtesy of Pozzoni LLP

WATER CONSERVATION

In order to reduce water consumption, graywater tanks have been installed to store water obtained from rainwater harvesting.

ENERGY CONSERVATION

In order to reduce operational costs and to meet with required Eco Homes Standards, the scheme has employed the use of Borehole Geothermal Heating to heat the circulation areas. Unfortunately, ongoing maintenance problems have been reported in this system. The use of broad areas of natural lighting provided primarily along the corridors has been very successful, reducing the requirement for electrical lighting to be on during the daytime. This design provides pools of natural light enhancing the quality of the corridor environment and acts as focal points highlighting the incidental meeting areas along the corridor.

Outdoor Living

Garden

Does the garden support principles of care?

The garden area at the Brook is one of its most successful features. The treatment to the building's elevations along the sloped property provides a pleasing and interesting backdrop, and the arrangement of buildings allows for a variety of external spaces. Paths lead around the garden, with resting areas along the path routes. One can loop around the garden or purposefully walk to the spiritual center or the café. Wayfinding is enhanced by the surrounding buildings forming strong visual cues. Their bays and changes in façade material of stucco, brick, and stone provide additional cues set into the landscape. Old-fashioned lampposts, a water stream, hard and soft landscaping all add to the pleasant garden experience.

The structure orientation takes full advantage of light and sunshine, but both shaded and covered areas are provided to accommodate different resident preferences. Areas for planting have been provided enabling residents an opportunity to tend to their nearby garden surroundings. The design emulates private gardens, with open lawns and flower beds. All bedrooms, without exception, have been designed to look onto landscaped gardens. The high-dependency resident unit has access to a landscaped courtyard offering a relaxed and alternative environment to the internal spaces.

FIGURE 20-10 Point of reference along a walking route. *Courtesy of Pozzoni LLP*

FIGURE 20-11 External seating area for the café. *Courtesy of Pozzoni LLP*

Project Data

DESIGN FIRM

ASI Architects, Ltd.
2–4 Shipquay Place
Londonderry
BT48 7ER
United Kingdom
http://www.asi-architects.com/

AREAS/SIZES

- Site area: 56,800 square meters (611,390 square feet)
- Building footprint: 17,308 square meters (186,301 square feet)
- Total building area: 16,176 square meters (174,117 square feet)
- Apartment sizes: 44.8 square meters (482 square feet)
- Bungalow sizes: 64 square meters (689 square feet)
- Bedroom sizes: 18.8 square meters (202 square feet)

PARKING

There are 20 surface parking spaces for residents, staff, and visitors.

COSTS

- Total building cost, Phase one: £2,300,000 ($37,128,687 USD)
- Total building cost, Phase two: £3,501,481.24 ($5,727,916 USD)
- Total building cost: £5,801,481 ($9,375,946 USD)
- Cost per square meter: £358.65 ($579,445 USD per square meter)
- Cost per square foot: £32.95 ($54 USD)

RESIDENTS' AGE

Ages range between 50 to 90 years

RESIDENT PAYER MIX

Funding streams include housing benefit and supported people start-up costs and funding. This enables socioeconomically vulnerable people who may not qualify for a community care grant to still have access to the scheme.

Sir Moses Montefiore Home is a large residential aged care facility that reflects the cultural heritage and expectations of the Jewish community. *Brett Boardman Photography. Courtesy of Calder Flower Architects*

Southwood is a nursing home for people with dementia and consists of six cottages that are designed to look and operate like suburban Australian homes. *Courtesy of HammondCare*

Wintringham's Port Melbourne Hostel supports older people who were previously homeless or at risk of homelessness. *Martin Saunders Photography*

Tjilpi Pampaku Ngura Aged Care Facility is located in an Aboriginal community in very remote South Australia and provides respite care, allowing older people in the Anangu communities to remain in their lands for as long as possible. *Courtesy of Kirsty Bennett*

Tinglewood cottage at Brightwater Onslow Gardens supports fifteen people with complex care needs and has a large garden designed to give a sense of delight to residents. *Courtesy of Brightwater*

Himawari Group Home in Ofunato City was one of the first group homes opened in Japan. *Courtesy of Stephen Judd*

Akasaki-cho (Kikuta) Day Care, a century-old restored Japanese home used as a day center for older people with dementia, Ofunato City, Iwate prefecture. The tsunami of March 2011 completely destroyed Kikuta with only the stone gate posts surviving. *Courtesy of Stephen Judd*

NPO Group Fuji is set in a Tokyo suburb with similar scaled apartment buildings. *Courtesy of NPO-Fuji*

Gojikara mura is an organic care community that pays homage to traditional Japanese architecture. *Courtesy of Emi Kiyota*

A view of Tenjin no Mori from the nearby river. *Courtesy of Tenjin no mori*

Neptuna viewed from the sea wall with Calatravas "twisting torso" building beyond.
Photograph by David Hughes

Salem Nursing Home's winter garden and balcony. *Photograph by David Hughes*

Wiekslag Krabbelaan seen from the public garden with a children's playground opposite the street. *Courtesy of Jeanine de Zwarte*

Wiekslag Boerenstreek seen from the roundabout. *Courtesy of Jeanine de Zwarte*

In De Hogeweyk the buildings embrace the streets and gardens. *Courtesy of Molenaar & Bol & VanDillen architects*

The sheltered housing apartments at Weidevogelhof have their own balcony or garden. This building houses child day care and three households for dementia care. *Courtesy of Jeanine de Zwarte*

The main entry to Belong Atherton. *Courtesy of Damian Utton*

Stained glass window bringing vibrancy to the Brook Coleraine spiritual center. *Courtesy of Pozzoni LLP*

Heald Farm Court's principle façade facing Sturgess Street. *Courtesy of Damian Utton*

Sandford Station has created a continuing care retirement community on an old railway station site and has refurbished many of the buildings for resident use. *www.zedphoto.com*

The main entry to Leonard Florence Center. *Robert Benson Photography*

The Foulkeways building layout creates intimate garden spaces for the residents. *Courtesy of Jeffrey Anderzhon*

Deupree Cottages has included a well-appointed garden between their households.
Tom Uhlman/www.tomuphoto.com

Montgomery Place takes advantage of Lake Michigan views with its roof garden. *Barry Ruskin Photography*

The Park Homes resident and preparation kitchen and dining room.
© *darussellphotography.com*

The entry courtyard for Childers Place. ©*Chris Cooper, Courtesy Perkins Eastman*

Part VII

United States Schemes

Chapter 21

A Study of Leonard Florence Center for Living

REASONS FOR INCLUSION OF THIS SCHEME

- This is a multistory household scheme in an urban context.
- This scheme is the first use of The Green House® concept in an urban context.
- This scheme uses a contemporary design palette in a nursing home household.
- This scheme integrates community spaces on a small, modified continuing care campus for the entire campus.
- The scheme provides care for a variety of resident needs (frail elderly, MS, ALS, and the disabled) within one household design.

Building Description

Name of Scheme: Leonard Florence Center for Living
Owner: Chelsea Jewish Nursing Home
Address:
165 Captain's Row
Chelsea, Massachusetts
United States
Occupied since: 2010

FIGURE 21-1 The Leonard Florence Center is a Green House© concept in an urban setting. *Robert Benson Photography*

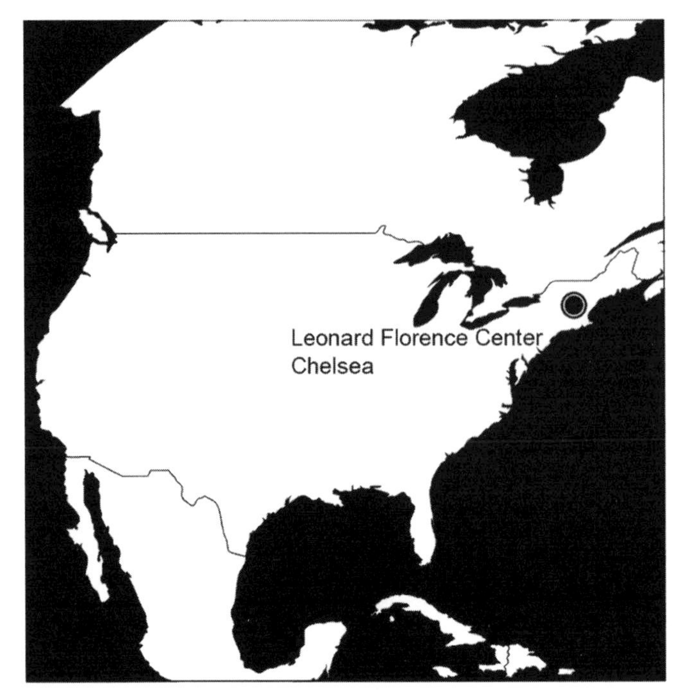

FIGURE 21-2 Scheme location. *Courtesy of Pozzoni LLP*

Leonard Florence Center: United States

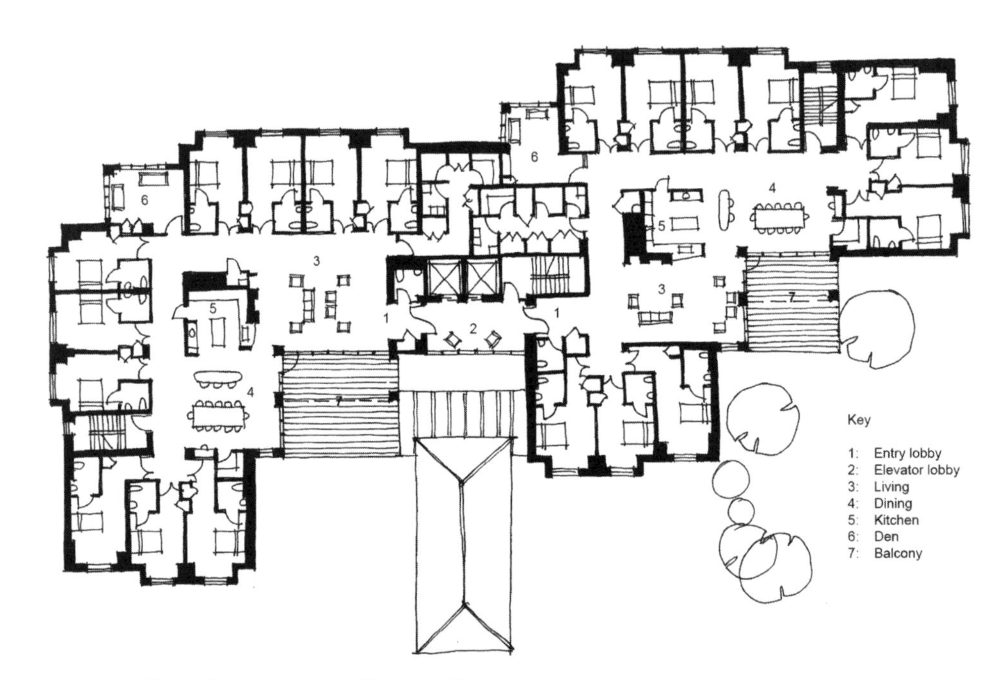

FIGURE 21-3 Floor plan. *Courtesy of Pozzoni LLP*

Description of the Type of Community, Including Number of Residents

Chelsea, Massachusetts, is an economically depressed urban neighborhood on the north side of Boston. It is here that the Leonard Florence Center for Living, a supportive community modeled after an urban apartment house, is located. The Florence Center provides skilled nursing care for 100 residents in an environment that bears little resemblance to traditional nursing homes or, for that matter, to the surrounding community. The project is the first "Green House®" community to be constructed within an urban setting in the United States, and, as such, has taken on a unique design unlike other Green Houses®, which are primarily located in less populated areas.

The Green House® concept, developed in the early 2000s, is a trademarked approach to the integration of nursing home design and care programming. Originally conceived as a way of integrating small, standalone nursing households into American neighborhoods within a single-level "home" that replicates so many American ranch homes, the program has expanded throughout the United States and has instigated a more focused attention to small-scale household person-directed nursing care. This concept provides a restriction on the number of residents to 10 within each household, provides guidelines for staffing and staff training, as well as a number of other requirements necessary to carry the Green House® name. The Florence Center has taken this concept into an urban neighborhood and has done so in a mid-rise multistory structure appropriate for its location.

The Green House® design concept, incorporated into the design of the Florence Center, follows the intuitive household typology of transition from public to private spaces within the defined household. Each household has a distinct front door, distinct social or public space, the living or hearth room and distinct private space, and the resident bedrooms. The Florence Center has two such households on each of five floors with the ground-level floor containing community social spaces as well as administrative spaces. The two households on each floor are separated by support spaces necessary for the functioning of the nursing home.

The design approach chosen for the Florence Center is a more contemporary articulation of the Green House® concept than might be typically found elsewhere. Combined with the size of the building, this rendering of the trademarked concept does not recall a single-family American home, but rather an apartment building that might appropriately fit into an urban setting. It could be argued that the simple fact that the building is not a standalone household, to which the Green House® concept originally aspired, defeats the purported tenets of that philosophy. However, when viewed outside the confines of these somewhat restrictive care and built environmental tenets, and as simply a nursing home, the design succeeds.

The Leonard Florence Center is the final piece of care provision on an elderly care campus located on Admirals Hill developed by Chelsea Jewish Nursing Home Foundation. In addition to this nursing facility serving 100 residents, there are 69 affordable assisted living apartments and 36 studio apartments for specialized elderly care. Intended to serve frail elderly from all economic backgrounds primarily from the local Jewish community, the Florence Center also serves younger residents with amyotrophic lateral sclerosis (ALS) who are aged 30 to 40 years, older residents with multiple sclerosis who are aged between 40 and 60 years, older residents with Parkinson's disease, and provides short-term rehabilitation services.

Geographics

Vernacular Design

How does the scheme/environment respond to the locality?

The Florence Center is the third building on this campus and is of a size that is complementary to the others, both on campus as well as the surrounding buildings in the community. While somewhat more "contemporary" in design and material selection than its neighbors, it is still aesthetically identifiable as a residence as opposed to a commercial building. The building's mass is broken up into smaller, more digestible components both through articulation and use of material. As the surrounding community consists primarily of similarly sized apartment buildings, this structure does not draw undue attention to itself, even given its prominent location on the highest topographical point in the community.

Care

Philosophy of Care

What is the operators' philosophy, and how does the building match this philosophy?

The Green House® concept is as much a philosophy of care as it is an environment in which to house that care. The objective is to provide as "home-like" an environment and care program as possible. Thus, care staff members are required to be trained as "universal" staff, called *shahbazim*, performing all the functions of running the household. This includes preparing and serving the meals from the open kitchen as well as providing nursing care. Medications are dispensed by licensed nurses, and dedicated housekeeping staff members provide necessary cleaning of the spaces. Each household is staffed with two universal staff members during the daytime shifts and one on the night shift. A registered nurse serves two or more households, depending on the shift. Specialists such as therapists, social workers, or doctors come to the households only when needed.

This staffing model can, at times, be challenging. As the residents are encouraged to follow their own individual schedules for activities of daily living, there are often multiple tasks that need to be accomplished simultaneously for the residents. However, with only 10 residents to care for, staff members are empowered to prioritize tasks and they are quickly accepted by the residents as members of the household family.

The household design is carefully crafted not only to enable this model of care provision, but to follow the requirements of The Green House® concepts. The small number of residents combined with the small number of staff allows residents to participate in activities that include the "family" of household residents and staff when and if they choose, but also to have their privacy within the household without the disturbance of loud noises or of staff intrusions.

When family members or friends visit residents, there is opportunity for them to go for an "outing" away from the household to the ground level where there is a bakery café, a deli, and a spiritual worship space. In addition, there is a well-appointed spa located on this ground level where residents can participate in massage therapy, a whirlpool bath, or simply obtain a haircut.

Community and Belonging

How does the scheme design and operation support this ideal?

FIGURE 21-4 Each private resident room has an en-suite bathroom. *Robert Benson Photography*

The Leonard Florence Center is the third and final building on this campus in Chelsea, and as such completes not only the land use but the somewhat abbreviated continuum of care. Each of the buildings is closely related to the others and the amenities included on the ground level of the Florence Center are open to all residents on campus as well as anyone from the surrounding neighborhood who cares to venture onto campus.

While the design of the Florence Center is unique in both layout and aesthetic, the material choices harmonize and complement the other buildings on this small campus. In addition, the siting of the building has created outdoor spaces that invite community participation and provide spaces for resident social interaction. The spiritual worship space on the ground level of the Florence Center was purposefully included to

FIGURE 21-5 On the ground level, there is a bakery café where residents and visitors can go for an outing. *Robert Benson Photography*

FIGURE 21-6 Community spaces on the ground level include a library for residents and visitors alike. *Robert Benson Photography*

enhance the Jewish experience for all campus residents and to encourage residents' ongoing religious practices within an organized structure, regardless of their religious affinity.

Innovation

If the operator pursues a policy of innovation and pursuit of excellence, how is this demonstrated?

The Chelsea Jewish Nursing Home, owner of the Florence Center and a well-established provider of traditional nursing care in the Chelsea area of Boston, chose to abandon the traditional delivery of long-term care and to provide care within the care model of The Green House® approach. While they are not the first to adopt this approach, they are the first to use the approach in a multiple-household urban setting that serves a substantial number of residents. Convinced that this model of care would enhance the privacy and dignity of their residents and would serve to increase their residents' independence and quality of care, the Florence Center undertook a substantial investment to manifest their commitment to their clientele and to do so regardless of ability of the resident to contribute to the cost of care.

But the use of The Green House® care program integrated with the built environment is not necessarily innovation, as this approach has been successfully accomplished previously. Using this model of care within a prescribed household environment and with so much that is formulaic with such a variety of special needs residents is unique and, some might say, quite courageous. Mixing these diverse populations within one community and sharing common social spaces is at once counterintuitive and borne of common sense. It is counterintuitive because the diverse care needs of the residents require the type of nonstandard care approaches that could lead to financial disaster. It is borne of common sense because the communities in which we all live are made up of such diverse populations as these and thus the sense of community within the Florence Center is more natural.

Neighborhood Integration

Community Involvement

Is the scheme and service designed to integrate successfully with the local community?

The Chelsea area of Boston is what might be referred to as a "blue-collar" area with a mixture of established, affordable housing, light commercial, and light industrial development. The Florence Center

FIGURE 21-7 Each household kitchen allows residents access to assist with meal serving and preparation. *Robert Benson Photography*

campus is located on a small area of land bounded to the east and north of the building by single-level industrial buildings, on the west and south by newer mid-rise multifamily residential developments. These residential developments, including the Florence Center campus, are examples of reclamation, and perhaps "gentrification" of the Chelsea urban fabric with attention being paid to the economic enhancement of this particular area.

With the ample number of residents in the surrounding developments, and with the mixture of income and age demographics of the immediate surrounding community, there would seem to be a wonderful opportunity to connect to the community. As the developments are yet to be firmly rooted, this opportunity has not reached its full potential. However, within the confines of the modified continuing care retirement campus and the extended community of resident family and friends, the addition of the Florence Center provides both interior and exterior spaces that lend themselves to successful community integration. With an appropriate approach to the neighboring buildings by administration, staff, or residents, these areas can serve to realize that as yet unmet potential.

Staff and Volunteers

Human Resources

Are policies and designs in place to attract good staff and volunteers?

Staff members are empowered to operate the household within a democratic framework and as chosen or directed by residents. They create the menus, assist in the provision of medications when necessary, and perform household cleanup tasks. They are also empowered to coordinate with residents, activities that are appropriate.

The total number of direct care staff for The Florence Center is 70 *shahbazim*, 20 nurses, and 10 clinical support team members, such as physical or speech therapists. Included on staff for the entire facility is a "sage" who provides advice to meet the recognized quality-of-life needs of the residents and family members. This translates to approximately eight direct care hours per resident per day, a fairly high number and one which, within a household environment, translates into significant attention paid to the residents. In addition to the direct care staff, there are 13 staff members in management, five

FIGURE 21-8 Universal staff members have a small and unobtrusive work space adjacent to the household dining room. *Robert Benson Photography*

FIGURE 21-9 Household hearth rooms are a place where families can gather for socialization. *Robert Benson Photography*

additional housekeeping staff, and two maintenance staff members. No staff members are directly attributable to food service as those tasks fall onto the shoulders of the *shahbazim* within the households.

- Direct care hours per resident per day: 4.0

Environmental Sustainability

ALTERNATIVE ENERGY SOURCES

There are no alternative energy sources used in this project.

WATER CONSERVATION

As mandated by government regulations, use of water-conserving fixtures throughout the project was a part of construction.

ENERGY CONSERVATION

The Florence Center is located directly opposite a city bus stop and thus has easy access for public transportation by residents, when needed, but more importantly for staff to arrive at the site. High-efficiency mechanical systems, including heat recovery units and energy-efficient lighting, have been used in the building's design. The building also uses a well-insulated exterior building skin and high-performance window systems. Large areas of windows allow substantial natural light without direct glare into the household social spaces as well as resident rooms, thus minimizing the need, at least during the daylight hours, of artificial lighting.

Outdoor Living

Garden

Does the garden support principles of care?

The Green House® concept promotes connection to nature and an openness to the households that lets ample natural light into the resident social areas. While this may be fairly easy to accomplish when the households are standalone single-story structures set on typical suburban sites, it is somewhat more difficult within an urban context. However, The Florence Center design provides for a very nicely sized secure balcony accessed from each household social space. These balconies can easily be viewed by residents through the large window areas in the dining or living rooms and thus there is also good visual access to the outdoors. Although the building is located on a very constricted site and shares that site with two other campus structures, there has been included in the design a well-designed "Peace Garden Terrace" adjacent to the grade-level bakery café and accessible through that social space. This exterior "room" provides a clear separation between The Florence Center and the nearest campus building, provides a well-conceived elevational transition, and contributes additional social spaces that can be used by any of the campus residents or the members of the surrounding community.

FIGURE 21-10 Each household has its own exterior balcony where residents can enjoy the outdoors. *Robert Benson Photography*

Project Data

DESIGN FIRM

DiMella Shaffer
281 Congress Street
Boston, MA 02210
United States
www.dimellashaffer.com

AREAS/SIZES

- Site area: 7,689 square meters (82,764 square feet; 1.9 acres)
- Building footprint: 1,356.38 square meters (14,600 square feet)
- Total building area: 8,732.89 square meters (94,000 square feet)
- Total area per resident: 87.33 square meters (940 square feet)

PARKING

There is surface parking for four automobiles directly adjacent to this building, however, there is surface parking for numerous other automobiles on the campus but constructed with the other building on campus.

COSTS (2010)

- Total building cost: $23,000,000 USD
- Cost per square meter: $2,634 USD
- Cost per square foot: $244 USD
- Investment per resident: $230,000 USD

RESIDENT AGE

Average age of elderly residents only: 86 years

RESIDENT PAYER MIX

Massachusetts Health and Medicaid, Medicare for short-term rehab, private care, and long-term care insurance; private insurance for the younger population.

Chapter 22

A Study of the Skilled Nursing Component at Foulkeways at Gwynedd

REASONS FOR INCLUSION OF THIS SCHEME

- Foulkeways used a unique approach to the design and care program for this nursing facility.
- The internal layout is an innovative approach to household nursing design.
- This building design completely blurs the line of distinct levels of care on a continuing-care retirement campus.
- The decentralized approach to nursing-care provision is enhanced by the attention to detail in the design.

Building Description

Name of Scheme: Foulkeways at Gwynedd
Owner: Foulkeways at Gwynedd, a not-for-profit, faith-based organization
Address:
120 Meetinghouse Road
Gwynedd, PA 19436
United States
Occupied since: 2001

FIGURE 22-1 Each household has an open-plan living room, and nurses work at a desk in the background. *Courtesy RLPS Architects/Larry Lefever Photography*

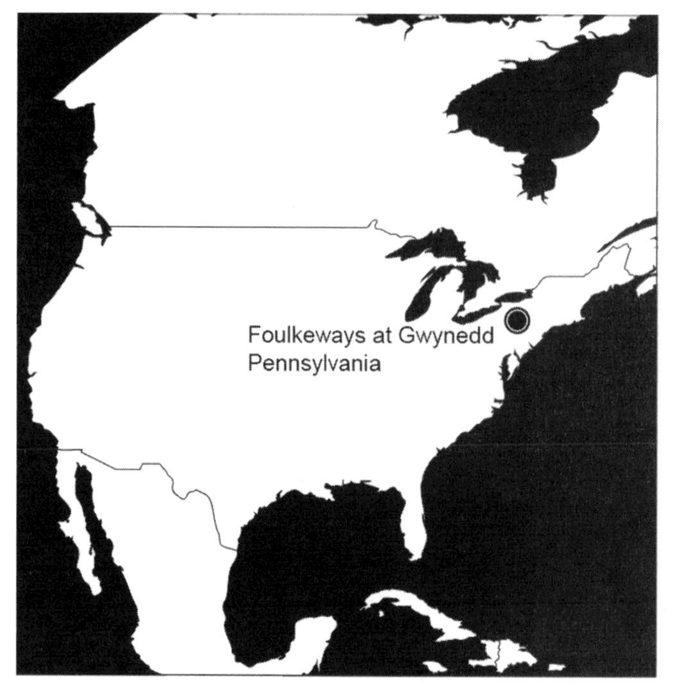

FIGURE 22-2 Scheme location. *Courtesy of Pozzoni LLP*

Foulkeways at Gwynedd: United States

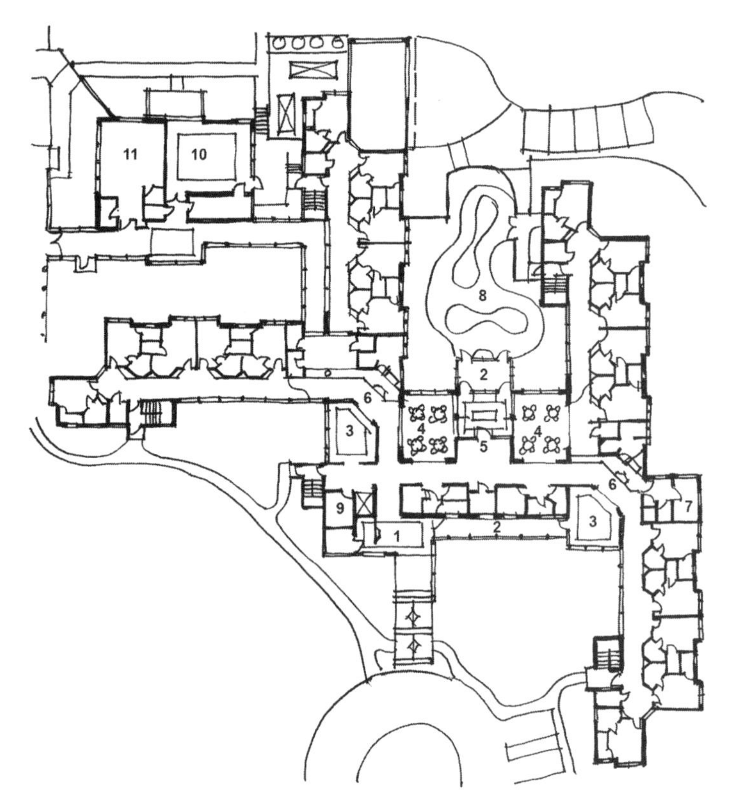

FIGURE 22-3 Floor plan. *Courtesy of Pozzoni LLP*

Description of the Type of Community, Including Number of Residents

Foulkeways at Gwynedd is a continuing-care retirement community established in 1967 in southern Pennsylvania's heavily wooded countryside just outside Philadelphia. The original community design included nursing rooms in a traditional, medical model design, and over the years, the commitment to excellence of services provided to clients eventually culminated in the decision to add assisted living and to construct 40 new nursing resident rooms. This decision incorporated a design that would provide a seamless transition from either the assisted-living or independent-living apartments and would provide for the residents of the new nursing home to maintain their connection to the remainder of the Foulkeways community's Quaker roots.

Foulkeways at Gwynedd: United States

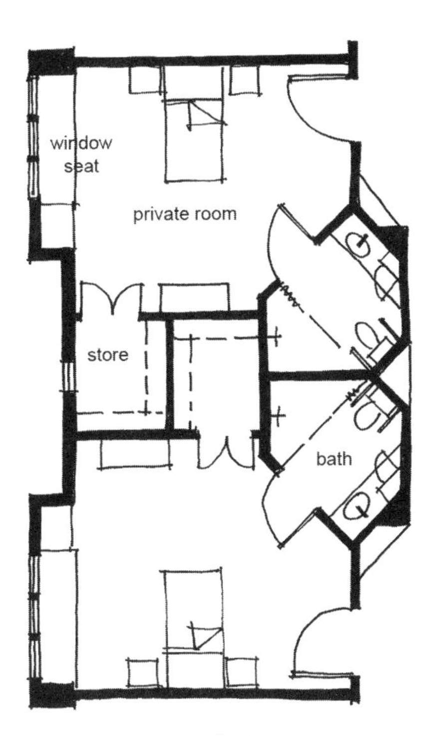

Typical skilled care private room

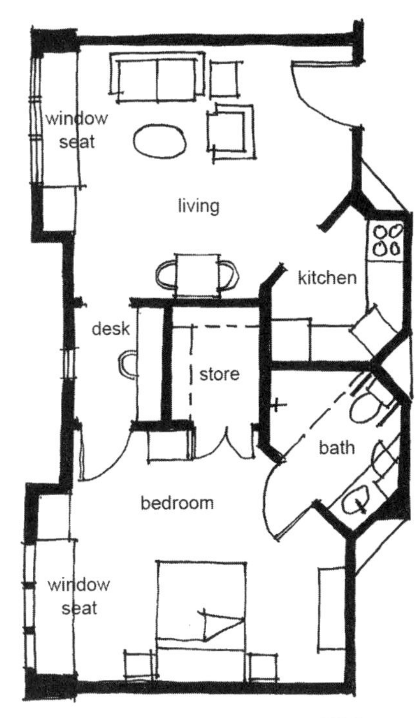

Conversion from skilled to assisted living

Apartment Plans

FIGURE 22-4 Resident rooms have storage for all medical supplies and can be converted to suites. *Courtesy of Pozzoni LLP*

Foulkeways began consideration of a new and innovative approach to the nursing component on its continuing-care retirement campus in the late 1990s with the formation of a "future care committee," the membership of which consisted of individuals from the not-for-profit board of directors, staff, and residents. Broad discussions over a five-year period of what an ideal nursing environment would look like and how the care would be structured ensued, culminating in a restructuring of the existing model of care and an embarkation of design for a new nursing structure on campus. The resulting design, ultimately constructed and occupied in 2001, consists of a two-story building, each story having two households of 10 residents each. However, each of those households is further delineated by having five private resident rooms along a corridor with the rooms on only one side of that corridor. The opposite side of the corridor opens to pleasant exterior views with large expanses of glass.

Each household has its own living room, but each pair of households come together at a dining room and resident kitchen, which in turn has access to each of the living rooms. The layout provides an open plan without barriers to resident movement between households or within each household. This design is quite residential in both its plan and in the finishes and furnishings that have been selected. There is no overt staff presence with the requisite nursing desk for each household being located conveniently near both the dining and living areas but done simply as a desk that is a part of the furniture one might find in one's home.

The private resident rooms are fairly large and each has an en suite bathroom and large exterior windows. As the nursing approach chosen was to decentralize the supply of nursing goods as well as medications, each resident room has a large walk-in closet in which that resident's particular supplies are stored and a medication cabinet in the bathroom where that resident's necessary medications are maintained. This approach, combined with the fact that there are only five rooms along a single corridor, has completely eliminated the need for institutional carts which, in other nursing homes, are constantly being pushed up and down corridors by staff.

Geographics

Vernacular Design

How does the scheme/environment respond to the locality?

The design of Foulkeways follows the Quaker tradition of simple forms and finish materials. Although the original campus buildings are somewhat dated, having been constructed in the late 1960s, this new building and its connection with the assisted-living structure complements and enhances the campus aesthetic without being overpowering or attempting to make a powerful architectural statement. In fact, the power of the architecture is in its understated simplicity, which also contributes to the residential nature of the building.

The two-story structure is neither massive nor institutional in appearance and expresses itself more as a large home than a skilled-nursing facility. Although fairly large, it is brought down to a residential scale by use of elements that would commonly be found on homes in the region such as porches, varying roofs, stone chimneys, clapboard siding, and simple wooden exterior detailing.

The building's design establishes the theme for the campus' future as this campus moves into repositioning in the coming years. That theme relates very well to both the Quaker fundamentals and to the nature of residential-scaled architecture. It also provides a base design palette that will completely blur the aesthetic demarcation lines between nursing, assisted living, and independent living. This was a goal as the design objectives of the "future care committee" were established in order to provide more consistency through that continuum of care.

This design philosophy carries through for the interior of the building, also. The building's layout, with its single-loaded corridors that include large windows to the exterior, is certainly unlike traditional double-loaded, medical model nursing home designs. This layout is reminiscent of perhaps an apartment structure or even hospitality design and is further enhanced by the inclusion of inset resident room entry doors, contrasting wood wall paneling and the use of wood trim, faux windows, and colors found in private residential architecture.

FIGURE 22-5 The exterior is understated Quaker in use of materials and forms. *Courtesy of Jeffrey Anderzhon*

FIGURE 22-6 Resident rooms are served by single-loaded corridors. *Courtesy of Jeffrey Anderzhon*

Care

Philosophy of Care

What is the operators' philosophy, and how does the building match this philosophy?

With the construction of the nursing building, as well as the adjacent community center, Foulkeways has made a very clear statement regarding its philosophy of care revolving around the resident lifestyle rather than staff convenience. This is evidenced in almost every design decision from the exterior noninstitutional massing and choice of materials down to the simple use of a roll-top desk used as a nursing station and which fits well with the household furnishings. But that philosophy is carried through in other ways that can be taken away from this study as valuable guides for future developments.

The care approach is completely and thoroughly decentralized. There are no carts used for medications or resident medical supplies. Each resident has a cabinet in the en-suite bathroom in which to store required medications. Additionally, there is a substantial walk-in closet where that resident's medical supplies can be stored for a period of time and easily replenished. Thus, each resident retains the dignity and privacy of accessing these materials and medications in the privacy of his or her own personal domain. Coupled with the fact that all of the personal hygiene needs can be accomplished in the generously proportioned bath, the design goes a significant distance in increasing the sense of self-worth and dignity for the resident.

The Foulkeways design takes very seriously the desire to completely eliminate delivery carts of any sort

FIGURE 22-7 Resident en-suite bathrooms include plenty of storage for medical supplies. *Courtesy of Jeffrey Anderzhon*

FIGURE 22-8 All deliveries are contained in lower-level corridors and support spaces to reduce resident anxiety. *Courtesy of Jeffrey Anderzhon*

from the entire household living area. Major supply deliveries are accomplished from the central stores to the household "back-of-house" areas by means of a series of basement delivery corridors accessible only by staff. Brought up to the household levels by means of service elevators, the deliveries become essentially invisible and certainly do not contribute to the disruption of the household daily operations.

The Foulkeways' staff recognizes the value of this privacy and strives to maintain it. They also understand that a preponderance of various staff members, each with his or her own particular assignment, would only serve to disrupt the residents' daily routine and probably provide too many individuals working within the household to maintain a calming influence. Staff members have fully embraced the modified universal worker concept as a part of the overall philosophy of care, and they enjoy the administration's full support in making this approach work to the benefit of the resident.

Community and Belonging

How does the scheme design and operation support this ideal?

The nursing facility at Foulkeways has been designed as an extension of the large community center, which connects the nursing building with the remainder of the campus. This community center includes spaces for activities of all campus residents, temporary artistic displays, a varying number of casual-dining venues, physical therapy, and most importantly, spaces where residents from the variety of housing alternatives on campus can come together for socialization. The community center is purposefully designed and located in such a way that there is no discrimination among the care levels or ambulatory abilities of any resident. It fully complies with the campus philosophy of breaking down the barriers, both physical and sociological, of a resident moving through the continuum of care from independent living to nursing care.

It is only a very short walk from the Foulkeways nursing building to the community center and, when accomplished, that walk feels as if one remained in the same building enclosure. But there is also an overriding sense of community and close community relationships when one remains within the nursing building itself. The distinct typology of the home is evident in the layout; however, the plan feels very open and welcoming, particularly with the multiple and varying views to the exterior around the building. These design devices also provide subtle but effective orientation and wayfinding cues to residents who may be somewhat affected by dementia and provides residents with a constant visual connection to the outdoors and to the changes of season, which can be dramatic in this area. In addition, the community center building acts

FIGURE 22-9 Foulkeways community center is adjacent to the nursing households for ease of resident access. *Courtesy of Jeffrey Anderzhon*

as a backdrop to several of the views to the exterior from the nursing building, reinforcing the sense of community by reminding the viewer there are additional spaces where socialization can take place.

Innovation

If the operator pursues a policy of innovation and pursuit of excellence, how is this demonstrated?

From the very beginning, Foulkeways approached the design and construction of this nursing facility with innovation in mind. The formation of the "future care committee" was a unique and innovative approach to the process, emanating from the ground up rather than dictated from administrative personnel. This approach considered resident needs first and staffing and financial considerations only after the resident needs were fully addressed. It also provided consistency across the campus from both an aesthetic perspective as well as accomplishing a complete blurring of the continuum of care. Having adopted this approach and having successfully implemented it in the nursing structure completion, residents on the Foulkeways the campus maintain the feeling of connection to the remainder of the campus regardless of where on that campus they may reside. It is even more commendable that this innovative approach was brought to full fruition without excessive interference by those who would want to "cheapen" the results through such actions as cost reductions or increasing the number of residents served in each household.

Neighborhood Integration

Community Involvement

Is the scheme and service designed to integrate successfully with the local community?

Foulkeways at Gwynedd is a large, full continuum of care senior-living campus with a substantial population of residents living in independent-living apartments. The health-care center is provided for both the convenience and security of the residents as their health or their spouses' health may begin to deteriorate. As such, it is a full community with amenities that match or exceed any other continuing-care retirement community. Additionally, Foulkeways is located in a fairly low-density suburban area near the metropolitan city of Philadelphia. Thus, there are many layers of community to which residents can subscribe, and each of those layers is fully and easily available to the residents.

The design of the nursing building, along with the adjacent community center, has been done in a way that does not isolate its inhabitants from the remainder of the campus community, but in fact, enhances the community experience of the entire campus at a location that is extremely convenient to the nursing residents. This community center provides many opportunities for campus community interaction, and the members of the surrounding community are also quite welcome to participate in community center activities. This does often occur particularly when exhibits are mounted that hold a broad interest beyond the campus borders. Foulkeways is a well-established community member and has maintained a place in the community that is respected and used by more than simply campus residents.

Staff and Volunteers

Human Resources

Are policies and designs in place to attract good staff and volunteers?

The administration at Foulkeways has worked diligently to maintain its position as an employer of highest choice. With the addition of the nursing structure and the unique care approach, that position has been, if anything, enhanced. The nursing staff members are encouraged and given the ability to resolve issues and solve problems which arise among themselves without bringing them to a higher level of administration. They have been empowered to provide the highest quality of care with the least amount possible of overt intrusion into the residents' lives. The building's design provides a workplace that is conducive to the care approach, a direct result of the process by which the project was conceived.

- Direct care hours per day per client: 5.20

Environmental Sustainability

ALTERNATIVE ENERGY SOURCES

The Foulkeways design does not incorporate alternative energy sources.

WATER CONSERVATION

Complying with established local and national regulations for water conservation in place at the time of construction, the design incorporates water-conservation fixtures into the building.

ENERGY CONSERVATION

Energy conservation is a part of the general design of Foulkeways including substantial insulation appropriate for the geographic region as well as energy-efficient mechanical and kitchen appliances.

Outdoor Living

Garden

Does the garden support principles of care?

From both a visual and interactive perspective, the gardens surrounding the Foulkeways nursing facility contribute to the sense of home and community for the residents. Although the building is a two-story structure, there is full visual access from household public spaces, corridors, and resident rooms on both levels. Two wings of each household, by their layout, form an enclosed garden area, which is easily accessed from a screened porch just off the common kitchen and dining area of the households on the ground level. This secured garden area is well landscaped and has a hard-surfaced walking path. The remaining household wings form intimate garden areas which, while not directly physically accessible by residents, are fully visible and their landscaping provides a variety of wonderful views onto these "pocket" gardens from resident rooms, household living rooms, or the open, single-loaded corridors on both levels of the building.

FIGURE 22-10 Exterior gardens provide seating areas and security from resident elopement. *Courtesy of Jeffrey Anderzhon*

Project Data

DESIGN FIRM

Reese, Lower, Patrick & Scott, Ltd.
1910 Harrington Dr.
Lancaster, PA 17601
United States
www.rlps.com

AREAS/SIZES

- Site area: 12,140.57 square meters (130,680 square feet; 3 acres, part of a 105-acre CCRC campus)
- Building footprint: 2,425.79 square meters (26,111 square feet)
- Total building area: 4,851.68 square meters (52,223 square feet)
- Total area per resident: 121.33 square meters (1,306 square feet)

PARKING

There are 38 parking places for staff and 24 parking places for visitors, totaling 62 automobiles all on surface lots for this building.

COSTS (2008)

- Total building cost: $10,730,072 USD
- Cost per square meter: $2,212 USD
- Cost per square foot: $206 USD
- Investment per resident: $268,252 USD

RESIDENT AGE

Average age of residents: 88 years

RESIDENT PAYER MIX

Foulkeways nursing facility is intended primarily for residents of the continuing-care retirement campus whose health needs require nursing care. Thus, the main payer source is individual private funds or long-term care insurance payments from policies owned by individuals.

Chapter 23

A Study of Deupree Cottages

REASONS FOR INCLUSION OF THIS SCHEME

- This scheme is a household nursing home designed to replicate residential standalone homes.
- The scheme uses a care approach change from the organization's previous, more staff-centered approach.
- The scheme reclaims a restricted site that was underutilized and that provided opportunity for the organization's expansion.

Building Description

Name of Scheme: Deupree Cottages

Owner: Episcopal Retirement Homes, a not-for-profit organization

Address:

3999 Erie Avenue
Cincinnati, OH 45208
United States

Occupied since: 2009

FIGURE 23-1 The Deupree Cottages, while connected, are designed as stand-alone houses. *Tom Uhlman/www.tomuphoto.com*

FIGURE 23-2 Scheme location. *Courtesy of Pozzoni LLP*

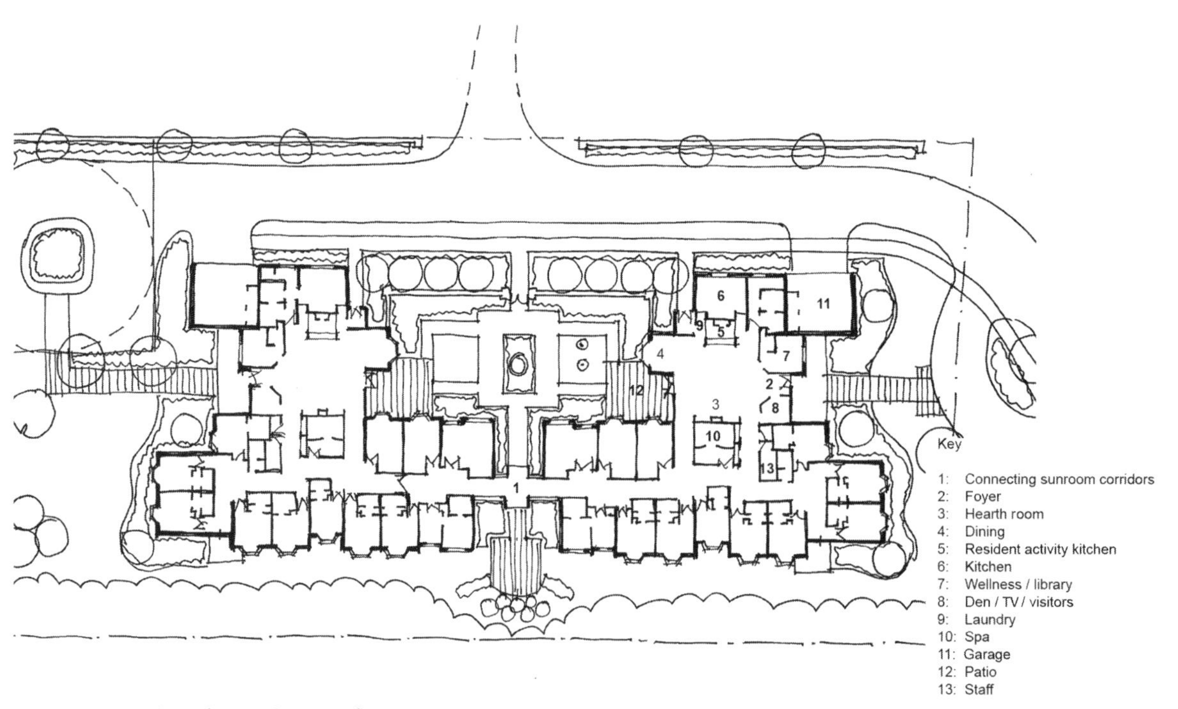

FIGURE 23-3 Site plan. *Courtesy of Pozzoni LLP*

Description of the Type of Community, Including Number of Residents

Deupree Cottages are two detached, single-story buildings and are a part of a larger continuing-care retirement community campus that is attempting to reposition itself. They represent a new person-centered nursing-care approach for the provider as well as a unique design in which to house that approach. Although the number of residents served by these two cottages housing nursing residents is fairly small, the commitment by the care provider is significant both in terms of resources and the change in the direction of care.

Each of the two households at Deupree Cottages house 12 nursing-care residents in private bedrooms. The bedrooms have been designed to include full en-suite bathrooms, complete with showers, and there are two differently designed bedroom layouts. One layout, the smallest of the two, is approximately 260 square feet (24.15 square meters), including the en-suite bathroom, in total space, while the larger is approximately 325 square feet (30.19 square meters) in total space, including the en-suite bathroom. The two differ in that the larger bedroom has a distinct living area separated from the bed area by a solid wall, while the smaller is simply a studio arrangement. The mix of bedrooms in each cottage is two of the larger bedrooms and 10 of the smaller.

The cottages are designed along an intuitive "home" typology with the private space of the bedrooms separated and behind the more public spaces of living, dining, and kitchen areas. These more public spaces are reached directly from the covered front porch and front door of each cottage. From this entry, one can see across the width of the cottage through the hearth room and

FIGURE 23-4 The households have been designed along an intuitive home typology that includes living or public space.
Tom Uhlman/www.tomuphoto.com

dining room and into the well-manicured, more formal garden area. The open plan of this public area allows residents to quickly and clearly see all the activities that may be under way in the social spaces, including cooking activities in the resident kitchen or a low-impact exercise class in the small wellness/library area. The more distracting activities such as watching television can take place in a separate den just off the front entry. In addition, there is also a wall-mounted flat-screen television in the centrally located hearth room just above the fireplace.

A unique design feature for these two cottages is the inclusion of an enclosed garage. This inclusion allows materials and food delivery to the cottages by means of a campus-owned vehicle from the main campus delivery point to the cottages without the unsightly trucks parked in front of the buildings. The delivery vehicle can pull into the garage and unload the materials in comfort even in inclement weather. Additionally, residents can enter transportation for outings while fully protected from the weather. The inclusion of this garage also adds a very home-like feeling to the exterior elevations of the building, bringing the typical American residential icon of a garage door into the design mix.

Beyond the garage are the "back-of-house" functions of the cottage, analogous to the "back door" and sort of family-only entry of the typology of home. At Deupree Cottages, this is where the clean and dirty utility rooms are located as well as the fully equipped preparation kitchen. While these functions are logically located here for convenience of staff and ease of materials and food delivery, it is somewhat disturbing that the dirty utility room location requires transportation of soiled garments across the social areas and in front of the main cottage entry.

Geographics

Vernacular Design

How does the scheme/environment respond to the locality?

Each of the cottages takes on its own architectural style, one being a neo-Craftsman style while the other tends to be traditional American suburban colonial. Quite different in architectural rendering and detailing, the cottages are connected by a gazebo-like structure that is neutral to both cottages' architecture and at first appears to be a separate structure. Either of the cottages would fit comfortably in a contemporary American neighborhood of single-story residences, albeit somewhat larger in size than the typical suburban home.

Unfortunately, the cottages have been sited on a parcel of land that is somewhat isolated from the remainder of the continuing-care retirement campus and is separated from the main campus by a waterway, but connected by a bridge. The continuing-care retirement campus is populated by fairly large buildings up to about six stories in height and provides a more urban background to the cottages than would be sympathetic to the suburban nature of the cottages. In addition, directly across the street from these cottages there is a light manufacturing district that includes three or four somewhat industrial buildings. Thus, the cottages, while pleasing architecturally, seem to be dropped into place and oddly residential in nature surrounded by nonresidential environs.

The layout of the cottages as an architectural unit takes as much advantage of the siting as possible, providing a formal and attractive landscaped garden in the void naturally created by the two buildings' shape. To the rear of the cottages, where they abut the waterway, the site is heavily wooded, giving some visual protection from the taller and more institutional buildings of the remainder of the campus and providing a visually attractive backdrop to building setting.

Care

Philosophy of Care

What is the operators' philosophy, and how does the building match this philosophy?

It has been the intent of Episcopal Retirement Homes to provide nursing care in a residential setting along with a care program that emulated, or at least came close to, a home-like setting. Additionally, the decision to develop the Deupree Cottages was intentionally made to construct them with a design as residential as possible in order to set the visual stage for the care that was to take place within that built environment.

Within the cottages staffing has been redefined from traditional care provision to what has been termed by Deupree as "versatile workers." Each staff member crosses delineated responsibilities in order to provide holistic care to residents. Thus, an individual who may be licensed to provide nursing-care assistance is also

FIGURE 23-5 Each household has its own kitchen used by residents and the "versatile workers." *Tom Uhlman/ www.tomuphoto.com*

expected to attend to housekeeping tasks when necessary, and to assist in the serving of resident meals. This dynamic approach that empowers the staff also provides consistent presence of that staff to interact with residents on various levels of care and the making of a home. Administration and staff are both committed to resident-centered care and have deliberately taken pains to shed the traditional nursing-care approach completely.

Community and Belonging

How does the scheme design and operation support this ideal?

Because of the somewhat isolated location of the cottages on a piece of land separated from the main retirement campus and across from a nonresidential area, both residents and staff are, by their immediate geography, disconnected from community and from an inherent sense of belonging. While this is generally a detriment to the sense of community and belonging, it does somewhat force the creation of a small-scale community composed of the cottages alone. The scheme design allows this to occur by providing a protected connection between the cottages, by providing a generous amount of social space in each of the cottages, and by providing nicely landscaped and secure exterior areas for socialization.

Innovation

If the operator pursues a policy of innovation and pursuit of excellence, how is this demonstrated?

Two levels of innovation are present in the Deupree Cottage scheme. First, there is the provision of a nursing home environment that is unique at least to the larger continuing-care retirement campus if not the surrounding community—that is, a household design that provides two distinct and separate home-like structures. Second, there is the provision of a restructured-care program—that is, a program that is resident-oriented rather than traditional, that integrates well with and complements the built environment, providing a care

FIGURE 23-6 The household dining room designs allow an abundance of natural lighting. *Tom Uhlman/www.tomuphoto.com*

approach that is both contemporary and well considered, keeping the resident foremost in the equation.

However, for a variety of reasons, the location of the cottages, at least to some degree, falls prey to the traditional approach of continuing-care retirement campuses of placing the highest level of health care at the most remote location on the campus. Although it is understood that this property became available to the provider for the construction of these cottages, it remains visually and somewhat physically remote from the remainder of the campus. While the remainder of the campus is fairly densely built upon, and the property for Deupree Cottages may have been located on the only logical place remaining on campus, it is at least somewhat isolated visually and socially from the remainder of the campus.

Neighborhood Integration

Community Involvement

Is the scheme and service designed to integrate successfully with the local community?

At the Episcopal Retirement Homes, a well-established senior living community, there is a very good history of community and resident involvement. Residents are encouraged to use their career talents by serving on a number of committees. This tradition of resident service and involvement with the community is more difficult to accomplish once a resident requires nursing care and becomes somewhat more isolated both socially and physically, as would be the case when residency at Deupree Cottages commences.

Regardless of their location, somewhat isolated from the remainder of the campus and in a nonresidential area of the larger community, Deupree Cottages is still an integral part of the larger continuing-care campus, as well as a recognized member of the surrounding community. This integration occurs through the concerted efforts of residents, staff, and family members and, at least to some degree, overcomes the barriers of the physical location. However, the local community involvement takes on more of an active and "destination" persona than had the cottages been alternatively located.

FIGURE 23-7 Social spaces in the households include a library where residents and visitors can visit. *Tom Uhlman/ www.tomuphoto.com*

FIGURE 23-8 There is a well-developed and accessible garden between the two households. *Tom Uhlman/www .tomuphoto.com*

Staff and Volunteers

Human Resources

Are policies and designs in place to attract good staff and volunteers?

Deupree Cottages defines care staff as "versatile workers." All traditional nurse aides are additionally trained in housekeeping activities and food service, and perform in all of these areas of caring for residents on a daily basis. The simple fact that Deupree Cottages provide a new and unique approach to care provision has attracted competent and committed staff. This care approach has empowered staff to reach their own potential and thrive as care providers in the cottages. The cottage design provides a noninstitutional and more staff-friendly setting for this provision to take place.

- Direct care hours per day per client: 6.4

Environmental Sustainability

The site on which Deupree Cottages are located is a former and reclaimed light industrial site that has been improved by a smaller building coverage as well as the inclusion of a natural green buffer strip behind the cottages and adjacent to the waterway. This buffer strip screens and softens the views from the cottages and also provides an improved stormwater quality from the former use of the site.

ALTERNATIVE ENERGY SOURCES

No alternative energy sources have been incorporated into the design of the cottages aside from high-efficiency appliances as mandated by government regulations.

WATER CONSERVATION

Low–water use plumbing fixtures are utilized throughout the cottages as mandated by government regulations.

ENERGY CONSERVATION

Energy conservation is accomplished in several ways; however, the most important is the use of daylighting for the living rooms and kitchen in order to minimize artificial lighting and energy use. This daylighting is accomplished by the layout of the plans and the large expanses of glass allowing natural light to penetrate these areas of the buildings.

Outdoor Living

Garden

Does the garden support principles of care?

One of the most significant features of the Deupree Cottages design is the creation of the exterior spaces as well as the access to those spaces, both visually and physically. The cottage footprints are "L"-shaped providing the void in the L to be located between the two cottages. This allows a large area for nicely developed

FIGURE 23-9 Each private resident room is large enough to accommodate resident furniture. *Tom Uhlman/www.tomuphoto.com*

gardens that are accessible by the residents either directly through each cottage living room or through the gazebo structure that connects the two cottages. These gardens include raised planting beds designed for individuals with movement restrictions and are accessible either from a wheelchair or standing position. Within these gardens, there are both hard and soft surfaces and landscaping that provides visual delight in all seasons. The hard surfacing provides both a patio for each cottage where residents can simply sit and enjoy the outdoors or where coffee or light meals can be shared. Additionally, there are hard-surface pathways that allow residents some amount of exercise while staying within visual connection to the cottages and care assistants as well asoutdoor dining and barbecue amenities.

On the opposite side of the gazebo structure, there is also a patio. Here, residents, when supervised by staff, can sit and enjoy the more heavily wooded and more natural landscaping along the waterway.

Project Data

DESIGN FIRM

SFCS, Inc.
305 South Jefferson Street
Roanoke, VA 24011
United States
www.sfcs.com

AREAS/SIZES

- Site area: 2.4 acres, 9,712.45 square meters (104,544 square feet)
- Building footprint: 1,029.37 square meters (11,080 square feet) for each cottage
- Total building area: 2,058.82 square meters (22,161 square feet)
- Total area per resident: 85.78 square meters (923 square feet)

PARKING

There are surface parking spaces for five automobiles specifically for the cottages. In addition, there is an enclosed garage attached to each cottage and additional surface parking elsewhere on the larger campus.

COSTS (2008)

- Total building cost: $5,000,000 USD
- Cost per square meter: $2,429 USD
- Cost per square foot: $226 USD
- Investment per resident: $208,333 USD

RESIDENT AGE

Average age of residents: 88 years

RESIDENT PAYER MIX

Deupree Cottages accepts private-pay residents as well as Medicare and Medicaid (U.S. government subsidy) residents.

Chapter 24

A Study of Montgomery Place

REASONS FOR INCLUSION OF THIS SCHEME

- This scheme is a major repositioning/refurbishment of an urban, high-rise continuing-care retirement community.
- This scheme refocuses the emphasis of care, creation of community, and creation of home on the resident and away from the staff.
- This scheme seamlessly added an assisted-living continuing-care component into an existing built environment.

Building Description

Name of Scheme: Montgomery Place
Owner: Montgomery Place
Address:
Montgomery Place
5550 South Shore Drive
Chicago, IL 60637
United States
Occupied since: 2009

FIGURE 24-1 Montgomery Place sits on a prominent location in Chicago's Hyde Park neighborhood. *Barry Ruskin Photography*

FIGURE 24-2 Scheme location. *Courtesy of Pozzoni LLP*

Montgomery Place: United States

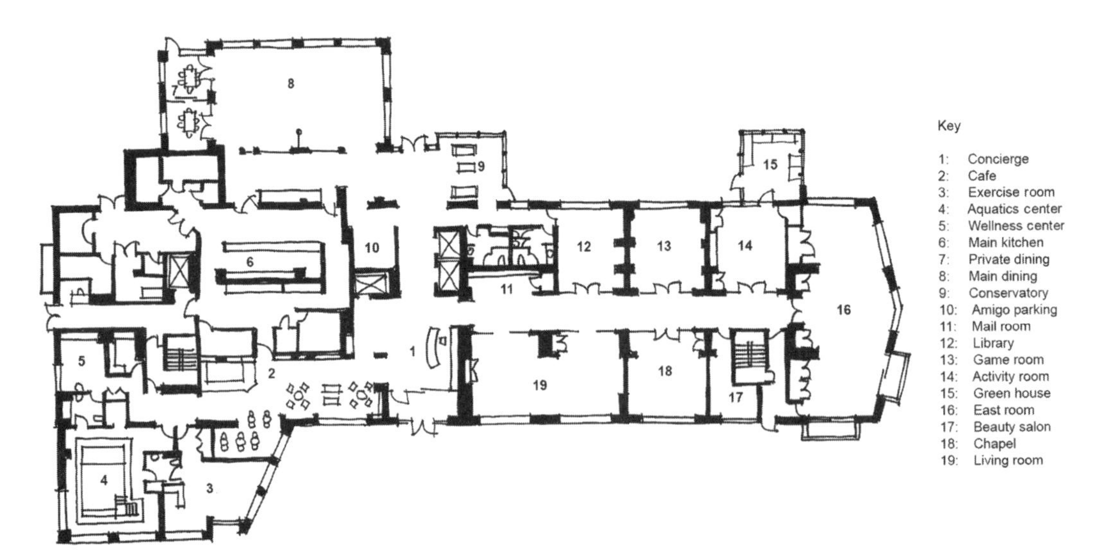

FIGURE 24-3 First-floor plan. *Courtesy of Pozzoni LLP*

Description of the Type of Community, Including Number of Residents

Located on prime real estate along the Lake Michigan shoreline just a short distance from downtown Chicago, Montgomery Place commands spectacular views of this Midwestern city and its surrounding natural amenities, including Lake Michigan. It also commands attention as a retirement community that has been popular because of its location and reputation, but has clearly understood the need to remake itself in order to maintain its premier status.

Montgomery Place is a complete continuing-care retirement community including 174 independent-living apartments, 12 assisted-living apartments, which have been added as a part of this repositioning project, eight apartments for dementia care, and 26 nursing-care places. Having been established at this location for several years, this vertical continuing-care retirement community has undergone a radical repositioning of its health-care component, which included the adding of the assisted living, as well as a major modernization of the independent-living apartments and public spaces, completed in 2009. Along with the physical repositioning of the health care, a new care approach was incorporated and complements the built environment.

The 14-story building sits on a very tight urban site in the heart of the well-established Hyde Park neighborhood of Chicago directly across from the famous Chicago Museum of Science and Industry, a very popular tourist destination. In order to preserve the open space of the small site but to maximize amenities of the facility, the repositioning design added a two-level structure near the building's main entry that visually realigns the building with the surrounding environmental urban

FIGURE 24-4 Much of the repositioning work addressed community spaces on the ground level. *Barry Ruskin Photography*

context. Additionally, as a demonstrative statement that the residents and their care program were at the center of Montgomery Place, the administrative offices were moved to a reclaimed portion of an existing under-building parking garage, to which light was provided by means of a large skylight well, providing additional and valuable above-ground portions of the building to dedicate to program and social space. The message was clear to the administrative and support staff that the repositioning work and new care approach were to place priority on residents.

With this repositioning project, most of the design work has taken place within the building itself. This design work has not only visually updated both the public and private spaces, but has done so in a contemporary choice of aesthetic finishes and furnishings. Additionally, this interior work reorganizes the existing spaces in a manner that feels comfortable to residents and, through the relocating and reorganizing of functions, emphasizes the newly established importance placed on the resident.

Most notable in this repositioning project is the creation of the new assisted-living care continuum within the existing building envelopment. This was accomplished by creating a dedicated household–concept assisted living on the third floor above ground level, which was originally traditional nursing care. This assisted-living floor includes the memory-support residents.

On the second floor above ground level, the renovations include restructuring the nursing care into a household model of 14 short-term residents who may need rehabilitation following a hospital stay prior to moving back into their apartment. In addition, there are beds here for 26 skilled-nursing residents within a newly designed household concept.

The independent-living apartments are located on the remaining 10 floors and have been each renovated with new kitchens, bathrooms, and added laundry areas. All renovation was done with a view toward the higher current average tenant age and aging-in-place requirements.

FIGURE 24-5 The nursing household includes a resident and preparation kitchen. *Courtesy of HammondCare*

Geographics

Vernacular Design

How does the scheme/environment respond to the locality?

As this project was predominantly a repositioning that only affected the exterior of the structure in minor ways, it is difficult to discuss the response to the local vernacular. The building is one high-rise in a block of high-rises and is neither obtrusive on the visual fabric, nor exceptional in original design. Without knowing its function, one would believe it was simply another high-rise apartment building that fills a space in the surrounding verticality of structure. However, the building addition near the front entry of the facility is complementary to the existing building's architecture and was designed in a manner that would enhance this entry and draw attention to the facility's new approach emphasizing the importance of the resident.

Care

Philosophy of Care

What is the operators' philosophy, and how does the building match this philosophy?

With the addition of assisted living and reduction in the number of nursing beds from the original during the repositioning, and the design of those assisted-living apartments and nursing beds into households, the philosophy of care within Montgomery Place was modified from a traditional hierarchical approach to a more resident-oriented approach. This change was not only desired by the administration, but essentially demanded by the residents. As their health began to decline, the assisted-living care model became the model of choice for residents: It meant that they were no longer forced to move directly from independent living to nursing care if they wished to remain in Montgomery Place. Along with the addition of the memory-support household, the continuum of care became more logical and more resident-friendly, particularly for those couples who needed this level of care for one spouse while the other remained completely independent.

Community and Belonging

How does the scheme design and operation support this ideal?

Montgomery Place is an excellent example where a repositioning design has been purposefully conceived to accommodate a new care approach. This approach has its focus on the resident, and the repositioning ensured

FIGURE 24-6 The new wellness center on the ground level allows passers-by to visually connect with residents. *Courtesy of Sylvia Gutierrez*

that there were care programs and amenities that would not only attract residents to Montgomery Place, but also enable them to maintain their residency for longer periods. This concept included a substantial increase in resident social and community spaces that would complement those offered in the surrounding urban neighborhood. A new informal café was included directly adjacent to the building's main entry to draw visitors and residents immediately together and to enhance the comfort of the entry sequence, providing a somewhat less formal, more inviting ambience.

A new resident wellness center also takes its place on the first floor in the front of the building. This area includes a small swimming pool that does not overwhelm residents with ostentation or extravagance but provides clearly what it was meant to provide: an opportunity for residents to exercise in comfort. This wellness center, complete with exercise equipment, and its prominent location within the building's layout, clearly makes a statement that Montgomery Place believes in resident physical and social well-being.

Montgomery Place is close to the University of Chicago and has appeal to former staff and associates of that university. This influence is seen in the remodeling of the first-floor "gallery," where there are nicely designed areas for art display, areas for both small-group and large-group meetings for those who share a wide range of interests as well as for social events. This influence is also evident in the fairly large library, which is well supported by many of the residents both in terms of contributions and patronage. All of these areas are easily accessible by residents as well as any visitors.

Innovation

If the operator pursues a policy of innovation and pursuit of excellence, how is this demonstrated?

It is very unusual for an operator of a continuing-care retirement community to revere the residents to the degree that Montgomery Place does. The general thinking when designing or redesigning such a facility is to place a lot of design and financial resources at the front entry to make a sort of "wow" first impression and to place the resident amenities around the back of the structure in order that visitors are not forced to see the elderly exercising or even relaxing with a cup of coffee. Montgomery Place has made a statement for all to see that the resident—the comfort and wellness of the

FIGURE 24-7 Community spaces include a library adjacent to a ground-level coffee shop. *Courtesy of Sylvia Gutierrez*

resident and the enjoyment of the resident—is what is important. This has been accomplished by taking the most valuable real estate of the building and dedicating it to these amenities and making certain that any visitor or even passers-by can see it for themselves.

Neighborhood Integration

Community Involvement

Is the scheme and service designed to integrate successfully with the local community?

Montgomery Place has been a part of the Hyde Park neighborhood of Chicago for many years and has established itself as an integral part of that neighborhood. The repositioning project serves to reinforce Montgomery Place's tie into the neighborhood fabric and, in fact, through its design, figuratively and literally, opens itself to community by placing resident amenities, which are available to other community members, right at the very front of the building. This has contributed to a perceived renewed interest in the facility by residents of the larger community, an increased sense of pride by residents of Montgomery Place, and enhanced pride of workplace by staff and administration.

Staff and Volunteers

Human Resources

Are policies and designs in place to attract good staff and volunteers?

With the introduction of assisted-living apartments and the repositioning of the nursing residence, a new, more resident-oriented philosophy of care had to be introduced into Montgomery Place. For the most part, existing staff accepted these changes, and the new staff necessary to accommodate the transformation were carefully selected to fulfill this philosophy. Overall, the staff training focuses on placing the residents first, regardless of their current residency. This integrates well with the building design approach, which also places residents first.

- Direct care hours per day per client: 3.7

Environmental Sustainability

ALTERNATIVE ENERGY SOURCES

No direct alternative energy sources were used on this project.

WATER CONSERVATION

The design of this project included the use of water-conservation measures that have been mandated by federal and state regulations including low water–usage plumbing fixtures.

ENERGY CONSERVATION

The repositioning design followed the principles and guidelines of the Leadership in Energy and Environmental Design (LEED). However, the facility owners chose not to obtain certification. Thus, wherever possible, the design complied with acceptable sustainability practices including the selection of high-efficiency appliances. In addition, the city of Chicago requires that 75 percent of all flat or low-sloping roofs on new construction be designed as "green" roofs. Two accessible green roofs were included in this design, one above the existing, refurbished dining room on the north side of the building, designed as a therapy garden, and the other over the newly constructed wellness center, designed as a dementia garden.

FIGURE 24-8 The repositioning included the design of a "gazebo" space with access to the north gardens. *Barry Ruskin Photography*

Outdoor Living

Garden

Does the garden support principles of care?

Despite the limited amount of land on this urban site, the repositioning work has creatively worked to ensure as much access to outdoor spaces as possible. In addition to retaining and refurbishing the existing garden at ground level, two rooftop gardens were created to provide dedicated outdoor spaces. The new work on the site also included a conservatory and greenhouse, which connect well with the existing garden spaces.

The renovated social spaces on the ground level are very well connected to the fairly substantial garden space created on the building's north side, opposite the main entry. This connection is both visual and physical and, as such, is quite welcoming. This garden space, while surrounded by adjacent high-rise structures, provides the user with at least a partial sense of being away from an urban area and in a natural setting that enhances contemplative activity.

FIGURE 24-9 The north garden area, above the parking garage, provides contemplative spaces away from the city noises. *Barry Ruskin Photography*

Project Data

DESIGN FIRM

Dorsky Hodgson + Partners, Inc.
23240 Chagrin Blvd., Suite 300
Cleveland, OH 44122
United States
www.dorskyhodgson.com

AREAS/SIZES

- Site area: 6,070.284 square meters (65,340 square feet; 1.5 acres)
- Building footprint: 1,860.66 square meters (20,028 square feet)
- Total building area: 21,033.25 square meters (226,400 square feet)
- Total area per resident: 1,029 square feet per resident and apartment

PARKING

Although specific parking information is not available, there are sufficient parking spaces under the building for the independent-living apartments.

Montgomery Place: United States

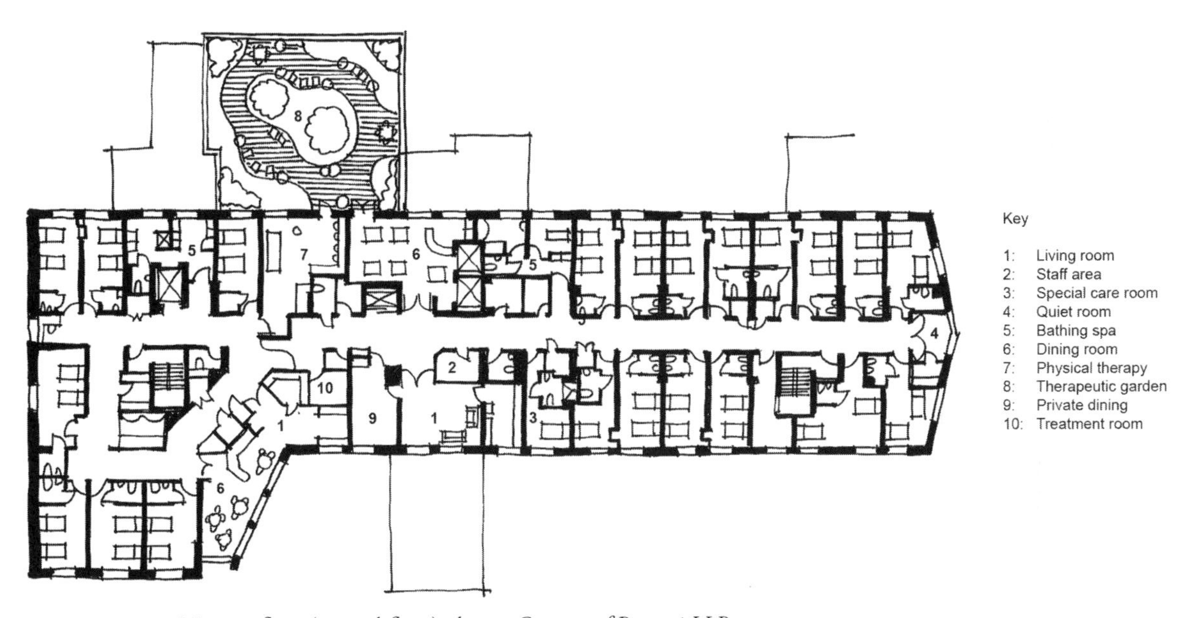

FIGURE 24-10 Nursing-floor (ground-floor) plan. *Courtesy of Pozzoni LLP*

COSTS (2009)

- Total building cost: $12,300,000 USD (Note: This project was a repositioning/refurbishment project; thus, the overall costs reflected here are for this portion of the work and do not include original construction costs.)
- Cost per square meters: $585 USD
- Cost per square foot: $54 USD
- Investment per resident: $55,909 (Note: This investment per resident includes 174 independent-living apartments, 12 assisted-living residents, eight special-care dementia residents, and 26 nursing residents for a total of 220 residents used in this calculation.)

RESIDENT AGE

Average age of residents: 83 years

RESIDENT PAYER MIX

Residents within the independent-living retirement apartments can either pay an entrance fee or a straight monthly rental fee. Residents in the assisted-living and nursing-care units are either individual private pay or covered by individual long-term insurance.

Chapter 25

A Study of Park Homes at Parkside

REASONS FOR INCLUSION OF THIS SCHEME

- This scheme provides a design for stand-alone nursing households clustered around a central support and social building.
- This scheme took design cues from the care program that was established for the environment.
- This scheme provides a radical change in nursing-care approach, particularly for a conservative region of the United States.
- This scheme fits well within the context of the surrounding neighborhood of single-family homes.

Building Description

Name of Scheme: Park Homes at Parkside
Owner: Parkside Mennonite Retirement Community, a not-for-profit faith-based organization
Address:
Parkside Homes, Inc.
200 Willow Road
Hillsboro, KS 67063
United States
Occupied since: 2007

FIGURE 25-1 The scheme's exterior design blends with the surrounding single-family housing. *Courtesy of Lu Janzen*

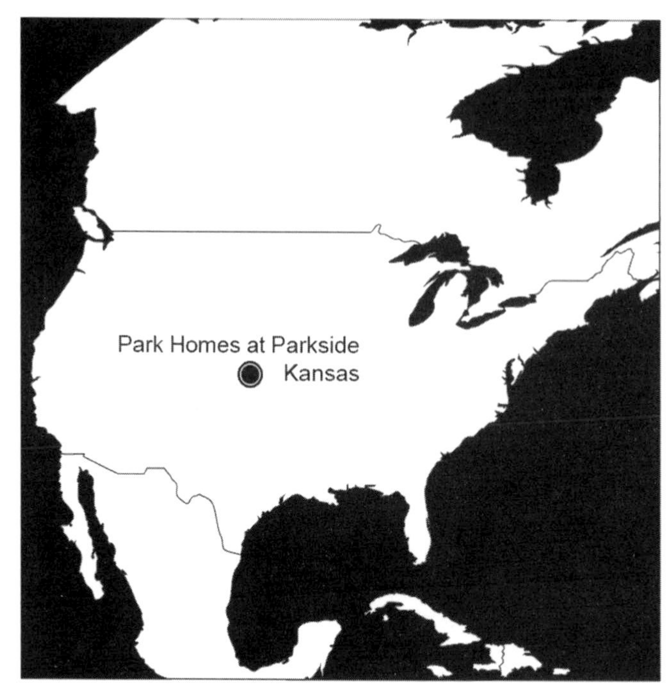

FIGURE 25-2 Scheme location. *Courtesy of Pozzoni LLP*

Park Homes at Parkside: United States

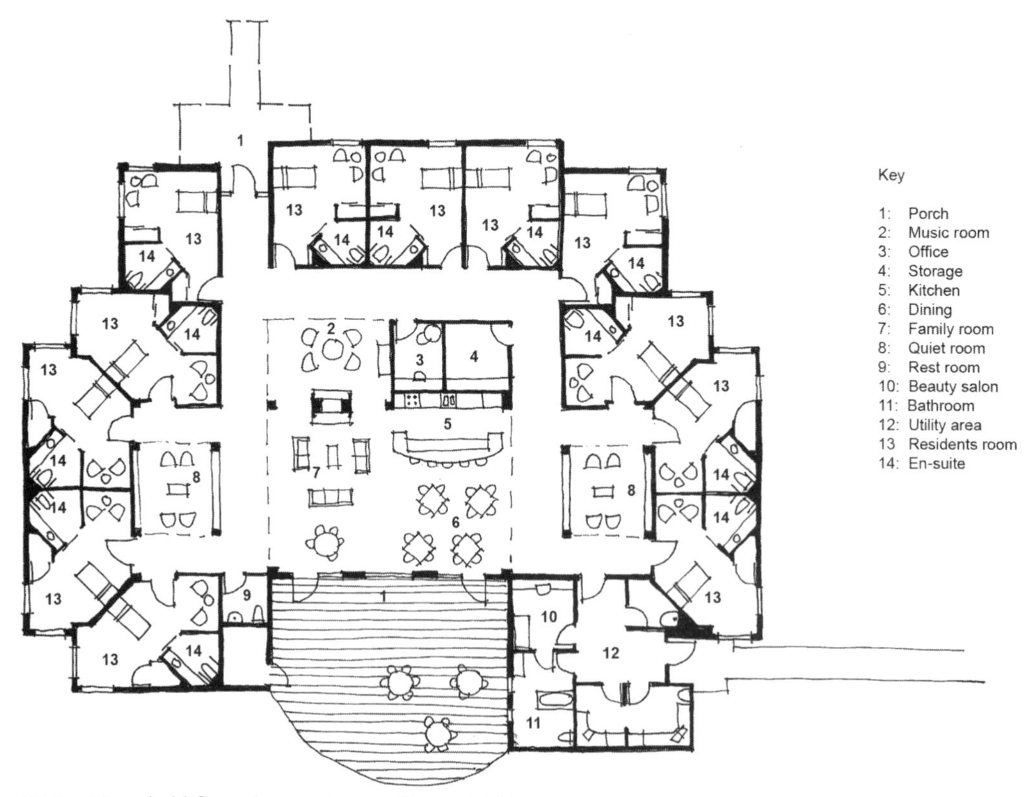

FIGURE 25-3 Household floor plan. *Courtesy of Pozzoni LLP*

Description of the Type of Community, Including Number of Residents

Established in the mid-twentieth century, Parkside is a modest retirement community located in a small rural town on the plains of the central United States. The community includes—besides nursing care—assisted-living apartments and independent-living apartments in separate structures.

The nursing scheme has places for 24 residents within the first building phase, divided into 12 nursing residents in each of two stand-alone households. These are the first two of five planned stand-alone households. They are meant to be replacement aged-care beds for nursing beds that were constructed in the 1960s, 1970s, and 1980s in a medical model arrangement.

The development of the project also entails the conversion of the old, medical model nursing structures into a community center that will house the main commercial kitchen, laundry, meeting rooms, library, and bistro café.

The household concept, called Park Homes, was purposefully designed as large houses for a number of reasons. The surrounding neighborhood consists primarily of single-family, single-story homes in a typical American suburban layout. Additionally, the care provider wanted to make a significant and demonstrable visual break from the traditional nursing home with its institutional aesthetic and to break new ground in the care program by radically altering the environment in which it is provided. Finally, Parkside wished to provide a model of both care and environment from which they could learn, through evidence-based design, and could use those lessons as they moved into the next phases of their overall campus repositioning strategy.

Geographics

Vernacular Design

How does the scheme/environment respond to the locality?

Being located within a small community and being surrounded by a subdivision, it was important to be complementary to the surrounding built environment. There was no question of making an architectural statement beyond stating that Park Homes is a good neighbor and an important part of the community. The exterior design of the households is intentionally replicative of single-family homes not only to make the residents feel that they are their own "home," but to make the neighbors feel comfortable as they enter the larger neighborhood.

Care

Philosophy of Care

What is the operators' philosophy, and how does the building match this philosophy?

The philosophy of care at Park Homes is intricately connected to the built environment of the Homes. In fact, it was that philosophy of providing an experience of care for the residents within an environment that approximated their own homes that drove the design brief. Of course, it was impossible to re-create each resident's home environment, but the design of the households takes into account the typology of home, at least as experienced in the United States, with clear definition of household "public" space, shared "public-private" space, and clearly "private" space.

The public spaces in this design, which include the main entry and living room, provide areas where residents and visitors can interact. The public-private spaces allow residents to invite more well-known visitors or perhaps family into a more casual setting where the social interaction may take place. The private spaces include primarily the resident bedrooms where visitors are rarely invited, as this is the exclusive domain of the residents themselves.

The underlying principle throughout the design and care programming process was to provide both the typology and aesthetic iconography that would provide the resident, the care staff, and visitors an intuitive sense of the place as home. However, it was also important to easily enable residents to visually access the more public spaces of the household in order that those who may be experiencing some level of dementia could connect with any activities that may be taking place in these public areas. This is accomplished by providing transitory

FIGURE 25-4 Transition spaces allow residents additional privacy and social interaction adjacent to their bedroom entry. © *darussellphotography.com*

spaces that separate the private and public spaces without having resident room doors open directly into the living or public spaces. These transitory spaces serve the added purpose of acting as a sort of personal living room for the residents whose rooms abut the space. They are used for individual conversations with neighboring residents and for activities, such as watching television, which may be disruptive to other residents.

In addition to the delineation of the household areas, a concerted effort was made during the design process to provide ample private space for the residents, not only to allow them to make this room their own by enabling the inclusion of significant amounts of personal items and furniture, but also to provide enough space for couples to feel completely comfortable. This also allowed a level of financial security for the owner, as these rooms are sized to be easily convertible and licensable as assisted living in the event that nursing-care demand waned. An added benefit to the increased room size is that staff assistance space, when required for such things as transfers, is increased and thus provides a greater ease for these tasks.

Each resident room has an en-suite bathroom that contains significant storage cabinets and lavatory counter space for residents' personal items and toiletries. A wall cabinet is provided for storage of resident pharmaceuticals except for scheduled drugs or those needing refrigeration. Full accommodation for residents needing ambulatory assistance is provided in the bathrooms with a permanent grab bar incorporated into the countertop adjacent to the toilet as well as a swing-down grab bar on

FIGURE 25-5 Resident bedrooms are large enough to allow variety in furniture selection and placement. © *darussellphotography.com*

the opposite toilet side, which can be used when in the roll-in shower or while on the toilet. The countertop grab bar can easily double as a towel bar and is readily available for the resident who may need minor balance assistance while at the lavatory. When it is not necessary to have wheelchair access to the lavatory, a cabinet face is in place, allowing storage beneath the sink area. This cabinet can be easily removed by staff when access is required.

This attention to detail that is reflective of the detail of care also carries through the seemingly minor details. Most resident rooms have multiple windows on more than a single wall allowing visual access to several exterior views; there is in most rooms a built-in window seat that not only allows an additional seating area but is the location for storage when the window seat is lifted up; each room has easily interchangeable electrical junction boxes that allow staff to move the regulatory required over-bed light, allowing residents free choice in furniture arrangement in their private space.

The elements of home and iconography of a stereotypical U.S. home have been integrated into the design through careful selection of furnishings and finishes, inclusion of warm wood trim throughout and a visually centered fireplace. Additionally, the open plan includes a preparatory kitchen, available to residents at any time, that allows cooking aromas to waft throughout the house as meals are prepared. More importantly, this allows residents who are predominantly female, to take part in the meal preparation either actively or vicariously, and in doing so, provides a connection to their former home and former activities.

FIGURE 25-6 En-suite bathrooms provide ample storage and maintain resident dignity and privacy.
© *darussellphotography.com*

Community and Belonging

How does the scheme design and operation support this ideal?

The community of Hillsboro, Kansas is a tightly knit rural town of about 5,000 residents. Most of these residents have spent the majority of their lives living and working within the community and are at least acquainted with many of their fellow Kansans. Thus the objective of Park Homes is to maintain the community connection that residents have developed over many years and to establish a cohesive community of campus residents as a sort of subcategory to the larger surrounding community.

FIGURE 25-7
The household kitchen encourages resident participation in meal preparation and serving.
© *darussellphotography.com*

This task was undertaken in a variety of ways, which critically informed the design and planning of the repositioned campus to include the stand-alone nursing households. The operator's decision to include unconnected households, even in the sometimes harsh climate of the central United States, was an important element and one that was discussed with the design team at length. In the end, the decision not to physically connect the homes was based on the intended experience of residents, staff, and visitors living in a home, leaving that home for social outings and firmly underlying the fact that these structures were indeed the residents' homes. Additionally, the placement of the homes around the converted original building in order to create two defined and secured exterior spaces—one contemplative, the other for activities—reinforces the nature of community and, with unsupervised access to these exterior spaces by residents, provides another comforting aspect of home.

Parkside is located in a residential portion of the community and is surrounded, at least on three sides, by single-family homes on suburban-sized building lots. As originally designed in the mid-twentieth century, the structures of Parkside were quite institutional in their aesthetic and, frankly, did not fit in well with their architectural context. While the exterior design of Park Homes is not contemporary or avant-garde, it is residential in scale and detailing, and does take its contextual design from the neighborhood and from the midwestern United States.

The sense of home is pervasive within these constructed households, if perhaps not elsewhere on campus. Keeping in mind that these households represent the first phase in a long-range plan to reposition this campus as a resident-centered care organization, this sense of home is rather intuitive to anyone who enters the buildings beginning with the building organization and continuing with the entire residential aesthetic carefully carried through the design. The care program complements and contributes to this sense of home with staff presence being noninvasive. There is easy camaraderie among staff and residents and an obvious freedom of choice given to residents in their activities of daily living.

Innovation

If the operator pursues a policy of innovation and pursuit of excellence, how is this demonstrated?

For Park Homes, innovation in providing long-term nursing care was a goal that was inclusive of both the environment and the care program. Emulating the experience of home for the residents while simultaneously providing the necessary nursing care was a concept that was embraced by the administration, board members, and the surrounding community. Convincing staff to abandon their vertically integrated tasks for a more universal-worker approach was a completely different story.

Over the short life of this project, it has been difficult to convince staff members that their old approach to care—that is, compartmentalizing tasks based on job titles—would simply not provide the type of long-term care envisioned by the administration and manifested in the built environment. While these issues were being addressed, they became more complicated by the fact that in the rural Midwest, competent and appropriate care staff are difficult to both obtain and retain. It appears that, until the "buy-in" of staff is complete, Park Homes will fall somewhat short of the mark of excellence that is

FIGURE 25-8 The household living room provides a space for quiet and intimate social interaction. © *darussellphotography.com*

evidenced in the concept's potential. Certainly, however, there is a policy of innovation in place, even if it is difficult to enforce, and certainly, there is a pursuit of excellence demonstrated in the commitment of the project, both environmentally and programmatically, to a more human approach to nursing care.

Neighborhood Integration

Community Involvement

Is the scheme and service designed to integrate successfully with the local community?

Both the design scheme and the program concept were conceived to be totally integrated within the community of the campus and the larger community and to allow residents to maintain their community connections as well as the overriding feeling of being at home. You can imagine that when the additional three households are completed and the existing nursing building is remodeled into a nursing community, the full involvement of both residents and staff will be facilitated by the built environs. It should allow residents to experience all the aspects of home while still receiving nursing care within a licensed environment. It will be interesting to visit the campus again to witness whether the vision of the administration has fully caught hold by then.

Visitors and local community residents are encouraged to visit the households by the provision of a variety of comfortable and easily accessed environments that promote social interaction with the residents. Because the surrounding community is one with which residents are closely intertwined socially and professionally, this seems to be a natural community in which to provide such arrangement. Thus, the community and Park Homes seemed to be made for one another. When the issues with staffing accepting a broader approach to the provision of care are resolved, the connection with the community is bound to be strengthened.

Staff and Volunteers

Human Resources

Are policies and designs in place to attract good staff and volunteers?

Certainly, the environmental design is intended to attract the best staff available. Not only is it a new and comfortable environment, but it is staff-friendly—intended to allow more expedient care of residents by staff, which also allows a higher quality of care by a limited number of staff. It is also true that the staffing at Park Homes is probably the best and most qualified available to that rural location. However, unlike a more urban location, the available staff pool is quite limited, resulting in some amount of resistance to the vision of staff functioning by the administration. This is an issue that is being addressed by the administration, but with limited success due to the availability of staff. It is believed that as staff turnover occurs at Park Homes, more "open-minded" employees will be brought to the households, and as applicable training occurs, this issue will be resolved.

Without question, the Park Homes have attracted a higher-quality and broader number of volunteers. Perhaps because there is not as much required from volunteers and the simple fact that, as volunteers, they can set their own schedules and, to some degree, tasks, this segment of the campus population has thrived and will undoubtedly continue to do so as the remaining phases of the project are completed.

- Direct care hours per day per client: 3.4

Environmental Sustainability

ALTERNATIVE ENERGY SOURCES

While initial budgetary concerns meant that no cutting-edge environmental innovations or alternative energy sources could be incorporated into the design, there was attention paid to more passive sustainability approaches. In particular, the incorporation of a variety of both natural and artificial lighting sources was paramount. Regulatory requirements mandated particular light levels at various locations, including the kitchen counter work surface and the resident bed, as these are considered task locations for care staff. The lighting design approach allows a good deal of natural lighting in both public and private spaces but also provides artificial lighting controllable in various levels, depending on either the time of day or the activities that may be occurring.

WATER CONSERVATION

Water conservation is an important community issue in central Kansas, which is in the high plains and a somewhat arid area of the United States. Most potable water is provided by way of extraction from deep aquifers either by the municipality or by privately dug wells. In deference to an ingrained social attitude as well as mandated conservation regulations,

FIGURE 25-9
The combination of natural and artificial lighting allows a variety of lighting levels.
© *darussellphotography.com*

Park Homes is fitted with low–usage plumbing fixtures and appliances.

ENERGY CONSERVATION

The detailing of Park Homes includes the maximization of insulative building materials and construction methods, including highly insulated windows and doors. Highly energy-efficient heating and air-conditioning equipment were chosen, and zoning of these systems was designed to allow varying comfort levels for residents within the household.

Outdoor Living

Garden

Does the garden support principles of care?

The building arrangements, as well as the buildings themselves, are situated in order to allow residents full, unrestricted access to the exterior. The courts, which are created by the buildings, are secured and are designed for both contemplative and active usage. The household design provides access to these courtyards through the family room/dining room areas, first into a covered patio and then into the courtyard itself. The covered patio, with its large overhang, allows residents to use the exterior even when it may be raining and also provides a shaded area that can be used even when the summer sun is hot.

Currently, the contemplative garden has been completed while the activity courtyard will be created during a subsequent phase of construction. As an added benefit to this first courtyard, a kitchen garden is available not only as a meaningful activity for the residents but also for use by the food service staff in meal preparation. Plantings have been chosen not only for their attractiveness, but to bring birds and butterflies into the courtyard for the enjoyment of the residents.

When residents are on an "outing" to the nursing community building, they pass through the courtyards as the most direct route as well as the most secure. This provides familiarity of the exterior spaces for residents and promotes the use of the courtyard and its amenities.

FIGURE 25-10 The covered back patio provides shade and protection during rain. *Courtesy of Lu Janzen*

Project Data

DESIGN FIRM

Crepidoma Consulting, LLC (design architect)
4123 Trowbridge Street
Fairfax, VA 22030
United States
www.crepidoma.com
Invision Architecture (architect of record)

AREAS/SIZES

- Site area: 29,350.0 square meters (315,920.77 square feet; 7.25 acres)
- Building footprint: 793.2 square meters (8,538 square feet)
- Total building area: 1,586.4 square meters (17,076 square feet; two households, 8,538 square feet each)
- Total area per resident: 66.10 square meters (712 square feet)

PARKING

For the first phase of this project (two households), there are 22 hard-surface parking spaces, including two handicapped-accessible spaces. These spaces are conveniently located near the front doors of the households and are specifically for visitors to the households. Staff parking has been provided prior to this project elsewhere on the campus.

COSTS (MARCH 2006)

- Total building cost: $2,600,000 USD
- Cost per square meters: $1,639 USD
- Cost per square foot: $152 USD
- Investment per resident: $108,333 USD

RESIDENT AGE

Average age of residents: 85 years

RESIDENT PAYER MIX

A mixture of private pay and Medicaid reimbursement makes up the resident payer mix. This ratio between private/Medicaid varies on a regular basis. Park Homes does not distinguish between either environmental or programmatic provision based on source of payment for these services.

Chapter 26

A Study of Childers Place

REASONS FOR INCLUSION OF THIS SCHEME

- This scheme is the manifestation of the philosophy of universal workers into the built form.
- The scheme's design incorporates abundant natural lighting to the benefit of residents.
- The utilization of resident access to the exterior spaces is particularly encouraged through the design and services.
- The incorporation of commercial space as an approach to creating community is innovative.
- The use of local materials and a contemporary design palette provides an aesthetic that is comforting without being contrived.

Building Description

Name of Scheme: Childers Place

Owner: Mary E. Bivins Foundation, a not-for-profit, faith-based organization

Address:

6600 Killgore Drive
Amarillo, TX 79106
United States

Occupied since: 2007

FIGURE 26-1 The exterior design is contemporary but also calming.
©Chris Cooper, Courtesy Perkins Eastman

FIGURE 26-2 Scheme location. *Courtesy of Pozzoni LLP*

Childers Place: United States

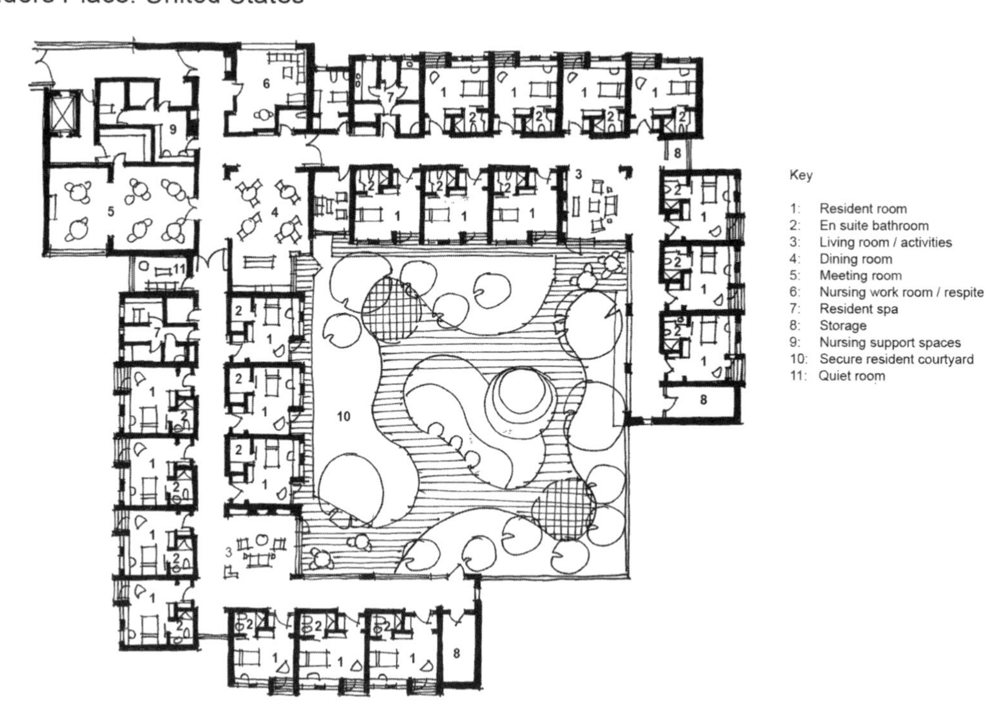

FIGURE 26-3 Household and courtyard floor plan. *Courtesy of Pozzoni LLP*

Description of the Type of Community, Including Number of Residents

Located in the often forgotten panhandle of Texas, The Bivins Foundation has created with Childers Place, a skilled nursing facility that is at once welcoming and tranquil even in the sometimes unforgiving climate of the vast high plains of the United States. The Foundation provides a variety of aged-care and housing services to the residents in the Amarillo area within a variety of venues. This addition to the Foundation's care program provides nursing care in a residential setting for 60 residents, all within quite large private rooms that have full en-suite bathrooms and ample space to arrange a variety of furniture. These 60 individuals reside in six households consisting of 10 residents each. Each two households, while they have distinct living spaces, are connected with a common social and dining space located near both the entry to the households and their connection to the remainder of the facility spaces. The households are fully connected to the remainder of the building, which houses larger social and amenity spaces fully accessible by the residents and by the members of the larger community of Amarillo.

Childers Place stands in contrast both in care programming and aesthetics to the adjacent traditional nursing home, also part of a larger but somewhat inconsistent Bivins Foundation campus. The contemporary building forms and layout provide a visual and harmonious link to the geographic region through its sympathetic forms and material use while remaining clearly residential in execution.

But Childers Place is more than a simple nursing home. It has been designed to contribute to a feeling of community for the residents and to entice the larger Amarillo community to use the structure and interact with the residents. The building takes advantage of the site topography to provide a two-story structure on the south and west portions of the building while maintaining a single level on the north and east portions. This siting not only allows for a smaller and more sustainable building footprint by allowing a functional lower level, but also maximizes the amount of natural light that penetrates the building spaces.

In addition, the building design includes approximately 8,000 square feet (743.22 square meters) of leasable space intended for use by elder-care agencies or elder-care resource providers. This not only initiates visits to the community and adds revenue to the program, but provides a very convenient location for those services most needed by the residents and their family members. This design addition and its use also provide a subtle marketing tool for Childers Place. As the scheme remains relatively new, this space has yet to be leased and its financial or programmatic success untested.

Geographics

Vernacular Design

How does the scheme/environment respond to the locality?

The use of materials and collaborating colors that are familiar to this area's population serves to deinstitutionalize the building as it is first seen. While the design has a character of its own, it can be called neither purely residential nor institutional, and as such piques the human curiosity to explore the building. It has a sense of calmly having been in this location for some time, yet is refreshingly new and somewhat intuitive to the observer.

One of the building program objectives was to create a tranquil and therapeutic atmosphere. This objective is evidenced in the design throughout the site and the building. The main building entrance provides appropriate, understated protection but requires the visitor to visually take in the building's forms and finishes during the entry sequence. Once inside, the abundant daylight not only floods the common spaces, but draws the eye upward to the volume ceilings and clerestory windows and also outward to the defined and developed courtyards formed by the creation of the facility's residential households.

FIGURE 26-4 The interior common spaces are flooded with natural daylight. *© Chris Cooper, Courtesy Perkins Eastman*

The site for Childers Place is suburban, with surrounding development being recently completed and controlled by means of government zoning restrictions. A fairly large water feature is located to the southwest of the building across the main access road and provides some interest of view for four of the six households. The building, as well as the adjacent Bivins Nursing Home, is surrounded by a manicured lawn; however, the small amount of vertical landscape material is concentrated near the building. While this planting remains somewhat immature due to the age of the construction, the courtyards at Childers are well landscaped and inviting, and each contains its own series of raised planters, lawn furniture, or garden feature.

Care

Philosophy of Care

What is the operators' philosophy, and how does the building match this philosophy?

FIGURE 26-5 A household living room designed to a residential scale. ©*Chris Cooper, Courtesy Perkins Eastman*

One of the significant differences between Childers Place and the adjacent, more traditional Bivins Nursing Home is the philosophy of care and how that philosophy influenced and informed the design of the building. The designers were charged with creating a "center of excellence" for nursing and memory care for the aged. In collaboration, the designers and owners attempted to redefine nursing care into more of a hospitality approach, while retaining the ability to ensure safety and community engagement for these long-term elderly residents.

Childers Place staff members are considered modified universal staff, each providing services that cross over distinct staff position descriptions. This is intended to foster, within the household design, a sense of family between residents and staff. This approach not only encompasses staff, but includes family members as an integral part of the overall care program for each resident. Additionally, the facility's recognition of the importance of what the universal staff does is demonstrated by the inclusion of significant areas for ongoing training purposes and the location of staff functional areas in what might be described as premium real estate.

The design of the building clearly followed the creation of the care program and was done with specific attention to maximizing staff efficiencies without sacrificing attention to the resident needs. As one studies the design with the care program overlain, one can soon see that care was given in each design decision to accommodate the resident first, the program second, and the efficiency of the staff. This was all accomplished not only in the design layout, but in the incorporation of technology that functions specifically to allow staff to provide quality care more efficiently and expeditiously. This technology is targeted at easing staff tasks while at the same time familiarizing them with an individual resident's daily rhythms. It also allows staff to understand and coordinate schedules of residents around those rhythms rather than the convenience of the staff member.

Community and Belonging

How does the scheme design and operation support this ideal?

With the approach to care provision initiated by the Bivins Foundation, the sense of belonging for the residents as well as the staff has increased. Although the transition from a traditional staffing model to a universal worker approach has, by the Foundation's own admission, proven somewhat difficult for staff, the staff members have, in the end, fully accepted this care approach and in doing so, are assisting in the creation of a community within Childers Place.

Having an established reputation and presence in Amarillo, the Foundation has, over the years, created a community of its own. Childers Place is an extension of that community, and residents enter the facility already somewhat inured to belonging to that community. However, the building's design enhances and reinforces that sense both through its layout of households and community space and its selection of familiar finishes and materials. This sense of belonging and of community is subtly underpinned by the design's lightness. By not being overtly institutional, by the introduction of a large amount of natural light and by the openness of the plan, the design is certainly not oppressive, and thus the resident or visitor does not have "institution" within their thoughts, allowing those thoughts to turn to socialization—to making the most of the time spent in the building and to living within this community.

Innovation

If the operator pursues a policy of innovation and pursuit of excellence, how is this demonstrated?

With the opening of Childers Place, the Bivins Foundation has made a commitment to innovation that benefits its residents. It is manifest in the full

FIGURE 26-6 Community rooms provide spaces for residents and visitors to meet. *©Chris Cooper, Courtesy Perkins Eastman*

FIGURE 26-7 Household spas allow residents a place to pamper themselves. *©Chris Cooper, Courtesy Perkins Eastman*

collaboration and full understanding of programmatic goals by the designer and care provider prior to the initiation of the design. It is manifest in the introduction of advanced technologies that aid in care provision, not simply to make life easier for staff. It is also evidenced in the introduction of natural light and ease of access to outdoor spaces. In short, the pursuit of excellence at Childers Place is embodied in a well-coordinated and well-considered holistic and integrative approach to design as it pertains to long-term nursing care.

Neighborhood Integration

Community Involvement

Is the scheme and service designed to integrate successfully with the local community?

The location of Childers Place requires visitors and guests to travel by automobile to the facility, being located in a suburban development. Thus, integration into the neighborhood is somewhat problematic. However, the building's design takes into account the need for involvement of members from the larger community and has included a substantial area intended to be leased to organizations that cater to the needs of the aged community. This is an innovative gesture not only to the commitment of Childers Place to the aged clients it serves, but to the broader aged community in and around Amarillo. While the space has been slow to lease up, it will in time. When it is fully rented, it will provide a purpose for visiting Childers Place as well as necessary services for those who are either residents of Childers Place or those from outside the facility who simply require assistance.

Staff and Volunteers

Human Resources

Are policies and designs in place to attract good staff and volunteers?

When Childers Place was envisioned by the Foundation, it deliberately undertook a new model of aged care and, with that model, a new approach to staffing. This approach encompassed a change from traditional staffing with specific and limited duties to a modified universal-staffing approach where staff members perform a variety of tasks that cross over those traditional boundaries.

FIGURE 26-8 Secured exterior courtyards allow free resident access. ©*Chris Cooper, Courtesy Perkins Eastman*

As with many providers who transition to this care approach, there was some initial resistance as well as some significant training involved for Childers Place staff. However, the system initiation has been successful, and residents, staff, and administration are all proponents of this universal staffing approach, believing it creates a more collaborative and familial feeling within the households.

- Direct care hours per day per client: 4.8 hours

Environmental Sustainability

ALTERNATIVE ENERGY SOURCES

No direct alternative energy sources were incorporated into the design of Childers Place.

WATER CONSERVATION

Mandatory low–water-usage plumbing fixtures have been used in the design.

ENERGY CONSERVATION

The site design of Childers Place was manipulated in order to severely limit the disturbance of the site and to fully balance the cut and fill of the earth for the building. By locating the service and storage areas required for the building in earth-insulated spaces, lower energy consumption was achieved. The maximization of natural daylight combined with deep roof overhangs to control direct sunlight is a significant design feature that serves to minimize artificial lighting and its energy consumption. An increased amount of natural landscaping covering has been accomplished by using

FIGURE 26-9 Each resident room is full of natural light, and many have easy access to the exterior. *©Chris Cooper, Courtesy Perkins Eastman*

land-banked parking, which involves identifying areas of the site that could accommodate additional parking, grading that land for future use, and retaining existing landscape elements for that area until the additional parking is necessary. At that time, a pervious paving solution will be used for this new parking area.

Outdoor Living

Garden

Does the garden support principles of care?

It seems that the outdoors is but a few steps away regardless of where one might be within the building. This is often quite literally true as the exterior spaces, which are enfolded within the arms of the resident households, are as carefully designed as those households themselves. Large expanses of windows, carefully shaded from the often hot Texas sun by broad roof overhangs, often lead the eye to the exterior courtyards, gardens, and exterior social spaces. These spaces are not only easily accessed visually, but physically, with doors seemingly from every interior space extending the invitation to participate in an outdoor activity.

One benefit of Childers Place is the accessibility of residents, or at least some residents, to the outdoors directly from their bedrooms. Of course, this outdoor space is secured from resident elopement by both the building itself and by connecting decorative fencing, but it provides a way for residents to feel less confined and certainly less restricted. In those rooms that are fortunate enough to have direct access, the room itself seems to flow without interruption of walls to the exterior. This invites residents to participate in whatever activity is taking place in the courtyard or simply sit quietly, without staff supervision, on their private patio and enjoy the surroundings. This design feature provides reinforcement to both residents and family members that the residents are indeed living their life as they choose, not as the care provider may deem appropriate.

FIGURE 26-10 Household kitchens encourage resident participation in meal preparation. *©Chris Cooper, Courtesy Perkins Eastman*

Project Data

DESIGN FIRM

Perkins Eastman
1100 Liberty Avenue
Pittsburgh, PA 15222
United States
www.perkinseastman.com

AREAS/SIZES

- Site area: 56,205.69 square meters (604,993 square feet; 13.89 acres)
- Building footprint: 6,317.41 square meters (68,000 square feet)
- Total building area: 9,754.82 square meters (105,000 square feet)
- Total area per resident: 162.58 square meters (1, 750 square feet)

PARKING

Surface parking for 77 automobiles.

COSTS (2007)

- Total building cost: $18,607,000 USD
- Cost per square meter: $1,907 USD
- Cost per square foot: $177.21 USD
- Investment per resident: $310,117 USD

RESIDENT AGE

Average age of residents: 80 years

RESIDENT PAYER MIX

Childers Place participates in the Medicaid and Medicare programs as administered by the state of Texas. In addition, it accepts private pay and long-term care insurance.

Conclusions

This book contains 26 examples of older persons' housing in seven different countries. The authors' purpose was to celebrate unique concepts in the approach to housing, mostly with care options, in several different countries. We believe that the chapters unfold a delightful consistency in the approach of committed individuals or small teams. In almost every instance we find a passion for excellence. This passion ignites an unstoppable thrust taking the development process through obstacles that would often have been easier to accommodate with inevitable compromise to the overall vision.

A few examples are brand new and a few quite older. Like a good song though, quality endures and these older developments provide an important backdrop to the picture we have tried to paint.

It is important to stress again that, although some of the buildings illustrate good architectural design—sometimes contemporary, sometimes eclectic—still others appear perfectly plain and perfunctory. This is fundamentally a refreshing aspect of the selections. Some of the Japanese schemes, for example, could not possibly be included in any debate which focuses strictly on architecture. Their inclusion owes more to the service they provide in a country leading the way into the world's aging demography. The world's population is growing older, but the huge variety of specifically designed buildings to accommodate this can appear confusing. Apart from small pockets of relative wealth, societies now generally recognize that they can only offer accommodation to elderly individuals with very particular needs in residencies which address broader elderly issues only. Inevitably entry levels will change from country to country, but the recent world economic downturn has placed a spotlight on the expense of aging. Countries do respond in different ways, often, but not always, to very similar criteria. We have seen the search for the right answers grow increasingly diverse over the last 15 years. Schemes focusing on dementia, on integration and, conversely, on isolation, have all been pursued and are included as examples in this book.

What are some of the common themes of these case studies?

First, producing good design for older people is not a question of money. What is evident from these case studies is that they were, first and foremost, focused on the person. They were not first and foremost driven by a financial model. That is not to say that budgetary issues were not an issue, because they were. But so often we as authors have seen other aged care projects that have started from an "economic" operational model or from a fixed capital cost and then the operator and architect have tried to shoe-horn any stray philosophy or beliefs that they might have.

The case studies in this book have approached their challenge from a completely different perspective. While the range of capital cost in these services differs enormously, all of these examples have started with a philosophy of care that is demonstrably focused on the person. They have been designed with that philosophy at the forefront of their thinking, and then and only then have they addressed the financial issues with which all providers have had to contend. By this method they have given their philosophy of care a fighting chance to prevail and to prosper. And it is our judgment that they have been successful.

Second, and closely related to the first point, is the very evident passion of the owner and service provider of these services. These schemes have been very much driven by their owners. At Gojikara village in Japan, or de Hogeweyk Village in The Netherlands, or Belong in England, or Wintringham in Australia, or Park Homes in the United States, the drive and the vision behind them and the determination to see that vision expressed in a physical form has come from their owners and this is a common theme throughout these case studies. That is not to say that the architects have been unimportant. To the contrary, the architects on these case studies have had the pleasure of working with clients who have a clear and uncompromising view of what they want to achieve and are determined to achieve it.

Third, regulatory and planning challenges are not the exclusive burden and challenge for any one country alone. Regulatory and planning hurdles are common to the seven countries which are featured in this book. However, a constant theme in these case studies is the impressive determination of the designers and owners of these services to overcome hurdles that may confront them. These hurdles might be fire regulations or they might be planning constraints or they might be prescriptive funding rules. What characterizes these case studies is not simply the determination to prevail but the ingenuity with which they have done so. We believe that the reason they are successful is that the whole scheme was grounded in a philosophical base that was person-focused. Regulations or planning hurdles were perceived as challenges to be overcome, not elements to divert or distort their envisioned plan.

Four, context does matter. While there are common design principles, designing for older people is not a generic exercise. Templates or trademarks should not prevail over the specific context and the specific group for whom you are designing. What these case studies share is a focus on the particular people for whom they were designing and the context in which they live. This means that, while there were common design principles, the case study of a service that works superbly for people with dementia in Weesp in The Netherlands would be entirely inappropriate for indigenous Australians in the middle of the Australian desert. It means that a scheme that works superbly in Chicago would be entirely inappropriate if located in rural Japan. In all case studies, universal design principles have been intelligently applied to the context. Visual access in the center of the desert has been expressed as a view to the mountain ranges whereas in an urban environment it has found expression in a view of the kitchen or a garden path leading back into the house.

Five, the idea of "community" cannot be stereotyped, but rather can be expressed in so many different ways. One case study has seven different "lifestyles" so that residents can share common interests. Many case studies cater especially to a specific ethnic group and that determines the daily rhythms of the service and the connections that the service has with the wider community. Many of the schemes have encouraged strong linkages between residence and neighborhood. And, yet, the expression of community and the idea of connection to community are very different for a scheme designed for a middle-class denizen of the suburbs compared to a scheme for people who are homeless or at risk of homelessness.

In the 1830s, at the dawn of the railway age, a standard gauge of 4 feet-8½ inches was adopted. Some countries, like Ireland, chose to ignore that standard for a more generous wider gauge. Elsewhere, such as in the mining industry, the more economical narrower gauges were commonly used. In many ways, we have highlighted in this book the advantages and disadvantages of many of the different "gauges" now being adopted in older persons' housing. Debate is intense between providers and users across many nations. We are hopeful that this book, which embraces the luxurious as much as the incredibly humble (sometimes within a single continent), may just open other avenues of thought and exploration as architects, designers, owners, and providers continue to seek to build environments for older people which are both therapeutic and prosthetic; environments for older people in which they can truly belong; and environments about which older people can truly say "This is my home."

Definitions

Adapted Housing:
General needs housing that has been adapted in one form or another (e.g., installation of an entry-level shower room) to meet the specific needs of its resident.

Source: U.K. HAPPI Report 2009

Adult Day Care:
Daily structured programs in a community setting with activities and health-related and rehabilitation services to elderly who are physically or emotionally disabled and need a protective environment. This care is provided for during the day, the individual returning home for the evening.

Source: U.S. Senior Housing and Care Glossary of Terms

Affordable Housing:
A general term applied to public and private sector efforts to help low- and moderate-income people with their payment for housing. The housing costs may be subsidized through government payments directly to the developer or tenant, or the housing construction costs, and thus the required payments by tenants may be subsidized through taxing credits, enhanced lending terms, or direct payments to the developer by government entities.

Source: Crepidoma Consulting, LLC

Aging in Place:
A concept that advocates allowing a resident to choose to remain in his/her living environment despite the physical and/or mental decline that may occur with the process of aging.

Source: U.S. Senior Housing and Care Glossary of Terms

Allied Health:
A group of collaborating clinical health-care professionals such as occupational therapists, speech pathologists, and physiotherapists.

Source: HammondCare

Ambulatory:
Describes ability to ambulate, walk around, and not be bedridden or hospitalized.

Source: U.S. Senior Housing and Care Glossary of Terms

Assisted Living:
1. Assisted Living: In general, state-licensed program offered at a residential community with services that include meals, laundry, housekeeping, medication reminders, and assistance with Activities of Daily Living (ADLs) and Instrumental Activities of Daily Living (IADLs). Generally regarded as one to two steps below skilled nursing in level of care. Might also be referred to as Personal Care, Board and Care, Residential Care, Boarding Home, and the like.

Source: U.S. Senior Housing and Care Glossary of Terms

2. Assisted living residences or assisted living facilities (ALFs): provide supervision or assistance with activities of daily living (ADLs); coordination of services by outside health-care providers; and monitoring of resident activities to help to ensure their health, safety, and well-being. Assistance may include the administration or supervision of medication, or personal care services provided by a trained staff person. Assisted living as it exists today emerged in the 1990s as an eldercare alternative on the continuum of care for people, normally seniors, for whom independent living is no longer appropriate but who do not need the 24-hour medical care provided by a nursing home. Assisted living is a philosophy of care and services promoting independence and dignity.

Source: http://en.wikipedia.org/wiki/Assisted_living

3. Also known in the HammondCare context as "hostel" or "low care." Permanent or respite residential care for people who are able to mobilize independently and do not require intensive skilled nursing care. Residents receive assistance with all aspects of daily living including medication management and clinical care.

Source: HammondCare

4. Also known in the United Kingdom as "extra care" or "very sheltered housing." See definition of **extra care**.

Source: Pozzoni

Assistant in Nursing:
A person without a medication qualification employed in a limited nursing role. Assistants in nursing provide personal care, assistance with activities of daily living, and some clinical care. In the United States, often referred to as Certified Nursing Assistant (CNA).

Source: HammondCare

BPSD:
Behavioral and psychological symptoms of dementia.

Source: HammondCare

Care Home:
A generic term to include accommodation where residents are expected to be provided with a bedroom, meals, help with personal care such as dressing, supervision of medication, companionship, and someone on call at night. Care homes providing personal care give care during normal short illnesses but do not provide constant nursing care.

Source: U.K. Elderly Accommodation Counsel

Care Hotel:
Offering temporary accommodation and 24-hour care and services, care hotels combine aspects of hotels with care facilities.

Source: www.kcwz.nl

Close Care:
Housing for older people adjacent to a care home that will deliver personal care services to the residents and/or will facilitate a possible transition to the care home if needed. This form of housing, be it sheltered, retirement or extra care, may be a preferred choice for couples with different care needs, or a person with a degenerative health condition.

Source: U.K. Elderly Accommodation Counsel

Cohousing:
1. Cohousing: Cohousing is a type of collaborative housing in which residents actively participate in the design and operation of their own neighborhoods. Cohousing residents are consciously committed to living as a community. The physical design encourages both social contact and individual space. Private homes contain all the features of conventional homes, but residents also have access to extensive common facilities such as open space, courtyards, a playground, and a common house.

Source: www.cohousing.org/what_is_cohousing

2. Cohousing (More general definition): A cohousing community is a type of intentional community composed of private homes with full kitchens, supplemented by extensive common facilities. A cohousing community is planned, owned, and managed by the residents—groups of people who want more interaction with their neighbors. Common facilities vary but usually include a large kitchen and dining room where residents can take turns cooking for the community. Other facilities may include a laundry, pool, child care facilities, offices, Internet access, guest rooms, game room, TV room, tool room, or a gym. Through spatial design and shared social and management activities, cohousing facilitates intergenerational interaction among neighbors, for the social and practical benefits. There are also economic and environmental benefits to sharing resources, space, and items.

In cohousing there is a strong emphasis on creating community. Members cook and share meals in the common house on one, two, or more nights a week. Shared child care, gardening, and other activities, as well as shared governance all foster a sense of community. Generally, consensus is used as a means of decision making. That is, the effort is made to hear all voices in the community, and to make major decisions only with the agreement of all members.

Source: http://en.wikipedia.org/wiki/Cohousing

Community Service Center/Multifunctional Center:
Community service centers provide facilities for housing, care, and welfare in the district and often also offer additional amenities such as health-care center, child care centers, and a grand café.

Source: www.kcwz.nl

Congregate Housing:
See *Independent Living* (may be also referred to as supportive housing).

Source: U.S. Senior Housing and Care Glossary of Terms

Continuing Care Retirement Community (CCRC):
1. Housing planned and operated to provide a continuum of accommodations and services for seniors including, but not limited to, independent living, congregate housing, assisted living, and skilled nursing care. See also **Life Care Community**.

Source: U.S. Senior Housing and Care Glossary of Terms

2. CCRCs are designed for older people and encompass the spectrum of independent living, extra care/assisted living and higher dependency care in one location, often across several buildings on one site in a campus format. Residents living at a CCRC can take advantage of a full range of care services and community facilities. Residents may initially move to the independent living units and, if desired, relocate to an onsite higher-dependency accommodation should their needs change. Some operators, however, prefer that residents have the choice to remain in their original "home" with the building and care adaptable to the resident's needs.

Source: Pozzoni Architects

Continuum of Care:
Full spectrum of care available at continuing care retirement communities, which may include independent living, assisted living, nursing care, home health, home care, and home and community-based services.

Source: U.S. Senior Housing and Care Glossary of Terms

Convalescent Home:
See **Nursing Home**.

Source: U.S. Senior Housing and Care Glossary of Terms

Day Care:
See **Adult Day Care**.

Dementia:
Progressive neurological, cognitive, or medical disorder that affects memory, judgment, and cognitive powers.

Source: U.S. Senior Housing and Care Glossary of Terms

The term *dementia* is used to describe a syndrome that may be caused by a number of illnesses in which there is a progressive decline in multiple areas of function, including decline in memory, reasoning, communication skills, and the ability to carry out daily activities. Alongside this decline, individuals may develop behavioral and psychological symptoms such as depression, psychosis, aggression, and wandering, which cause problems in themselves, which complicate care, and which can occur at any stage of the illness.

Source: U.K. Department of Health: National Dementia Strategy

Dementia is an umbrella term to describe the symptoms that occur when the brain is affected by certain diseases or conditions. There are many different types of dementia although some are far more common than others. They are often named according to the condition that has caused the dementia, e.g., Alzheimer's disease, vascular dementia, dementia with lewy bodies, fronto-temporal dementia, Korsakoffs syndrome, Creutzfeld-Jakob disease.

Source: U.K. Alzheimer's Society

Dementia Care:
A care service and housing component that is specifically designed and operated to mitigate the manifestations of Alzheimer's disease and other dementias.

Source: Crepidoma Consulting, LLC

Dementia Specific:
A service entirely for people with a diagnosis of dementia.

Source: HammondCare

Extra Care
Also known as assisted living, very sheltered housing, or frail elderly care. Essentially self-contained flats accessed from a communal corridor in a single building. There are shared lounge and other communal facilities and 24-hour staff. Care is brought to the residents as needed and the building is adaptable to change should an individual's needs and care requirements change. Some private sector developments eschew the term *extra care*, as it is usually associated with social housing.

Source: Pozzoni Architects

Extra care housing is housing to rent or to buy, designed with the needs of frailer older people in mind and with varying levels of care/support available onsite. People who live in extra care housing have their own self-contained homes, their own front doors, and a legal right to occupy the property. Facilities may include a laundry restaurant/dining room, domestic support, personal care, lounges, and 24-hour emergency support. Properties can be rented, owned, or part owned/part rented.

Source: U.K. Elderly Accommodation Counsel

Extra Service:
There are a small number of "extra service" residential aged-care services that are permitted to charge more than the standard resident fee. They must offer a higher standard of accommodation, food services, and lifestyle activities. Extra service residential aged-care services constitute about 5 percent of the total number of places available in HammondCare, and the number of places is tightly regulated. In this book, only the Montefiore facility has "extra service" status for its nursing home and dementia unit and can therefore charge an additional daily fee.

Source: HammondCare

Fokus Housing:
Apartments for people with severe physical disabilities that provide independent living with activities in daily life (ADL) support. Twelve to eighteen of these apartments are gathered within an area of 350 meters (1,148 feet) from an ADL-support unit. At the ADL-support unit the technical infrastructure, through which the client may initiate the delivery of ADL-support, is provided. This support is always given on request (not planned). The ADL-unit has a central bathing facility that can be used after having made an appointment. Workers are present 24 hours a day, 7 days a week. They are able to assist in the ADL activities of dressing, transfers, eating and drinking support, sanitary functions, and to give simple nursery assistance. The housing is generated through cooperation with an independent housing association.

Frail Elderly Housing:
Also known as extra care.

High-Dependency Care:
A generic term to cover nursing care, dementia care, and other levels of care where residents require assistance in everyday tasks.

Source: Pozzoni Architects

Home Health Care:
Provision of medical and nursing services in the individual's home by a licensed provider.

Source: U.S. Senior Housing and Care Glossary of Terms

Hospice Care:
Palliative care and comfort measures provided to those with a terminal illness and their families. It can include medical, counseling, and social services.

Source: U.S. Senior Housing and Care Glossary of Terms

Hostel:
Also known as "assisted living."

Source: HammondCare

Households:
1. This housing solution involves a situation in which a small group of people in need of intensive care and assistance live in a group home, enabling them to live as normal a life as possible.

Source: www.kcwz.nl

2. A generalized term used to describe, in the United States, a physical environment and care program for a small group of assisted living or nursing residents and containing social spaces such as living and dining rooms as well as resident bedrooms. A noninstitutional, nonmedical model of design and care provision providing a replicated home-like environment for residents.

Source: Crepidoma Consulting, LLC

3. Household model is generally called unit care in Japan. This model aims to provide domestic care of the kind found in group homes even in a large facility. Units are estimated to consist of 6 to 15 private rooms, with the appropriate scale depending on the condition of residents, quality of care, and architectural arrangement of space. With unit care, meals are eaten in a living room in accordance with the daily living patterns of residents. Meals are cooked in units, with residents taking part in serving and clearing up to encourage them to participate in everyday activities.

Source: Institute for Health Economics and Policy in Japan, 2007

4. Also sometimes known as "units," "pods," or "clusters." In the United Kingdom, used to describe a small group of people living as a self-contained "household" sharing lounge, dining, kitchen, activity, assisted bathing, and external facilities. A large care development may be divided into several households.

Source: Pozzoni Architects

Housing with Care:
A generic term to include extra care, assisted living, very sheltered housing, frail elderly care, close care, retirement villages, and CCRC. Self-contained accommodation where care is brought to the residents as and when needed.

Source: Pozzoni Architects

Independent Living:
Multiunit senior housing development that may provide supportive services such as meals, housekeeping, social activities, and transportation (see also **Congregate Housing, Supportive Housing, Retirement Community**). Independent living typically encourages socialization by provision of meals in a central dining area and scheduled social programs. May also be used to describe housing with few or no services (senior apartment).

Source: U.S. Senior Housing and Care Glossary of Terms

Also known as sheltered housing or retirement housing, self-contained apartments with access to communal facilities. There may be an emergency call to an on, or off, assistance. In broad terms, sheltered housing often refers to the social housing sector (for rent) and retirement housing to private sector (for sale).

Source: Pozzoni Architects

In-Home Care:
Also known as "community care." Services delivered into a person's home by skilled and unskilled workers. Support is provided at varying levels for personal care, medical management, clinical care, meal preparation, household management, and transport. In-home care services are significantly subsidized by the Australian government.

Source: HammondCare

Integrated Neighborhood Services:
Occupying a district or village either in part or in whole, areas with integrated neighborhood services offer optimum conditions for housing combined with a whole spectrum of care and welfare services including 24-hour care that can be scheduled and are generally organized around a community service center or regional care center. "Integrated neighborhood services" is also used as a general term referring to all initiatives relating to adapting regular districts so that care and welfare services can be provided to those in need of them.

Source: www.kcwz.nl

Intermediate Care:
A service provided on a short-term basis either at home or at a care facility for people who require some degree of rehabilitation and recuperation. The aim is to prevent unnecessary admission to hospital, facilitate earlier discharge from hospital, and prevent premature admission to residential care.

Source: Pozzoni Architects

Intermediate Nursing Home (*kaigo roujin hoken shisetsu*):
One of the three types of long-term care facilities for elderly in Japan. The other types are skilled nursing home and sanatorium medical facility for the elderly. An *Intermediate Nursing Home* provides care to elders whose medical conditions are stable, and who need rehabilitation to return home. This facility provides elderly residents a stay of three to six months for the purpose of completing rehabilitation.

Source: M. Masud, 2003: Wakariyasui Kaigo Hoken Ho, Yuhikaku, Japan

Life Care Community:
A Continuing Care Retirement Community (CCRC) that offers an insurance-type contract for residents and provides all levels of care. It often includes payment for acute care and physician's visits. Little or no change is made in the monthly fee, regardless of the level of medical care required by the resident, except for cost of living increases.

Source: U.S. Senior Housing and Care Glossary of Terms

Life Cycle Homes/Lifetime Housing:
A home is defined as a "life cycle" home if it can be lived in during each stage of a person's life without major physical exertion or a high risk of injury. New homes must meet the requirements of the WoonKeur certificate; existing homes must meet those of the Opplussen certificate.

Source: www.kcwz.nl

Lifetime Homes:
Housing designed to meet access and adaptability standards for everyone including older people.

Source: U.K. HAPPI report 2009

In the United Kingdom, there are a set of criteria for new-build houses to comply with in order to meet with the "Lifetime Homes" standard.

Source: Pozzoni Architects

Lifetime Neighborhood:
Occupying a district or village either in part or in whole, areas with integrated neighborhood services or lifetime neighborhood; offer optimum conditions for housing combined with a whole spectrum of care and welfare services including 24-hour care that can be scheduled and are generally organized around a community service center or regional care center. *Integrated neighborhood services* is also used as a general term referring to all initiatives relating to adapting regular districts so that care and welfare services can be provided to those in need of them.

Source: www.kcwz.nl

Long-Term Care:
Provision of services to persons of any age who are afflicted with chronic health impairments.

Source: U.S. Senior Housing and Care Glossary of Terms

Nonambulatory:
Inability to ambulate, walk around, and usually bedridden or hospitalized.

Source: U.S. Senior Housing and Care Glossary of Terms

Not-for-Profit:
Status of ownership and/or operation characterized by government taxation standards and operated by community-based boards of trustees who are all volunteers. Board members donate their time and talents to ensure that a not-for-profit organization's approach to caring for older people responds to local needs. Not-for-profit homes and services turn any surplus income back into improving or expanding services for their clients or residents. Many not-for-profit organizations are often associated with religious denominations and fraternal groups.

Source: U.S. Senior Housing and Care Glossary of Terms

Nursing Home:
1. A facility that provides 24-hour nursing care, room and board, and activities for convalescent residents and those with chronic and/or long-term care illnesses. Regular medical supervision and rehabilitation therapy are mandated to be available.

Source: U.S. Senior Housing and Care Glossary of Terms

2. Also known in the Australian context as "high care." Permanent or respite residential care for people with a greater degree of frailty and in need of continuous skilled nursing care. A registered nurse is available in Australian nursing homes 24 hours a day.

Source: HammondCare

3. In the United Kingdom, a care home registered for 24-hour nursing care. Currently known as "care homes with nursing."

Source: U.K. HAPPI report 2009

Nursing Care:
Provide personal and nursing care 24 hours a day for people who are bedridden, very frail, or have a medical condition or illness that means they need regular attention from a nurse. There is always a qualified nurse on duty.

Source: U.K. Elderly Accommodation Counsel

Palliative Care:
Palliative care is the active holistic care of patients with advanced progressive illness. Management of pain and other symptoms and provision of psychological, social, and spiritual support is paramount. The goal of palliative care is achievement of the best quality of life for patients and their families.

Source: U.K. National Institute for Clinical Excellence

Person-Centered Care (see also Resident Directed Care):
An ethical approach to caring for people with dementia that has been very influential in the aged care sector. Person-centered care emphasizes the importance of valuing the person regardless of the level of dementia, treating them as individuals, looking at the world from their perspective, and providing a positive environment that supports well-being. The approach was formulated by Tom Kitwood (1997) and elaborated on by Dawn Brooker (2004).

Source: HammondCare

Personal Care:
Provision of nonmedical care and help with everyday tasks, e.g., bathing, dressing, eating.

Rehabilitation:
Therapeutic care for persons requiring intensive physical, occupational, or speech therapy.

Source: U.S. Senior Housing and Care Glossary of Terms

Residential Care:
See **Assisted Living**.

Source: U.S. Senior Housing and Care Glossary of Terms

In the United Kingdom, Residential Care Homes are generally referred to as *care homes*. A care home is a residential setting where older people live with access to onsite services. A home registered as a care home will provide personal care only—help with bathing, dressing, eating, and so forth. Some care homes are registered to meet a specific need, e.g., dementia or a terminal illness. Care homes may also be registered as a "care home with nursing."

Source: Pozzoni Architects

Resident-Directed Care
(see also Person-Centered Care):
A health and personal care program, either in an assisted living or nursing home setting that is collaboratively chosen by residents, family members, and staff. Each resident generally chooses the daily routines and services he or she wishes to receive. Staff place supreme value on listening and knowing resident backgrounds and personal preferences, while educating residents about concerns related to their care and health.

Source: Crepidoma Consulting, LLC

Respite Care:

1. Temporary relief from duties for caregivers, ranging from several hours to days. May be provided in-home or in a residential care setting such as an assisted living facility or nursing home.

Source: U.S. Senior Housing and Care Glossary of Terms

Retirement Communities:

These can be a large development of sheltered housing or extra care that is large enough to sustain its own community. When different levels of care are combined into a single facility, the term "continuing care retirement community" is often used.

Source: Pozzoni Architects

Retirement Village:

Also known as Continuing Care Retirement Communities (CCRC), these are large developments (often 100+) with a range of housing types and levels of care and support (sheltered, extra care, nursing care) on one site.

Source: U.K. HAPPI report 2009

However, among some U.K. operators, retirement villages refer to developments that comply with the above definition but without the nursing care or care home facility.

Source: Pozzoni Architects

Sanatorium Medical Facility for the Elderly (*Kaigo ryouyou gata iryou shisetsu*):

One of the three types of long-term care facilities for elderly in Japan. The other types are Skilled Nursing Home and Intermediate Nursing Home. Long-term care facilities for elderly that provide both care and clinical treatment. This type of facility is a part of a hospital and highly resembles an acute care hospital. The service provided is mainly for rehabilitation with minimum clinical care.

Source: M. Masuda, 2003: Wakariyasui Kaigo Hoken Ho, Yuhikaku, Japan

Senior Apartment:

Age-restricted multiunit housing with self-contained living units for older adults who are able to care for themselves. Usually no additional services such as meals or transportation are provided.

Source: U.S. Senior Housing and Care Glossary of Terms

Sheltered Housing:

1. Sheltered housing consists of independent housing complexes which are designed with safety and shelter in mind. Each complex is subject to an agreement for the provision of care and services, although the provision of housing, care, and services are clearly separated contractually. The homes meet the requirements for adaptable housing. Such a complex can function as a service center in an area with integrated neighborhood facilities for the surrounding community.

Source: www.kwz.nl

2. Sheltered housing is often called "retirement housing." The majority of sheltered/retirement housing schemes have a scheme manager/warden and emergency alarm service. There are often communal facilities such as a lounge, laundry, guest flat, and garden. Meals are not normally provided but a few schemes include a restaurant or can arrange a hot meal. There are many different types of sheltered/retirement housing, to rent, to buy, or part-buy. Developments may be self-contained apartments, bungalows, or luxury apartments. There is a minimum age, usually 60. Sheltered or retirement housing appeals to people who like living independently but want the reassurance of knowing that assistance is on hand if there is an emergency, or who expect to be away from home for long periods and need to know their home is safe.

Source: U.K. Elderly Accommodation Counsel

Skilled Nursing Home (*tokubetsu yogo roujin home*):

1. One of the three types of long-term care facilities for elderly in Japan. The other types are Intermediate Nursing Home and Sanatorium Medical Facility for the Elderly. A skilled nursing home provides support for ADL and IADL, rehabilitation, and clinical support for elders in order that they can go back to their home, though many spend their end of life in the facility. In Japan only local municipalities and social welfare corporations can provide this service.

Source: M. Masuda, 2003: Wakariyasui Kaigo Hoken Ho, Yuhikaku, Japan

2. In the United States, skilled nursing homes are commonly referred to as simply nursing homes, see **Nursing Homes** definition.

3. In the United Kingdom, known as "Nursing Homes" or "Care Homes with Nursing."

Social Role Valorization:
A philosophy of care formulated by Wolf Wolfensberger in the 1980s that aims to create, support, or recognize socially valued roles for people who are devalued or at risk of being devalued in society. In this book, this philosophy strongly influenced Brightwater's Onslow Gardens.

Source: HammondCare

Supported Housing:
A generic term to describe any form of housing whose residents require some form of care and/or support due to their physical or cognitive condition.

Source: Pozzoni Architects

Universal Staffing Approach:
Also known as *multiskilled staffing* or *universal worker*. Traditional distinctions between care roles are disregarded. For example, a staff member may be trained as a nursing assistant but also provide housekeeping services or food preparation assistance. This approach in care provision is thought to provide a more intimate and understanding relationship between the care provider and the resident, particularly within a household environment.

Source: HammondCare

Very Sheltered Housing:
Also known as **extra care**.

Index

D

G

T

Y

Z